UNIVERSITY OF MIAMI

Integrating the Americas:
Shaping Future Trade Policy

Edited by

Sidney Weintraub

Transaction Publishers
New Brunswick (U.S.A.) and London (U.K.)

The mission of the North-South Center is to promote better relations and serve as a catalyst for change among the United States, Canada, and the nations of Latin America and the Caribbean by advancing knowledge and understanding of the major political, social, economic, and cultural issues affecting the nations and peoples of the Western Hemisphere.

Library of Congress Cataloging-in-Publication Data

Integrating the Americas: shaping future trade policy / edited by
   Sidney Weintraub.
       p.   cm.
   At head of title: North-South Center, University of Miami.
   Includes bibliographical references.
   ISBN 1-56000-769-9
   1. Latin America--Commercial policy. 2. United States--Commercial
policy. 3. Free trade--America. 4. International economic relations.
 I. Weintraub, Sidney, 1922- . II. University of Miami. North-South Center.
HF1480.5.I519 1994
382'.3'097--dc20

                                      94-38585
                                         CIP

ISBN 1-56000-769-9

Printed in the United States of America

00 99 98 97 96 95 94 7 6 5 4 3 2 1

Contents

Acknowledgments

The editor gratefully acknowledges the financial and intellectual support given to this research and outreach project by the University of Miami's North-South Center, the Inter-American Dialogue, and the Center for Strategic and International Studies.

The sponsors wish to express their deep appreciation for the contribution of Peter B. Field (1935-1993), whose vision of free trade and economic integration in the Western Hemisphere and tireless work at the U.S. Department of Commerce and the North-South Center's Enterprise of the Americas Program gave birth and momentum to this project.

Foreword

Over the past ten years, there has been a dramatic transformation in the attitudes of Latin American and Caribbean countries toward international trade. These countries have demonstrated increasing interest in forging agreements to secure access to U.S. and local markets, and they have been encouraged by the signing of the North American Free Trade Agreement (NAFTA). Economic policy attention is now focused on ensuring their insertion into the world economy, while taking advantage of regional markets. Although NAFTA provides a model for future arrangements, there are still many unexplored trade policy options confronting the nations of the Western Hemisphere. Questions remain as to the appropriate balance between deepening the integration process within NAFTA and other subregional trade arrangements, on the one hand, and proceeding toward some form of hemispheric free trade, on the other. These options are of special importance on the eve of the December 1994 Summit of the Americas and will play an important role in defining hemispheric relations in the future.

On March 2, 1994, the Inter-American Dialogue joined with the Center for Strategic and International Studies and the North-South Center of the University of Miami to sponsor a three-day conference on the future of Western Hemisphere economic and trade relations following the ratification of NAFTA. The central purpose of the conference was to explore and illuminate the trade policy options confronting the nations of the hemisphere, with particular emphasis on the direction in which countries should steer their trade policies: whether a deepening or widening of NAFTA should be pursued; what mechanisms, institutions, procedures, and timetables are necessary or desirable for this process; and how much effort should be placed on forging a single, integrated hemisphere.

This meeting was part of the Dialogue's ongoing project on Western Hemisphere economic integration. In June, conference directors Peter Hakim and Sidney Weintraub traveled to Latin America to meet with senior public officials and business leaders to report the results of the March conference and to discuss recent developments in U.S. trade policy. The objective of the trip was to exchange information and ideas on the many issues that must be addressed in moving toward some form of hemispheric free trade area and to gain a full and accurate sense of the thinking among key Latin Americans.

The Inter-American Dialogue's research and publications are designed to improve the quality of public debate and decision on key issues in the Western Hemisphere. The Dialogue is an independent, nonpartisan center for policy analysis on U.S.-Latin American economic and political relations. Its one hundred members — from the United States, Canada, Latin America, and the Caribbean — include former presidents and prominent political, business, labor, academic, media, military, and religious leaders. At periodic plenary sessions, members analyze major hemispheric issues and formulate recommendations for policy and action. The Dialogue presents its findings in comprehensive reports circulated throughout the hemisphere. Its research agenda focuses on four broad themes — democratic governance, inter-American cooperation, economic integration, and social equity.

The Inter-American Dialogue wishes to express its gratitude to the North-South Center of the University of Miami and to the Center for Strategic and International Studies for their financial support and work toward the promotion of democracy and economic relations in the Western Hemisphere.

Peter Hakim
Inter-American Dialogue

Contributors

Albert Fishlow is the former dean of international and area studies at the University of California at Berkeley. He was also a professor of economics at the same institution. From 1978 to 1982, he was director of the Concilium on International and Area Studies at Yale University. In 1975 and 1976, he served as deputy assistant secretary of state for interamerican affairs. Dr. Fishlow is an authority on Brazil and international financial issues.

Ambassador **Joseph A. Greenwald** specializes in international negotiations, trade law counseling, and litigation; representation in the United States and abroad on international economic issues and business transactions; and advisory services for multilateral trade negotiations.

Ambassador Greenwald served as assistant secretary of state for economic and business affairs (1975-1976), U.S. ambassador to the European Community (1972-1975), and U.S. ambassador to the Organization for Economic Cooperation and Development (1969-1972). He has represented the United States at numerous international meetings and played a leading role in the Kennedy Round of the General Agreement on Tariffs and Trade negotiations (1961-1967). He headed the U.S. delegation to the Second United Nations Conference on Trade and Development in New Delhi in 1968. He negotiated the generalized system of preferences for developing countries (1964-1968). For many years, he was responsible for the formulation and implementation of U.S. foreign economic policy in the Department of State.

Ambassador Greenwald received a B.A. degree in economics from the University of Chicago, an L.L.B. from Georgetown University, and an M.B.A. from Michigan State University. He is now an adjunct professor at the American University Law School.

Since April 1993, Dr. **Eckart Guth** has been head of Unit 1.B.1, Unit for Relations with the United States of America, Directorate B-External Economic Relations, in the European Commission in Brussels. From October 1990 until March 1993, he was head of Unit 1.A.2, Agriculture and Fisheries, in the Directorate General for External Relations. Previously, he served in the European Commission's Division on Agriculture and Fisheries. From February

1979 until December 1984, he was a member of the cabinet of Vice President Haferkamp in the European Commission. He was minister of agriculture in Bonn from December 1974 until January 1979.

Dr. Guth received his Ph.D. from the University of Göttingen in Germany and was a postdoctoral fellow at Michigan State University. His studies at the University of Göttingen were in agriculture and agricultural economics.

Peter Hakim is president of the Inter-American Dialogue and authors a regular column for *The Christian Science Monitor.* Mr. Hakim was vice president for research and evaluation at the Inter-American Foundation (1981-1984) and previously worked for the Ford Foundation (1968-1980). He has taught at the Institute of Human Nutrition of Columbia University (1975-1980) and the International Nutrition Program of the Massachusetts Institute of Technology (1974-1975). Mr. Hakim is principal author of *Development, Reform and Malnutrition in Chile* and co-editor of *Direct to the Poor: A Reader in Grassroots Development.*

Nora Lustig is a senior fellow in the foreign policy studies program at the Brookings Institution. From 1975 to 1991, she was a professor of economics at El Colegio de Mexico's Center of Economic Studies in Mexico City. She was a visiting scholar at the Massachusetts Institute of Technology's department of economics in 1982 and a visiting professor at the University of California at Berkeley in the department of agricultural and resource economics in 1984. She has also served as a consultant for the Mexican government, the Inter-American Development Bank, and the World Bank and has worked for the Economic Commission for Latin America.

Dr. Lustig is currently vice president of the Latin American and Caribbean Economic Association and co-director of the "Washington Exchange," a Washington-based forum to discuss economic issues affecting Latin America. She is also a member of several editorial boards.

Dr. Lustig's research has focused on the economic restructuring of Mexico during the 1980s, NAFTA and other economic integration initiatives in the Americas, and income distribution and poverty in Latin America. Born in Buenos Aires, Argentina, she has also lived in Mexico and the United States. She received her B.A. and Ph.D. in economics from the University of California at Berkeley.

María Beatriz Nofal received her Ph.D. from Johns Hopkins University in 1983 with specialization in development economics and planning. She received postgraduate diplomas in development planning from the École des Hautes Études en Sciences Sociales, University of Paris, France (1977) and the Institute of Social Studies, The Hague, Netherlands (1976).

Since 1989, she has been working as partner and principal consultant in Beatriz Nofal & Asociados on economic and management consulting for private firms in Argentina and for international firms and international financial institutions. Since 1991, Dr. Nofal has been an external consultant to the Inter-American Development Bank. While in the United States, she was an assistant professor at the Massachusetts Institute of Technology and at Johns Hopkins University, as well as a consultant for the World Bank.

From January 1986 to December 1988, Dr. Nofal was under-secretary of industrial development at the Secretariat of Industry and Foreign Trade in the Ministry of Economy of Argentina. From July to December 1985, she was an adviser to the under-secretary of economic policy, and from July to December 1984, she was an adviser to the under-secretary of development programming.

Dr. Nofal has authored several publications in Argentina, Brazil, and the United States. In 1989, she was awarded the Order of Rio Branco by the government of Brazil in recognition of her "excellent performance in the Argentine-Brazilian Integration Program."

Moisés Naím holds a Ph.D. and an M.S. degree from the Massachusetts Institute of Technology. In 1978, he became a professor at IESA, a business school and research center located in Caracas, Venezuela, where he served as dean from 1982 to 1986. From February 1989 to September 1990, he was Venezuela's minister of industry and trade. He was executive director at the World Bank until 1992, when he became a senior associate at the Carnegie Endowment for International Peace. Dr. Naím also teaches at Johns Hopkins University's School of Advanced International Studies. He is a member of the U.S. Academy of Science/National Research Council Committee on Economic Reform and Democratization and a fellow of the World Economic Forum in Geneva.

Carlos A. Primo Braga is an economist with the International Trade Division of the World Bank. Before joining the World Bank, Mr. Primo Braga was an assistant professor of economics at the University of São Paulo and senior researcher at the Fundaçao Instituto de Pesquisas Económicas (FIPE), São Paulo, Brazil. Since 1988 he has also been a visiting professor at the Johns Hopkins School of Advanced International Studies, Washington, D.C. Since 1984 he has served as an economic consultant to many private companies, multilateral agencies, and governmental institutions in Brazil and abroad — including the World Bank and the Organization of American States. During 1987-1988, he was joint coordinator of the Brazilian team working on a Rockefeller Foundation project on "Multilateral Trade Negotiations and the Developing Countries." Among Mr. Primo Braga's publications are *Brazil e a Rodada Uruguai* (co-editors, C.L. Martone and E.R. Pelin, IPE/USP, forthcoming); "NAFTA and the Rest of the World," in *North American Free Trade: Assessing the Impact* (1992); and "The North South Debate on Intellectual Property Rights," in *Global Rivalry and Intellectual Property* (1991).

Leonard Waverman is a professor in the department of economics, University of Toronto and director of the university's Centre for International Studies.

He received his B.Comm. and M.A. from the University of Toronto (1964 and 1965, respectively) and his Ph.D. from M.I.T. in 1969. He has been a visiting scholar at the University of Essex, Stanford University, and the Sloan School at M.I.T.

Dr. Waverman specializes in international trade, industrial organization, and antitrust, energy, and telecommunications economics. He has authored numerous scholarly works, was a board member of the Ontario Energy Board, and currently is a board member of the Ontario Telephone Service Commission. He has consulted widely in Canada, the United States, and Europe.

He is editor of the *Energy Journal*. He has also been an associate editor of the *Canadian Journal of Economics* and has served on the executive committee of the European Association for Research in Industrial Economics.

In 1991, he was a visiting professor at INSEAD in Fontainebleau, France. He is a research associate at ENSAE-CREST (Ecole Nationale de la Statistique et de l'Administration Economique, Centre de Recherche en Economie et Statistique) in Paris.

Recent works include an examination of costs and productivity in the United States, Canadian, Japanese, and German automobile industries (Cambridge University Press); analyses of the impact of U.S.-Canada-Mexico free trade; an analysis of costs and regulation in European satellite service provision; and an examination of the system of international telecommunications pricing (for OECD).

Sidney Weintraub holds the William E. Simon Chair in Political Economy at the Center for Strategic and International Studies and is also Dean Rusk Professor of International Affairs at the Lyndon B. Johnson School of Public Affairs, the University of Texas at Austin. Prior to joining the LBJ School, Dr. Weintraub was a career foreign service officer of the U.S. Department of State working primarily on issues of international trade, finance, and development. He has written extensively on North American economic integration, including a book published by the Brookings Institution in 1984 with the prophetic title *Free Trade between Mexico and the United States?* His book *A Marriage of Convenience: Relations Between Mexico and the United States*, published by Oxford University Press in 1990, has just come out in a Spanish edition published by Editorial Diana in Mexico City under the title *Matrimonio por Convenienca*.

Ippei Yamazawa is a professor in the department of economics at Hitotsubashi University in Tokyo, Japan. He is an adviser to the Ministry of International Trade and Industry (Textile Council and Coal Council), the Ministry of Foreign Affairs, the Ministry of Finance, and the Economic Planning Agency. Since 1968, he has been working on Pacific economic cooperation and is a regular member of both the Pacific Trade and Development Conference and the Pacific Economic Cooperation Council. He is the Japanese representative on the Asia Pacific Economic Cooperation's Eminent Persons Group.

Dr. Yamazawa studied both at Hitotsubashi University and at the University of Chicago, receiving his Ph.D. in economics from the former. He has also taught at Thammasat University in Thailand and at the University of Sheffield in the United Kingdom. His areas of expertise are international economics, trade investment, industrial adjustment, and trade policy. He is a member of the Association of National Universities, the Foreign Student Council, and the Ministry of Education and is secretary of University Mobility of Asia Pacific.

Dr. Yamazawa has published several books and journal articles including *Economic Development and International Trade: The Japanese Model* (1990), *Vision for the Economy of the Asia-Pacific Region in the Year 2000 and Tasks Ahead* (1992), and *Economic Integration in the Asia-Pacific Region and the Options for Japan* (1993).

Introduction

Sidney Weintraub

For many years, Latin America and the Caribbean (LAC) were considered the backwater of the global trade policy arena. The region looked inward, and the prevailing philosophy was to belittle the role that exports might play in stimulating economic growth. Export pessimism dominated: Why bother, economists said, because the center, to use the terminology of the United Nations Economic Commission for Latin America (ECLA), would act, in any event, to stifle any export progress made by the periphery? Among the world's developing countries, playing in the world trade game was left to the Asian nations.

Leaders in the LAC region recognized that most of their national economies were too small to generate substantial markets, and efforts were made to stimulate regional economic integration. These efforts were structured to be consistent with the accepted regional wisdom of using import substitution to generate an industrial base. LAC countries therefore joined together behind high border barriers to limit what imports could enter from the outside. The inherent inconsistencies of these schemes led uniformly to their stagnation or collapse. They created some benefits for the more economically advanced Latin American countries, but at the expense of the weaker. The weaker countries paid higher prices for goods than were charged on the world market — a classic form of trade diversion — while the more economically advanced were enabled to find markets despite inefficiencies.

During the years when the LAC region was looking inward, the difference in trade growth between LAC countries and developing countries in East Asia was startling: The average annual growth in exports from 1970 to 1980 was -0.1 percent for LAC countries compared with +9.5 percent for East Asian and Pacific countries. The export growth figures for the years 1980 to 1991 were 2.9 percent a year for LAC and 10.2 percent a year for East Asia and the Pacific.[1] During the 1970s, growth in gross domestic product (GDP) held up reasonably well for the LAC region, at 5.5 percent a year, only marginally lower than for developing countries in East Asia, at 6.6 percent a year. But LAC growth during the 1970s was built on a house of cards — favorable terms of trade for some oil-exporting countries and a foreign and domestic debt buildup for almost all LAC countries — and this defect had its consequences in subsequent years. GDP growth in the LAC region from 1980 to 1991 was only 1.7 percent a year, or less than population growth, compared with 7.7 percent a year for East Asian developing countries.[2]

The purpose here is not to compare East Asia with Latin America, but rather to contrast the remarkable change of thinking from what existed in the LAC region then to what prevails now. LAC countries now actively promote exports. Import barriers have been reduced unilaterally in country after country in the region in order not to burden producers with high costs for imported inputs and to encourage competitive rather than protected markets. Regional integration schemes have been reborn or been created anew based on today's ECLAC (a *C* for "Caribbean" has been added) doctrine of "open regionalism."[3] Free trade with the United States was unthinkable a decade ago; now it is actively sought by a number of LAC countries and is being considered by all of them.

The United States, for its part, underwent its own shift in philosophy. Until the 1980s, those who made U.S. trade policy focused almost exclusively on the multilateral structure that existed under the aegis of the General Agreement on Tariffs and Trade (GATT). To the extent that the United States looked regionally, it was to Europe and, increasingly, to Asia; Latin America hardly existed in U.S. trade policy formulation.

The prospect of a North American Free Trade Agreement (NAFTA) was inconceivable at the end of the 1970s. The suggestion that the United States might even contemplate free trade with Mexico, a low-income, highly insular country, would have been outlandish. But here we are: NAFTA is in effect, and consideration is being given to a wider Western Hemisphere free trade area (FTA).

This book is an outgrowth of these changes in outlook both north and south of the Rio Grande/Río Bravo. Every book has its time. This is the time to concentrate attention on economic integration in the Americas.

The Project

A n ongoing series of meetings on economic integration in the Americas has been arranged by three cooperating institutions — the Center for Strategic and International Studies (CSIS), the Inter-American Dialogue (IAD), and the North-South Center at the University of Miami (N-S Center). This book is the first work to result from these sessions. Other publications will examine hemispheric integration as seen from the United States and from major Latin American countries. The overall project is designed to bring together scholars — plus policy officials and key players in the private business communities — from all parts of the hemisphere, as well as senior officers of international organizations active in the Americas.

Our purpose is to inform the publics in the hemisphere and to have some influence on economic policy decisions. Nineteen ninety-four has been a watershed year for policy making. A number of forcing situations coincided. The main event is the summit of the heads of government in the Americas in December 1994 in Miami. The Southern Cone integration arrangement, MERCOSUR (Mercado Común del Sur), which includes Argentina, Brazil, Paraguay, and Uruguay, must carry out decisions on January 1, 1995, on the content of their effort — whether they truly wish to become a customs union, a choice that can have significant implications for the integration architecture of the hemisphere. The U.S. administration and the Congress must decide whether they wish to expand NAFTA to other countries and at what speed or whether the preference is for the United States to proceed through a series of bilateral FTAs. There is a third option of doing nothing formal for the time being.

The December summit will call for conscious decisions. An agenda will be needed; this may be the single most important determination that must be made. Other substantive themes may be finessed, such as the expansion of NAFTA, the form this expansion will take, the terms for entry, and the relationship between NAFTA and other subregional integration agreements. MERCOSUR may fudge its choice on its proximate content but still go ahead with reducing trade barriers among the member countries. The U.S. administration may delay any formal accord on the next steps after NAFTA.

However, even these actions will have consequences. Decisions will be made, expressly or by delay. Facts will assert themselves, and in the absence of conscious decisions, they will determine the nature of trade and economic relationships in the hemisphere. Standing still is a formal option, but not one that exists in the real world. Too much has happened during the past few years to put everything on hold. This is one of the messages we hope to send through our tripartite project.

Contents of This Book

The present book contains eight chapters on hemispheric integration by nine scholars — one paper is jointly authored. The writers are from Argentina, Brazil, Canada, Mexico, the United States, and Venezuela, plus one each from Japan and the Commission of the European Union (EU). The effort was to obtain a variety of views both from within the Americas and from the two main centers outside the hemisphere. Yet as is clear from a reading of the chapters, an author's nationality is not a basis for predicting the substantive content of his or her work. The views expressed are by no means uniform.

Joseph Greenwald examines the historical pillars of U.S. trade policy and then speculates about the direction of future U.S. policy. He notes the centrality of the GATT in U.S. policy starting after World War II and then discusses the questioning of the GATT effectiveness because of a series of developments starting in the mid-1970s — the expansion of the European Community (EC); the growth of competition from new actors, especially in Asia; changing trade patterns; and the weakness of the GATT in handling disputes. The Uruguay Round of Multilateral Trade Negotiations (MTN) addressed a number of issues, such as agricultural trade and better dispute settlement procedures, that had been dealt with inadequately earlier but also tackled what have since come to be called "new" issues — the protection of intellectual property rights, trade in services, and trade-related aspects of investment. One of the outcomes of the Uruguay Round, if the agreements are implemented, is that the GATT will be replaced by a World Trade Organization (WTO), the first permanent trade organization that the United States will have joined.

As he looks ahead, Greenwald says that trade negotiations will increasingly take place on many levels — bilaterally, regionally, and globally. The content of these negotiations will cover not only traditional areas, such as market access or lowering border barriers, but also the new areas, plus other themes that have emerged just recently — the latest new areas are trade and the environment, trade and labor standards, and trade and competition.

The trade agenda has become quite complex. When the Uruguay Round was launched in Punta del Este in 1986, there was no clear indication what the end result would be when it was concluded in 1993. Similarly, as we examine the themes on the potential agenda for the WTO and look at bilateral and subregional bargaining, it is most uncertain how they will evolve. International trade negotiations used to refer to the movement of goods across borders. Future negotiations will encompass much more than that.

Nora Lustig and C.A. Primo Braga study recent developments in trade policy in Latin America, and they speculate about future directions from that vantage. They highlight four recent developments in the region — unilateral trade liberalization, increased adherence to multilateral trade discipline as exemplified by increased membership in the GATT, the emergence of subregional trading arrangements on the new basis of open regionalism, and the willingness to enter into preferential arrangements with the United States.

They note that there is evidence of "adjustment fatigue" in a number of countries in the hemisphere (they cite Brazil and Venezuela, specifically). However, they conclude that the danger of recidivism to protection is not high because there are now growing domestic constituencies in favor of openness and a series of commitments made in the Uruguay Round with regional trading partners and with multilateral financial institutions, especially the World Bank.

Lustig and Primo Braga see the subregional trading groups in Latin America more as building blocks toward greater regional integration than as stumbling blocks. The future of regional integration, they conclude, depends crucially on the position of the United States — whether NAFTA will be open to new members and under what terms. They cautiously suggest the establishment of a trade-monitoring agency for the region, what they call a mini-GATT, to promote convergence among the various subregional integration groupings and to pave the way for hemispheric free trade.

Moisés Naím deals directly with the uncertainty about prospects for free trade in the hemisphere. He says that the prospects for achievement are better than ever but that the confusion about trade relationships is also higher than ever. He lists what he refers to as misconceptions about free trade in the hemisphere. His analysis is that while some Latin American governments have embraced hemispheric free trade, not all of them have. FTAs with the United States, he says, will not increase the region's exports to the United States in the short run; FTAs are much more about investment than trade; the terms that Mexico accepted in NAFTA cannot be a model for most other countries because the degree of integration that existed between Mexico and the United States is generally absent elsewhere in Latin America; and subregional agreements in Latin America are more likely to be stumbling blocks than building blocks to hemispheric free trade. On this last point, Naím's position is different from that of Lustig and Primo Braga.

Naím reviews the remarkable progress in achieving subregional integration in Latin America since the late 1980s. He then argues that despite this sweeping liberalization, grass roots support for open markets is superficial. With the exception of Chile and possibly Mexico, stable political coalitions to consolidate the recent reforms are lacking. His conclusion is that it would be a mistake to overload trade negotiations with excessive conditions because this could create intolerable political burdens. He says that hemispheric free trade can be achieved, but only if key assumptions that have guided recent actions — by which he presumably means the extent of the commitment to free trade that now exists in Latin America — are discarded.

Leonard Waverman states that the NAFTA agreement as it now exists represents an "unstable equilibrium" that could unravel unless a number of items of unfinished business are attended to. These include more expeditious customs procedures and harmonizing or mutually recognizing product standards among the three participating countries — the United States, Canada, and Mexico.

The central theme of the chapter, however, is about the potentially disruptive effects of current antidumping (AD) and countervailing duty (CVD) laws and procedures in North America. His starting point is that in an FTA, there should be no difference between the treatment of a product shipped from Canada to the United States as compared with the same product moving within the United States, whereas, in fact, the former falls under U.S. AD laws and the latter, if there is predatory pricing, under competition policy. Waverman criticizes both Canada and the United States for their AD actions, but he emphasizes their greater impact on Canada and Mexico, which each send about 70 percent of their exports to the United States compared with much lower proportions of U.S. exports moving in the other directions.

He assumes that wholesale removal of AD is unlikely, at least immediately, and suggests instead some remedial measures, such as the reimbursement of all costs if an AD action fails and the adoption of the principle that decisions in cases under chapter 19 of NAFTA serve as a precedent for future cases. Chapter 19 permits appeal to a binational panel rather than the courts to determine if national laws were followed when an AD or CVD was imposed.

Waverman devotes the final part of his chapter to arguing against the suggestion that Canada should fix its exchange rate to the U.S. dollar, as has been proposed by at least one prominent Canadian economist.

The novel suggestion of Albert Fishlow's chapter is that a major U.S. policy goal should be to obtain a firm commitment of Brazil's adherence to NAFTA and that Brazil, in turn, should not strive toward forging South American solidarity but rather seek early membership in NAFTA. His reasoning is that Brazil is too important for the United States to omit in its free trade efforts; and for Brazil, a commitment to NAFTA could assure the success of Brazilian stabilization efforts.

Procedurally, in the interest of speed, Fishlow proposes a U.S.-Brazilian FTA. He argues that while his type of hub-and-spoke arrangement violates economic principles, the losses to Canada and Mexico would be marginal and would not persist for very long in that the end objective is the full adherence to NAFTA of Brazil and, subsequently, other hemispheric countries. Fishlow proposes that the United States should make this strategy a centerpiece of the hemispheric summit in December.

María Beatriz Nofal examines the progress made to date in MERCOSUR, particularly in trade between Argentina and Brazil, and then speculates about the group's next steps. The original goal of the grouping was to achieve a common market (CM) by January 1, 1995, that is, free trade plus free movement of factors of production (labor and capital). That will not occur, she says. She predicts that, as of that date, an FTA will be achieved or perhaps what she calls an imperfect customs union (CU), by which she means free trade plus a common external tariff (CET) and a common commercial policy. Nofal makes clear that her preference is for an FTA precisely because it does not require a CET and a common commercial policy, which she argues could convert MERCOSUR into a closed trading bloc. She says that an FTA, by contrast, would facilitate the incorporation of both MERCOSUR and NAFTA into hemispheric-wide free trade.

Nofal points out that tariff reductions for trade within MERCOSUR are already extensive and will most likely reach 100 percent by January 1, 1995. She traces the trade outcomes between Argentina and Brazil from the time their economic integration program started in 1986 to the formation of MERCOSUR in 1991, with the addition of Paraguay and Uruguay. From 1986 to 1990, there was a sustained increase in bilateral trade, particularly from Argentina. In 1991, the balance shifted in favor of Brazil, and in addition, there was a decline in Argentina's exports of high value-added products, such as industrial and agroindustrial goods. There was a partial rebalancing in Argentina's favor in 1993.

Equally important, the two countries followed divergent macroeconomic policies; for example, Brazil's inflation was accelerating while that in Argentina was declining. This divergence, Nofal points out, makes it virtually impossible to have a CM and most difficult to have a CU but does permit forming an FTA under which each country retains its independent commercial policy toward nonmembers.

Ippei Yamazawa constructs a detailed matrix showing trade figures within the main regions — East Asia, the EU of 12, and the NAFTA 3 — and also trade between the regions. The share of intraregional trade increased in all three groups between 1980 and 1990 — most strongly among the EU12 and roughly similarly at a lower level for East Asia and the NAFTA 3.

He states that NAFTA was received calmly in Japan but with considerable concern over potential trade diversion elsewhere in East Asia. He reports on surveys of Japanese firms by the Japan External Trade Organization (JETRO) and Japan's Export-Import Bank; both sets of surveys show little change in overseas investment but some heightened interest in the enlarged North American market.

Finally, Yamazawa speculates about techniques to make NAFTA's preferential arrangement consistent with the nonpreferential regionalism of the Asia Pacific Economic Cooperation (APEC), of which all three NAFTA countries are members. This can be done, he says, if NAFTA countries liberalize trade and investment rules on a nonpreferential basis as Mexico has done in its new foreign investment act.

Eckart Guth, of the European Commission, devotes his chapter mainly to developments within Europe, namely, the challenges of the Maastricht Treaty and the enlargement of the EU, including relations with countries in Eastern Europe. In the concluding part of his chapter, he addresses the same new issues raised by Greenwald, namely, trade and competition, trade and the environment, and trade and social issues. He says merely that he does not see unilateral measures as being appropriate in these areas, suggesting rather a cautious multilateral approach. Guth says that the EU supports regional integration agreements in the Americas as long as they are in conformity with GATT provisions.

Some Personal Views

As the countries of the hemisphere look ahead, I see five questions that must be answered:

1. Is hemispheric free trade a meaningful objective?

2. If so, what policies are needed between now and the time this can be achieved?

3. Is the proliferation of subregional and bilateral preferential agreements in the hemisphere a building block or a stumbling block to hemispheric free trade?

4. If there is a conflict between subregional and hemisphere-wide integration, which should take precedence?

5. What are the separate parties — the United States and the other countries of the hemisphere — prepared to do to achieve hemispheric free trade?

There are different answers to these questions in the several chapters. Naím believes that hemispheric free trade requires some loosening of the conditions that exist in NAFTA to facilitate incorporation of most other LAC countries. Lustig and Primo Braga assert that the subregional agreements in the hemisphere will prove to be building blocks to hemispheric free trade. Fishlow argues that the best approach is first to establish a bilateral FTA between Brazil and the United States. Nofal is convinced that MERCOSUR and NAFTA can get together, especially if MERCOSUR chooses the FTA version of integration and not a CU. And Waverman doubts that even NAFTA is durable unless there are improvements in dealing with AD and CVD issues.

In no case, however, is there an explicit argument against the idea of hemispheric free trade. This fact, in light of the great differences among the chapters in other respects, is remarkable. Our authors unanimously favor the objective of hemispheric free trade. I share in this consensus. The authors differ widely, however, on how to reach that goal.

My own policy stress would be on the period between now and the time that free trade could be achieved, whether we get there or not. Chile is prepared to negotiate now for entry into NAFTA. Colombia has indicated that it is not far behind. Argentina has said something similar, but it is not clear whether this is a tactic designed to prod its MERCOSUR partner, Brazil, into taking steps to restructure and stabilize its economy or a true indication of a desire to accede to NAFTA. As Nofal's chapter makes clear, now that MERCOSUR opted for a CU with a common tariff against outsiders, it may be technically impossible for Argentina to enter NAFTA because that move would break the CET for the goods from NAFTA countries when they enter Argentina.

At any rate, beyond these potential entrants over the short term, most other countries in the hemisphere are not prepared to undertake the obligations required by NAFTA. I see little merit in weakening NAFTA discipline on this account. For the United States, exports to NAFTA countries represented almost 80 percent of all its merchandise exports within the hemisphere in 1993. Diluting these ties in favor of the remaining 20 percent makes little economic sense. The primary task, as I see it, is to strengthen NAFTA in all the ways that make deep integration welfare enhancing. These include many of the areas touched on by Waverman, including harmonization or mutual recognition of standards and more efficient customs procedures, plus additional measures such as working out the kinks in the environmental and labor commissions, raising sanitary standards, cleaning up the border between Mexico and the United States, and — of great concern to Waverman — improving the functioning of AD and CVD procedures.

If, without sacrificing NAFTA discipline, interim arrangements are needed for countries not prepared to undertake even the present NAFTA commitments, looser arrangements must be established for non-NAFTA countries. These can range from parity arrangements for key commodities of countries in Central America and the Caribbean to enhanced tariff preferences for Andean countries, with understandings short of free trade but dealing with the new issues of trade in services, investment, and perhaps intellectual property (although this last is controversial in much of the hemisphere).

The exact nature of these interim agreements can vary by country, but there are some principles that should be followed. The interim agreements should be fashioned to be beneficial if they become reasonably permanent. But they should also be constructed so that they do not impede a country's eventual accession to NAFTA. They should not contravene the GATT provisions; thus, for example, a preferential sectoral agreement should not be concluded, nor should a two-way FTA be considered, if it does not include substantially all trade in goods. The concessions given by the United States or by the NAFTA countries generally need not be nonreciprocal, although there can be cross-reciprocity, as in a U.S. or NAFTA tariff preference in exchange for greater protection of intellectual property or greater freedom for direct investment.

If I were the czar of inter-American trade policy, I would give greater stress to subregional integration than to accession to NAFTA. One reason for my taking this position is that most LAC countries are not ready to subscribe to NAFTA's provisions, and there is no reason to jettison the more promising subregional efforts now taking place.

But more meaningful in this context, I agree with Uruguay's president, Luis Alberto Lacalle, who told the *Financial Times* in June 1993 that regional integration is made real by geography.[4] Geography dictates much of the physical infrastructure necessary for deep integration and plays a big role in trade and investment flows. Reliance on trade with the United States diminishes the farther south a country is in South America. Chile is not a member of MERCOSUR, but its investments there are growing precisely because of geography. The U.S. FTAs (other than the one with Israel, which was determined more by politics than economics) are with its two neighbors.

If the Southern Cone countries seek one day to affiliate with NAFTA, their bargaining power would be more substantial if they negotiated as a successful MERCOSUR rather than country by country after a failed integration effort among themselves. Individual Central American countries have little bargaining power with the United States; as a unit, they would have much more.

The most important forcing event of 1994 is the hemispheric summit in December. That is not the place to conclude specific agreements, but it will be an ideal occasion to proclaim some hemispheric principles. I would like at least three principles to be endorsed:

1. Hemispheric free trade is the objective.

2. Within this context, priority should be given to subregional integration agreements.

3. Until such time as hemispheric free trade can be achieved, there should be flexible arrangements to mitigate economic damage to countries not yet ready to take on the obligations of more demanding integration agreements, but only if these arrangements do not prejudice the deepening of existing agreements and do not violate provisions of the GATT.

Machinery may have to be devised to make these principles operational, but for now I would settle for the principles.

Notes

1   World Bank, 1993, *World Development Report 1993* (New York: Oxford University Press for the World Bank), 265.

2   World Bank, 1993, 241.

3   United Nations, ECLAC, 1994, *Open Regionalism in Latin America and the Caribbean*, document LC/G.1801(SES.25/4) (Santiago, Chile: ECLAC).

4   *Financial Times*, 1993, June 7, 21.

Chapter 1

Future Directions of U.S. Global Trade Policy

Joseph A. Greenwald

Introduction

At this stage in the evolution of U.S. international economic policy, which is taking place in a changing global economic system, it is indeed a daunting task to provide an analysis of the future directions of U.S. global trade policy. The conventional summary is that the United States is moving from a policy of multilateralism to a multitrack policy that embodies unilateralism, bilateralism, regionalism, and multilateralism. This chapter will discuss each of these approaches, how they may or may not fit together, and what the impact will be on U.S. interests around the world.

Another shorthand usage that needs some elucidation is the term "trade policy." Over the past fifteen years, this term has grown to cover not only nontariff trade barriers (which are linked primarily to trade in goods) but also trade in services, "trade-related" investment measures, measures to enforce intellectual property rights, and other domestic policies and regulations that result in trade distortions.

The U.S. agenda for future negotiations expands the term "trade policy" to cover the effects of trade on the environment, trade and competition policy, and trade and labor standards. The substantive extension of trade policy for the future will also be discussed in this chapter.

Historical Pillars of Trade Policy

A brief review of post-World War II international trade principles and structure may provide a useful point of departure from which to move into the future directions of U.S. policy.

General Agreement on Tariffs and Trade (GATT)

After the failure of the United States to ratify the comprehensive Havana Charter for an International Trade Organization (ITO),[1] twenty-three countries negotiated GATT,[2] which was based on the commercial policy provisions of Chapter IV of the ITO Charter. The United States adhered to GATT as an executive agreement, using the president's authority granted by Congress to negotiate and implement reciprocal tariff concessions.

GATT thus became the main international trade policy institution. The fundamental GATT principles were unconditional most-favored-nation (MFN) treatment (nondiscrimination), removal of quantitative restrictions, national treatment, and reduction of tariffs through negotiated concessions.

The first six rounds of GATT negotiations were concerned primarily with the reduction of tariff duties. During this same period, economic recovery in Europe and Japan led to the removal of import restrictions applied for balance of payments reasons. The trade liberalization from these developments led to substantial increases in international trade and economic growth. The GATT system worked well and was generally supported in the United States and in most other developed, market-economy countries.

GATT Questioned

Starting in the mid-1970s, a series of developments raised questions about the efficacy and effectiveness of GATT and its principles. First was the expansion of the European Community (EC)[3] from the original six members to nine and then to twelve. This development took place under the GATT exception to the principle of nondiscrimination, which allows the formation of customs unions (CUs) and free trade areas (FTAs).[4] Further broadening and deepening of European integration extended the scope and area of discrimination and raised concerns about a "Fortress Europe" adversely affecting outside countries. The Kennedy Round[5] was directed primarily at reducing this discrimination by lowering the EC common external tariff. In the mid-1980s, these fears were intensified by the launching of a program to establish a single market in Europe with the free flow of goods, investment, services, and people.[6]

The second development raising questions about GATT was increased competition in world markets from a revived Europe and Japan and from low-cost exports of the newly industrialized countries, particularly the four Asian tigers. The perception grew in the United States that it was the only truly open market and the only one that observed GATT rules. In other words, there was not a "level playing field" for U.S. business. This perception led to the increased use of unfair U.S. trade laws (antidumping and countervailing duties) and voluntary export restraints. GATT permits the application of antidumping and countervailing duties in cases of serious injury.[7] But the "voluntary" restraint technique was a way of dealing with increased imports causing serious injury to a domestic industry circumventing the GATT escape clause or safeguard provisions, which allowed temporarily a higher level of protection for the domestic industry being injured. The proliferation of such measures was contrary to the spirit of GATT.

The third development was the structural change in industrialized economies and in the composition of international exchanges. High technology industries, services, and investment grew in importance. For high tech, the most critical subject was the protection of intellectual property rights, which were not effectively dealt with in GATT. Trade in services was not covered at all, and there were few provisions dealing with trade-related investment measures. Thus, GATT was perceived as not addressing the most significant current issues.

Finally, GATT was considered weak in the area of dispute settlement,[8] which had become increasingly crucial. In many cases, the process took an inordinately long time, and losing defending parties could block action.

In the early 1980s, the United States took the initiative in seeking a comprehensive round of negotiations to promote further liberalization, to update GATT, and to strengthen its operations. This effort led to the September 1986 ministerial meeting in Punta del Este to launch the Uruguay Round.[9]

The Uruguay Round

The successful conclusion of the Uruguay Round represents the high-water mark of the multilateral track of U.S. trade policy.[10] The Uruguay Round had a very ambitious agenda, and the outcome may not have satisfied everyone. But it is a major achievement and points the way to some of the continuing directions of U.S. global trade policy.[11]

The fact that the Clinton administration adopted the two major trade initiatives of the previous administrations — the North American Free Trade Agreement (NAFTA), albeit with modifications, and the GATT negotiations — and pushed them through suggests that "liberal" trade policy continues to have bipartisan support. Internationally, the participation of over one hundred countries in the Uruguay Round, plus the desire of other powerful countries like China and Russia to join, indicates that GATT is alive and well.

Agriculture

The negotiations were unduly, and perhaps unnecessarily, protracted at least in part because of a flawed U.S. strategy with respect to agriculture. At the outset, the United States put on the table a proposal that was clearly unacceptable to the other main party involved, the EC.[12] The United States held this position for a number of years without the negotiations really being engaged.

Considering that agriculture had been effectively taken out of GATT forty years ago when the United States obtained a waiver for certain agricultural import restrictions and removed primary products from the prohibition of export subsidies, it was unrealistic to expect anything in the Uruguay Round but a modest start in applying GATT disciplines to agriculture. The introduction of a highly protectionist and trade-distorting Common Agricultural Policy by the EC compounded the problem of bringing agriculture back into GATT. Not surprisingly, the outcome was an agreement that roughly matched what the EC had already decided to do in the context of the reform of its own system and what Congress had done in U.S. legislation. Nevertheless, it is most worthwhile to have agriculture subject to GATT rules.

Until the six-year agreement covering commitments on market access, domestic support, and export subsidies[13] has run out, it is unlikely that either the United States or the EC will be prepared to negotiate again on agriculture. The future direction may be more in the field of sanitary and phytosanitary regulations, a set of issues being pressed by environmental and consumer interests.

In retrospect, it was probably a mistake to give top billing to agriculture. From the overall U.S. point of view, the priorities should have been market access for goods, intellectual property rights, services, investment, and the operation of GATT. An analysis of how these subjects came out will help determine the future directions of U.S. global trade policy.

Market Access for Goods

There was an important breakthrough, with significance for the future, on the market access issue. With the support of interested industries, the United States proposed the elimination of duties in certain sectors by all major suppliers and users in each sector. This proposal was dubbed the zero for zero formula and proved to be surprisingly successful. For the Uruguay Round, it raised the overall level of liberalization achieved. But the longer-term consequence is that it points the way to what should be a key element in the multilateral track of future U.S. global trade policy.

With the decline in import tariff levels to 5 percent or less for many of the industrial sectors among the industrialized and industrializing countries (except, of course, for sensitive sectors like textiles and apparel), it would be a great boon to commerce to set a target for tariff elimination after the Uruguay Round cuts have been phased in early in the twenty-first century. Such a move would also help to avoid a complex set of tariff schedules. The combination of more free trade areas or customs unions and special duty-free treatment under programs like the generalized system of preferences (GSP) — assuming it is extended by the United States — means that tariff duties are becoming less significant as trade protection (and they should not, in any event, be used for revenue purposes, especially in developed countries).

Intellectual Property Rights

The Agreement on Trade-related Aspects of Intellectual Property Rights, including Trade in Counterfeit Goods,[14] met most of the U.S. objectives. It embraces a very high level of substantive norms and effective enforcement provisions. The lead in this case was taken mainly by an industry coalition.

It is likely that the main task for the future will be to monitor the application of the agreement, to bring it up to date where necessary, and to ensure that the same high standards or better ones are included in bilateral or regional arrangements.

Trade in Services

Not so successful was the extension of GATT to include trade in services. This disappointment was due not only to the inherent complexity (national and state intervention) and sensitivity of the services sector but also to a flawed conceptual strategy.

The negotiators decided to start with a framework agreement and then to fill in specific concessions. The obvious model was GATT. The first principle adopted was nondiscrimination, or the MFN principle. However, it apparently was not understood that the MFN principle (GATT Article I) cannot stand alone. It must be coupled with GATT Article II (Schedule of Concessions).

Nondiscrimination can be achieved by keeping everyone out of the market, but this is clearly neither the intent nor the objective of the agreement. Much time in the negotiations was spent on the nonapplication of MFN treatment to various sectors. It should have been explained at the outset that the principle had no meaning without an acceptable schedule of concessions.

Negotiations are in process to improve the concessions offered in the GATS (General Agreement on Trade in Services).[15] These negotiations will probably continue into the future multilateral track of global trade policy. In the meantime, however, the United States has adopted a policy of "conditional" MFN treatment; that is, its new liberalization measures will not be extended to other countries unless they provide reciprocity. This approach carries the risk of getting into the question of what kind of reciprocity is required, a problem that arose in connection with the Second Banking Directive of the EC. In the directive, the EC demanded "mirror" reciprocity, which U.S. laws precluded the United States from offering. The EC accepted the U.S. market as "open" to European banks (since the target was Japan), but this case reveals the problems arising in the reciprocity concept.

Services will undoubtedly continue to be pursued on the multilateral track of future U.S. trade policy, but a question has been raised as to whether the other tracks may not be more profitable.

Investment

Similarly, relatively little progress was made in expanding GATT coverage of investment issues.[16] Bilateral (for example, bilateral investment treaties) or regional (such as NAFTA) tracks may prove to be more effective.

World Trade Organization (WTO) and Dispute Settlement

The final element of the Uruguay Round package that is relevant for the direction of future U.S. global trade policy is the establishment of the World Trade Organization and the strengthening of dispute settlement provisions.[17]

Assuming this element of GATT is passed by Congress, the WTO will represent the first permanent international trade organization joined by the United States. There are two features of the WTO that could affect the direction of U.S. global trade policy. First, the agreement establishing the WTO is designed to deal with the "free rider" problem. Previously in GATT, contracting parties could pick and choose among the ancillary codes, for example, those on standards or dumping negotiated in the Tokyo Round. Under the WTO, membership requires acceptance of all the separate agreements or codes with the exception of four "plurilateral trade agreements," the most important of which is the Government Procurement Code. It remains to be seen how this requirement will affect national decisions on membership in the WTO. Countries that were GATT contracting parties will be able to maintain that status.

The second feature is the continuity provided by the establishment of a permanent organization. This development could make it easier to shift from a system of discrete negotiating rounds to a continuing negotiation. The main argument in favor of the change is the enormous amount of time and effort involved in mounting and carrying to a conclusion the separate rounds — the Uruguay Round being the most recent and horrendous example. On the other hand, experience has indicated that the prospect of a negotiating round or ongoing negotiations has served to contain pressures for protectionist actions; it has been argued in some cases that the problem can be dealt with in the negotiations. Another argument in favor of the old system is that it is necessary to have a fairly large agenda to find the trade-offs necessary to put together a final package acceptable to the negotiating parties. The answer to this question will probably depend on the nature of the subjects ripe for negotiation and the pressures for early action. It may also be possible to have a combination of continuing negotiations on some subjects and plurilateral negotiations on others.

The new dispute settlement system may turn out to be a mixed blessing. Under GATT, one party, including the defendant, can veto a request for a panel or the acceptance of a panel report. In other words, unanimity is not required. The new provisions turn this arrangement on its head and require unanimity to reject a request or a panel report. The new system also has set up strict and enforceable time frames designed to deal with earlier problems arising from the process dragging on for years.

These changes will presumably meet demands for a more certain and speedy adjudication. Moreover, the new system is intended to force the losing party to make prompt redress. To the extent that the United States is the winning party, this new system will please business interests and Congress. Acceptance of panel recommendations against the United States will depend, in part, on the quality of the report and the economic or political clout of the interested party.

To get the EC member states to accept the new dispute settlement process, the EC Commission said that it would restrain the use of Section 301 of the Trade Act of 1974[18] outside the GATT framework. The EC has announced that it will very carefully monitor the U.S. implementing legislation to find out whether any provision will undermine this expectation. The potential differences over the use of Section 301 lead into the following section on the unilateral track.

Unilateralism

Section 301

Section 301, as well as related sections, of the Trade Act of 1974 is the present-day archetype of U.S. unilateralism. Most of the country's trading partners look upon this legislation as the main instrument of U.S. application of power and pressure. Conversely, from the perspective of the U.S. Congress and business community, Section 301 has been a highly effective tool in the effort to open foreign markets and level the playing field.

Neutral observers consider that the previous U.S. administration used Section 301 with a good degree of care and finesse, recognizing that it is like an atom bomb: the game is usually lost when it has to be used. In most cases, GATT procedures were used when they were clear and effective. But even when GATT did not cover the measure (for example, adequate protection of intellectual property rights) and the United States felt it had to impose sanctions, if the affected country was a GATT contracting party, the matter was settled out of court.

Section 301 itself is not contrary to the existing GATT (its status under GATT 1994 is not explicit). Unless the United States changes the law to make it a per se violation of GATT, the problems usually arise when a specific action, such as increasing bound duties in retaliation for "violation of an agreement" or for "an unjustifiable" measure, is taken by the United States. Regardless of the legalities, the political reality is that Section 301 is here to stay, perhaps until the WTO and the world have changed enough to support reliance on international processes. In the meantime, the best hope is that unilateral actions by the United States are carefully crafted to serve the other aspects of future global trade policy.

The danger of less careful application of Section 301 than has been the case in the past is that it could lead to what is generally referred to in the press as a "trade war." This means that the Section 301 process — 1) a finding that an action by another country falls under one of the categories listed in the law; 2) the publication of a list of products as candidates for duty increases; 3) a hearing to obtain public views about the impact of higher duties on items in the list; or 4) a decision to increase duties on specified products when imported from the offending country — results in the violation of the binding U.S. commitment not to increase duties on items in its GATT schedule (practically all U.S. tariff is "bound").

If the country against whose trade Section 301 action is taken is a GATT contracting party, it can seek redress under GATT Article XXIII. If the GATT process goes to a dispute panel and the aggrieved party wins, the recommendation will likely be for the United States to restore the bound duties or to offer other tariff reductions to restore the balance of concessions. If the United States does not take either action, the complaining party would presumably be authorized to withdraw equivalent concessions. This "unraveling" process is the feared outcome of extensive and careless use of Section 301.

Antidumping and Countervailing Duties

Although the application of antidumping and countervailing duties is permitted under GATT Article VI (paragraph 1 states that dumping "is to be condemned" if it causes or threatens material injury), U. S. laws and procedures[19] are sometimes put in the category of unilateralism. The fact is, that while the United States is among the countries with the largest number of cases, other parties including Australia, Canada, and the EC resort as often to such "unfair" trade laws. In the United States, private parties have the right to bring an action, so the government does not control the number of cases. Secondly, the U.S. process is much more open and transparent; public awareness is greater compared with other countries, which deal with such matters behind closed doors. Finally, other countries have other methods of combating "unfair" trade practices.

A more justifiable accusation is that U.S. antidumping and countervailing duty law and practice encourage the filing of cases and make affirmative findings more likely, even in dubious cases. This was one of the factors driving the Canadian interest in a free trade agreement and resulted in the Chapter 19 binational dispute settlement provisions in the U.S.-Canada Free Trade Agreement.[20] U.S. law and practice have also been a long-standing issue in GATT. One of the hotly disputed subjects in the Uruguay Round was the revision of the GATT code. A compromise dealing with some of the complaints that the United States and other main users of antidumping duty laws did not apply their practices consistently with the spirit of GATT Article VI was struck.

The antidumping problem will probably not be solved until trade barriers are completely removed and it becomes possible to "dump back." Only at that point will it be feasible to substitute competition policy measures for border trade measures, as is the case within the single markets of the United States and the EC.

Bilateralism/Regionalism

The mid-1980s also saw a move into bilateralism with the negotiation of a free trade agreement with Israel. But this agreement was taken as more of a political measure than a trade policy departure.

The real bilateral/regional track began with the U.S.- Canada FTA in 1989 and gathered steam with the successful negotiation of NAFTA. By GATT standards established in the European Economic Community (EEC) and European Free Trade Association (EFTA) cases, the U.S. agreements are clearly GATT-consistent.[21]

More important from the point of view of fitting in with U.S. interests in an open trading system, these agreements did not raise barriers against outside countries. Further, except for some overly restrictive rules of origin, they did not establish any trade policy precedents that could undermine U.S. longer-term objectives on the multilateral track.

More serious problems may arise when the United States faces the question of extending NAFTA to other countries in the Western Hemisphere or beyond. The conventional wisdom (reflected as recently as an article in *The New York Times* on February 4, 1994) is that the first candidate for accession to NAFTA will be Chile, which already has made requests and which is generally considered economically and politically qualified to assume NAFTA membership.

Beyond Chile, there are questions about countries that are not yet in a position to take on full NAFTA obligations, countries that are in economic groups with free trade area or customs union pretensions and even countries outside the region. The U.S. administration is obviously aware of these problems and is taking a cautious approach.

Looking at the problems in terms of not prejudicing U.S. global interests, there are a few points to consider. First, any arrangements should be consistent with GATT, the main multilateral track for the United States. Second, agreements requiring less than full NAFTA accession should be worked out very carefully.

These cautions apply not only to the obligations undertaken by the other countries in the hemisphere but also to the benefits offered from the U.S. or NAFTA side. Less than fully GATTable agreements will become unfortunate precedents. To avoid this development, obligations and benefits should be sought outside trade measures as defined in GATT Article XXIV. That is, sectoral or partial trade agreements should not be offered. If interim agreements before full accession are deemed necessary, they should be in the form of framework agreements that deal with matters like intellectual property rights or the right of establishment, which were not traditionally part of trade agreements until NAFTA.

Another possibility for interim action as a step toward bringing other hemispheric countries into NAFTA would be to add a dispute settlement system along the lines of NAFTA (including the supplementary agreements on labor and the environment) to the framework agreements. These framework agreements have consultation provisions, and the United States would presumably be urging potential NAFTA candidates to make unilateral reforms as Mexico did. But these countries may be seeking something more from the NAFTA parties to make the reforms more palatable at home. The offer of binational dispute settlement might help politically to show the interest and good faith of the NAFTA countries and to further the process of getting candidates used to NAFTA disciplines.

In addition to the narrow trade policy issues, another pitfall to be avoided is accepting lower standards in fields like services, investment, and agriculture to prevent a watering down of what was achieved in NAFTA. One of the beauties of NAFTA is that it can be held up as a standard for agreements between developed and developing countries. It would be unfortunate to lose this advantage.

Future Agenda for U.S. Global Trade Policy

Beyond NAFTA and the Uruguay Round, what are the substantive issues to be taken up? There is general agreement, and President Clinton endorsed it in Brussels early in January 1994, that the top items for future negotiations, probably on both the multilateral and the bilateral/regional tracks, are trade and the environment, trade and competition policy, trade and labor standards, and investment.

Trade and the environment have been on the agenda for some time, particularly after the GATT panel report in the tuna/dolphin case.[22] Discussions at the governmental level have been under way in the Organization for Economic Cooperation and Development (OECD) and in GATT. An informal exercise between the business sector and government officials indicated that there would be no problem on the U.S. side in carrying over the environmental provisions from NAFTA into GATT. But it is doubtful whether the environmental community will now be satisfied with that plan, particularly in the areas of transparency and non-governmental organization (NGO) participation.

Trade and competition appeared on the agenda more recently. The issue has been discussed at the OECD in Paris, but the cross-education process is still in the early stages. The range of possibilities goes from the multilateralization of the EC-U.S. bilateral agreement on enforcement cooperation, through the idea of international antitrust codes (of various kinds), to the notion of using competition policy tools instead of (or with) trade measures to deal with unfair trade practices.

Trade and labor standards have been taken up in GATT for more than forty years without any solutions having been found. The new NAFTA Supplemental Agreement is a possible model.

In any event, political pressures will drive this agenda item, which has little hope of success. With regard to both environment and labor standards, the developing countries are suspicious of hidden protectionism, so progress on these issues may be more likely on the bilateral/regional track.

Investment was dealt with effectively in NAFTA as far as developing countries are concerned. But new issues such as participation in governmental research projects and other aspects of industrial policy are arising among the OECD countries. The question of piercing the corporate veil to look at ownership is likely to become a more important issue.

Conclusion

U.S. interests will be best served by maintaining the open, multilateral trading system as now embodied in GATT 1994. This policy will provide the stability of bound concessions and a set of rules under which trade and investment can flourish. In a world characterized by the internationalization of production, services, and investment, sustainable economic growth can be achieved most effectively by the free flow of goods, services, and capital.

As suggested earlier, unilateral measures should be used with care. Bilateral and regional policies should be applied in such a way as to minimize damage to the global system. Above all, this means not raising barriers against countries or groups outside the regional or bilateral arrangement — in general, following GATT 1994 rules. In GATT areas where the rules and commitments are not fully developed, like services and investment, outside countries should have the opportunity to obtain most-favored-nation or national treatment on reasonable terms.

An important step that should be taken after 1996 is to propose to the major trading countries that duties on all industrial products (with some sensitive exceptions, if necessary) be phased out among the developed countries. This step would not only lift a burden from traders but would also remove a source of friction and complication arising from the likely proliferation of bilateral and regional arrangements as well as existing preferences like the GSP and the Caribbean systems.

Since most countries in the Western Hemisphere have joined GATT and adopted outward-looking market policies, these conclusions should be understood and generally acceptable. The degree of acceptability will probably vary with the degree to which the countries have progressed toward implementing derestriction and open market policies. Most difficulties will probably arise in connection with subregional groupings that are not truly into free trade and able to negotiate as a unit. These are the cases where long transition periods may be necessary and where great care must be taken to ensure that the basic global policy is not undermined.

Notes

1   U.S. Department of State Publication 3206, Commercial Policy Series 114, released September 1948.

2   GATT/1986-4, 1986, (Geneva).

3   *Treaties Establishing the European Communities,* Abridged Edition, 1987 (Luxembourg: Office for Official Publications of the European Communities L-2985).

4   GATT Article XXIV.

5   John W. Evans, 1971, *The Kennedy Round in American Trade Policy* (Cambridge, Mass.: Harvard University Press).

6   *Treaties...* The Single European Act, 523-577.

7   GATT Article VI.

8   GATT Articles XXII and XXIII.

9   For the text of the ministerial resolution, see Annex A of Atlantic Council Policy Paper, "The Uruguay Round of Multilateral Trade Negotiations under GATT," 1987, (Washington, D.C.: Atlantic Council of the United States), November.

10   Testimony of Ambassador Michael Kantor, United States Trade Representative, before the House Ways and Means Committee, January 26, 1994, and the Senate Finance Committee, February 8, 1994.

11   Final Act Embodying the Results of the Uruguay Round of Multilateral Trade Negotiations (Version of December 15, 1993) (Washington, D.C.: Office of the U. S. Trade Representative, Executive Office of the President).

12   "The Uruguay Round...," 45-60.

13   Final Act, II Annex 1A3.

14   Final Act, II Annex IC.

15   Final Act, Annex 1B.

16   Final Act, II Annex 1A7.

17   Final Act, II and II Annex 2.

18   Public Law 93-618, approved January 3, 1975, 19 USC 2411.

19   U.S. Congress, Title VII of the Tariff Act of 1930 as added by the Trade Agreements Act of 1979 and amended by the Trade and Tariff Act of 1984 and the Omnibus Trade and Competitiveness Act of 1988, 1671 and 1673.

20   U.S. Congress, 1988, Communication from the president of the United States transmitting the final legal text, July 26, 100th Cong. 2nd sess. H. Doc. 100-216.

21   GATT Article XXIV.

22   U.S. Restrictions on Imports of Tuna, 1991, Report of the Panel (GATT: Geneva) September.

References

Evans, John W. 1971. *The Kennedy Round in American Trade Policy*. Cambridge, Mass.: Harvard University Press.

Final Act Embodying the Results of the Uruguay Round of Multilateral Trade Negotiations (Version of December 15, 1993). Washington, D.C.: Office of the U.S. Trade Representative, Executive Office of the President.

"Ministerial Resolution." 1987. *Atlantic Council Policy Paper: The Uruguay Round of Multilateral Trade Negotiations under GATT*. Washington, D.C.: Atlantic Council of the United States. Annex A. November.

Treaties Establishing the European Communities. Abridged Edition, 1987. Luxembourg: Office for Official Publications of the European Communities.

Chapter 2

The Future of Trade Policy in Latin America

Nora Lustig and C.A. Primo Braga

In the 1990s, trade policy in Latin America has so far been characterized by the following main tendencies: 1) the continuity of unilateral trade liberalization efforts (most of which were initiated in the 1980s); 2) an increased commitment to multilateral disciplines; 3) the emergence of new subregional trading arrangements and the revival of old ones; and 4) the willingness to negotiate preferential trading arrangements with the United States on a reciprocal basis. Of these four, the most significant one is the first because it is at the core of the change in the development strategy of the countries in the region. This new commitment to open trade regimes has shaped a more positive attitude toward the multilateral trading system (built around the General Agreement on Tariffs and Trade — GATT) and has fostered a new form of regionalism that is supposed to lock in liberal trade policies rather than reproduce protectionist practices on a larger territory.

This chapter will briefly review the results of recent unilateral liberalization in Latin America and pose the question of whether openness is currently

Presented at the conference "Future of Western Hemisphere Economic Integration," sponsored by the Center for Strategic and International Studies and the Inter-American Dialogue, Washington, D.C., March 2-4, 1994. Nora Lustig is a senior fellow at the Brookings Institution. C.A. Primo Braga is an economist with the International Trade Division of the World Bank. The authors are grateful to Sebastian Edwards, Antonio Martín-del-Campo, Rosalinda Quintanilla, Sylvia Saborio, and Jose Tavares for very useful conversations. All the usual disclaimers apply. The authors also want to thank staff members of the United Nations Economic Commission for Latin America and the Caribbean, the Inter-American Development Bank, the Mexican Secretaría de Comercio y Fomento Industrial, and the Latin America and Caribbean region at the World Bank for providing information. Gary Gordon provided excellent assistance. The findings, interpretations, and conclusions of this chapter are the authors' own and should not be attributed to the institutions with which they are associated.

at risk. Then, it will look into current regional integration initiatives and identify the predominant tendencies in them.

Trade Liberalization Is "In"

Although some countries, such as Argentina, Chile, and Uruguay, had liberalized their trade regimes in the second half of the 1970s, trade barriers were raised again (if not for long in Chile) with the onset of the debt crisis in 1982. Since the mid-1980s, however, outward-oriented reform has become pervasive in the region. These reforms have involved lowering tariffs, reducing or eliminating nontariff barriers (NTBs) to imports,[1] phasing out price and quantitative barriers to exports, and implementing or improving measures for export promotion.[2]

In country after country, nominal protection as measured by the average tariff has been reduced (Table 1). The tariff range and the number of tariff rates have also fallen, implying a smaller variance in protection among sectors. In addition, quantitative restrictions have been eliminated, by and large. Finally, most countries have confirmed their commitment to the multilateral system either by actively participating in the Uruguay Round of Multilateral Trade Negotiations (MTN) (as illustrated by Argentina, Brazil, Chile, and Mexico) or by acceding to the GATT and signing a number of GATT codes over the last eight years.[3]

Of course, not all the countries liberalized their trade regime at the same time, but by the early 1990s, practically all of them had made substantial progress in opening their economies. It is hard to establish a clear ranking of the countries according to the degree of "openness" or "liberalization." As Sebastian Edwards points out, there is no clear consensus on how to define a country's trade orientation or degree of liberalization.[4] It seems, however, that using the criteria suggested by Anne O. Krueger, most of the countries included in Table 1 could be characterized as "fully liberalized."[5] It is worth noting that trade liberalization and economic recovery have translated into a sharp rise in trade volume as a share of gross domestic product (GDP) in most countries of the region. For the region as a whole, the ratio rose by 24 percent between 1985 and 1992 (Table 2).

Despite the clear shift toward more open trade regimes in Latin America, there should be a few words of caution. First, in some countries, although the maximum tariff range is formally low, there are significant exceptions, especially in agriculture.[6] Second, although in most countries the tariff structure is substantially narrower than before, it still generates high levels of *effective* protection in certain cases. Jose Tavares estimates that in Ecuador, effective protection granted to the auto assembly industry is close to 247 percent.[7] Tariff escalation, therefore, remains a problem in some countries.

Third, despite the fact that in most countries the remaining quantitative restrictions are linked to health and public safety factors, there are forms of "sneaky protectionism" disguised as bureaucratic requirements. Also, there remain some significant cases of protected sectors. For example, the automobile sector in Mexico is still protected from competition by a series of rules involving local content and balance of payments requirements. Quantitative restrictions represent a coverage of 70.6 percent, weighted by output, in the automobile sector.[8] As of June 1993, the average coverage of these restrictions was 16.5 percent of the total output of the economy. These barriers will be phased out under the North American Free Trade Agreement (NAFTA) for imports from Canada and the United States. In the case of Brazil, despite the almost complete elimination of quantitative restrictions in the 1990-1992 period, high tariff protection still prevails in certain sectors. Motor vehicle imports, for example, faced an average nominal tariff of 34.2 percent at the end of the tariff liberalization program (July 1993).[9]

Fourth, there are some indications that neo-protectionist practices are on the rise, particularly in the form of abusing antidumping (AD) procedures. Latin American countries have become more sophisticated players in the international arena and are emulating the United States. This form of protectionism has the disadvantage of introducing significant uncertainty in trade relations. Moreover, some authors have estimated that the tariff equivalence of AD actions can be rather high.[10]

Finally, the subregional integration initiatives tend to have complex rules of origin (for example, the treatment of textiles and automobiles in NAFTA). Given their complexity, these rules conspire against the transparency of the trade regimes in the region, particularly, as countries become participants in overlapping arrangements. Moreover, they can be used to export protection within the preferential arrangement as discussed below.

Is Trade Liberalization at Risk?

The answer to this question requires first that the term "at risk" be defined. Does it mean a reversion to all-encompassing protectionist practices of the import substitution industrialization era? Does it mean a slowing down of the reforms in the trade regime? Does it mean the occasional use of higher tariffs and NTBs (including the use of AD practices) to stop the free flow of goods? Let's start by asking the question of whether a reversion to across-the-board protectionism is likely.

Concerns about the sustainability of trade reform are not unjustified. In the past, several countries that had engaged in trade liberalization programs had a relapse: Argentina, Brazil, Colombia, Chile, and Uruguay are some notable examples.[11] It can be argued that the main threat to the outward-oriented strategy in Latin America comes from left and center-left opposition groups. Trade liberalization is often perceived by these groups as a major cause of labor displacement and also as contributing to a loss of national sovereignty. Despite the fact that most economists insist, and most economic research shows, that trade liberalization is likely to be beneficial both from the efficiency and from the equity points of view, it is not clear that this view is shared by the electorates of the region.

Another factor that might encourage a reversion to protectionism is adjustment fatigue. The principal symptom of adjustment fatigue is a growing impatience with market-oriented reforms. Evidence of this phenomenon can be observed in countries where political hurdles make market-oriented reforms difficult to implement (as in Brazil) or where economic recovery is slow or is slow to reach the majority of the population (as in Venezuela). Such cases provide fertile ground for political groups who favor a return to the use of trade policy to promote specific economic sectors.

Nonetheless, it is apparent that the likelihood of major recidivism is smaller at present than in past liberalization episodes. The success stories of outward-oriented economies — the East Asian newly industrializing econo-mies in particular, but also Chile, an example closer to the region — have had an important demonstration effect. Furthermore, the debt crisis fostered a rising consensus against the previous inward-looking development model.[12]

In addition, today there are a number of factors that can counter or limit the influence of these protectionist tendencies. The following are worth mentioning: first, the existence of a growing domestic constituency that benefits from openness; second, the commitments made by individual countries in the context of the Uruguay Round; third, the commitments made with multilateral financial institutions (the World Bank, in particular) to implement trade liberalization programs; fourth, the commitments made to other trading partners as a part of the regional integration initiatives; and fifth, both the threat of retaliatory actions and the incentive provided by the prospect of negotiating a free trade agreement with a major trading partner such as the United States.

It would seem that the political clout and influence of the pro-openness constituency is in itself a function of the length of time in which an open economy strategy has been in place. During the early stages of trade liberalization, it is probably hard to find great public support for the new policies because of the dislocation costs they are perceived to bring. Perhaps it is no coincidence that in the past many trade liberalization efforts in Latin America were launched by authoritarian regimes: in Brazil in 1967, in Uruguay in 1974, in Chile in 1975, and in Argentina in 1977. Even if the actual dislocation costs are estimated to be small, the mere possibility of such costs tends to cause animosity toward the change in policy regime. The NAFTA debate in the United States was a good example of this.

If public support for openness is a function of time, then a reversal is less likely in countries like Bolivia, Chile, and Mexico, which were early reformers, than in Ecuador, which is a very recent reformer. However, the length of time that a reform has been in place is not the only relevant variable in this process. The probability of a policy reversal may also be linked to economic performance. Thus, in countries like Argentina, even if trade reform has been introduced more recently than in other countries, the impressive record in terms of inflation and growth may have galvanized the support of the population for the new policy regime.

Many countries in the region have borrowed from the World Bank to carry out structural adjustment programs. These loans commit the government of the borrowing country to follow a particular liberalization schedule lest the loan disbursements be suspended. World Bank conditionality can operate as an external source of pressure to keep the liberalization process on track even when domestic pressure goes in the other direction. Needless to say, this leverage is diminished once the loan is fully disbursed.

Perhaps of a more lasting effect are the commitments made by countries under the Uruguay Round of multilateral negotiations and to partners in regional integration initiatives. In the Uruguay Round negotiations, many of the countries in the region have committed themselves to maximum tariff rates that are well below their pre-reform maximums (Table 1). For example, Brazil offered to bind its entire tariff schedule for industrial products at 35 percent, whereas before the trade reform, the maximum bound tariff was 185 percent (and tariff bindings covered only 6 percent of its tariff schedule). Uruguay and Argentina also made offers to bind their entire tariff schedules (including agricultural products) at a ceiling of 35 percent. In acceding to the GATT, Bolivia bound its entire tariff schedule to a maximum *ad valorem* rate of 40 percent (a 30 percent ceiling applies for a few items) compared with nominal peaks of 100 percent before trade reform. Mexico, in turn, bound its maximum tariff at 50 percent in 1986, compared with the 100 percent maximum tariff that existed before.[13] It is worth noting that the maximum import duties prevailing in all these countries are substantially lower than the bound rates mentioned above (see Table 1). The expansion of binding commitments at the GATT level, however, provides a growing disincentive to a return to prohibitive tariff barriers in Latin America.

In addition, the commitments to phase out trade barriers within subregional trading arrangements, as well as the increasing overlap of such arrangements, can act as effective external constraints on domestic trade policy. This factor is particularly relevant for countries that have a clear regional orientation with respect to trade as exemplified by Mexico in the context of NAFTA and by Paraguay in the context of Mercado Común del Sur (MERCOSUR).

The stance adopted by the United States vis-à-vis its trading partners may also act as an effective restriction and as an incentive. On the one hand, the U.S. government is firmly committed to open external markets and is likely to use retaliatory measures (or the withdrawal of preferences) if countries go back to practices that conflict with U.S. interests. It is worth noting that practices perceived as unfair by the United States include not only conventional market access restrictions (that is, protectionist policies) but also domestic policies that are considered to discriminate against U.S. firms (for instance, weak intellectual property protection). Furthermore, in order to be considered as a candidate to join NAFTA or to sign a free trade agreement with the United States, a country must first have a liberal trade regime. For some countries in the region, the possibility of signing a free trade agreement with the United States has acted as an additional incentive to liberalize trade.

Even if a reversion to trade protectionism out of conviction is not likely, a relapse still may occur out of necessity. In the past, trade liberalization episodes were often aborted in the context of balance of payments crises. These crises were usually the result of a combination of macroeconomic excesses and external shocks. At present, most countries of the region are following prudent fiscal and monetary policies, and, therefore, it is hard to envisage a rerun of the debt crisis of the early 1980s.

Nevertheless, in recent years, Latin America has been the recipient of large capital inflows with a resulting appreciation of real exchange rates and a worsening of current accounts. Some authors and observers of the region are concerned about the countries' vulnerability to a sudden shift in investor preferences, a possibility that cannot be ruled out.[14] Portfolio equity finance is playing an important role in private capital flows to Latin America, and the volatility of these flows is a matter of concern. If a balance of payments crisis were to occur, there might be a temptation to reinstate some form of import and exchange controls instead of allowing equilibrium to be restored by adjustments in the exchange rate. This concern is particularly relevant to countries that have used the exchange rate as a nominal anchor for their stabilization program (such as Argentina) or are committed to a pre-announced crawl (such as Mexico).

However, there are reasons to believe that resorting to a widespread use of controls in the face of a balance of payments crisis is less likely today than in the past. First, several Latin American countries now practice a flexible exchange rate policy. Second, the fact that some countries have sustained a liberalization program for some time leads one to believe that restoring equilibrium with adjustments in the exchange rate would be less painful than in the past, when imports and exports were less responsive to changes in relative prices precisely because the countries followed an inward-looking development strategy.[15] Third, external commitments (as in the case of Mexico under NAFTA) limit the scope for protectionist practices.

All in all, it is safe to say that trade liberalization and the commitment to an outward-oriented strategy in Latin America are here to stay. The greatest risk to openness in the countries of the region, leaving aside the possibility of a balance of payments crisis, comes from the ad hoc use of targeted trade-restricting measures: for example, an abuse of antidumping and countervailing duty (CVD) actions, the application of discretionary import surcharges, or the setting up of unnecessary bureaucratic requirements. Table 3 shows that Brazil (AD and CVD investigations), Chile (CVD investigations), and Mexico (AD investigations) are already active in these practices. Moreover, AD legislation has been introduced recently or reactivated in Argentina, Bolivia, Chile, Colombia, Jamaica, Peru, Trinidad and Tobago, and Venezuela. Accordingly, even though neither the number of actions initiated nor the level of trade affected so far seems to be significant, this trend illustrates the potential for new forms of protectionism in Latin America.

To sum up, a dramatic reversal in trade policy strategy in Latin America seems unlikely. However, administered protection in the context of unfair trade practices may become a problem. Moreover, policy-driven regionalism may introduce new forms of discrimination against outsiders, such as overly restrictive rules of origin included in free trade agreements (FTAs) (for example, the case of textiles in NAFTA). It is conceivable that these arrangements could lead to free trade *within* participant countries but raise barriers for the nonparticipant countries or blocs. This question will be taken up in the next section.

Regional Integration in Latin America

Since 1990, throughout Latin America and the Caribbean (LAC), a number of new regional integration initiatives have been advanced, and a number of old ones have been revived (Table 4).[16] The following factors are often mentioned as contributing to the so-called new regionalism: the demonstration effect of unilateral liberalization, which called attention to the potential benefits of freer trade with existing partners;[17] problems with the multilateral trading system, as reflected by the difficulties in completing the Uruguay Round; the announcement of the Enterprise for the Americas Initiative (EAI) in June 1990; and Mexico's negotiation of an FTA with the United States (which became NAFTA when Canada joined the negotiations).

The specter of a possible failure of the Uruguay Round, plus the consolidation of large regional blocs (for instance, the European Union — EU — and NAFTA), fostered defensive strategies in Latin America. The conclusion of the Uruguay Round diminished the incentive for the creation of defensive arrangements in the region. Yet the market power of the large trading blocs and continued doubts about the capacity of the multilateral system in disciplining these actors will keep interest in regionalism alive. The lure of accession to NAFTA, for example, has created a constituency for regionalism among export interests in Latin American countries. It is also worth noting that the EAI acted as an additional incentive for regional arrangements because it was perceived that the United States would prefer to negotiate with fewer parties and that countries together could bargain more effectively with the United States as a group.[18] These considerations played a role in putting the Andean Common Market (ANCOM) and the Central American Common Market (Mercado Común Centroamericano — CACM) back on their feet and in launching MERCOSUR. Moreover, Mexico became an attractive partner for free trade negotiations (as illustrated by the agreements with Chile and Costa Rica and the negotiations with Colombia and Venezuela) to the extent that these agreements are perceived to enhance a country's chance of accession to NAFTA.

Is Latin America Moving in the Direction of Closed Trading Blocs?

The literature on regional integration arrangements emphasizes the danger posed by such arrangements because there are good reasons to believe that they may become effective impediments to global free trade, not to mention their second-best nature.[19] On the other hand, some authors have emphasized that the types of initiatives now observed in the Americas should be viewed as building blocks rather than stumbling blocks to freer global trade.[20] The consensus is that for regional initiatives to be compatible with global free trade, the regional blocs have to be *open*. For a bloc to be defined as open, at least two conditions have to be met: first, trade and investment barriers to nonmembers must not be raised; and second, new members who are prepared to abide by the same rules as the existing members should be easily accepted.[21]

The majority of the countries in the LAC region currently belong to one of four regional integration arrangements that group together neighboring countries and whose stated objective is to develop a common market: ANCOM, the Caribbean Community and Common Market (CARICOM), the CACM, and MERCOSUR. Mexico and Chile have followed a different path. Mexico decided to institutionalize its economic integration with its neighbors to the north and signed NAFTA. Chile would like to follow suit and, in the meantime, is signing bilateral free trade agreements with countries having a common objective in terms of trade policy principles (such as Colombia, Mexico, and Venezuela) but which are not its neighbors.

An interesting phenomenon is that the initiation and revitalization of regional trading arrangements have been accompanied by two processes that on the surface may seem either 1) redundant, such as the free trade agreements signed among a subgroup of the members of a larger trading arrangement, or 2) contradictory to the ultimate objectives of the original trading arrangement, such as free trade agreements signed by an individual or a subgroup of countries with a nonmember.[22] Among the examples of the first category are the free trade agreements signed by Colombia and Venezuela and by El Salvador, Guatemala, and Honduras. Instances of the latter type are the bilateral free trade agreements signed by Colombia and Venezuela with Chile, the future FTA between Costa Rica and Mexico, and the so-called Group of Three (Colombia, Mexico, and Venezuela).

Regardless of initial appearances, these agreements may be neither redundant nor contradictory. In practice, they have acted as sticks to goad more reluctant trading partners in the original regional bloc to proceed more rapidly with the establishment of free trade *within* the original arrangement. This has clearly been the case in ANCOM with respect to Ecuador, for example.[23] Costa Rica's impatience with the inability of other members of the CACM to implement agreed policies drove it to seek a bilateral free trade agreement with Mexico. Thus, the breakaways have not led to breakups of the original trading arrangement but, on the contrary, have acted as a fillip to lagging partners. Somewhat paradoxically, then, the proliferation of FTAs is speeding up liberalization both *within* the regional arrangements and *between* subgroups of the arrangements and nonmembers. However, this process of overlapping FTAs is far from ideal because it creates a morass of nonuniform, parallel bureaucratic procedures for enforcing commitments.

In principle, none of the regional integration arrangements is raising its barriers to nonmembers, and, thus, they fulfill one of the conditions for definition as open blocs. Nevertheless, there are some caveats to this proposition. First, in the determination of the common external tariff in the case of a customs union, the selected tariff for a product may be higher than that maintained by the member with the lowest tariff; second, protectionist elements may be introduced in the setting of rules of origin in the free trade areas.

The difficulties involved in determining the common external tariff in the cases of ANCOM, the CACM, and MERCOSUR point to the fact that convergence to the lowest tariff level is not always easy.[24] It is worth noting that the "Understanding of the Interpretation of Article XXIV" negotiated in the Uruguay Round helped to clarify GATT disciplines with respect to regional arrangements.[25] It provides guidelines for evaluating the general incidence of duties and charges before and after the creation of a customs union, based on the comparison of weighted average tariff rates and customs duties. Hence, from a "legal" perspective, a customs union could be characterized as an open trading bloc (GATT-compatible) as long as the weighted average trade barrier against outsiders does not increase with the formation of the customs union — even though increases may occur at the level of specific tariff lines. The new regionalism in Latin America complies in broad terms with this standard (particularly because of the impact of parallel unilateral liberalization efforts in the countries of the region). It may be preferable to pay the price of a "local" violation (at the tariff line level) of the first principle of open regionalism if the end result (a customs union) minimizes the need for complex and nontransparent rules of origin.

Rules of origin are the instrument used to determine which goods and services in a free trade area or in a customs union are entitled to preferential treatment. In customs unions, given the existence of a common external barrier, rules of origin are equivalent to domestic content requirements, being also used to determine quota eligibility when quantitative restrictions apply. In FTAs, however, the main role of rules of origin is to impede trade deflection schemes by which outsiders would use the partner in the FTA with the lowest trade barriers to transship their products to the more protected markets in the FTA. The rules of origin can, however, be used for export protection. In practice, this means that one FTA partner can effectively impose its higher external tariff on another partner, which has lower restrictions on an input used to manufacture a product qualifying for duty-free treatment within the FTA.[26] There is no evidence of the generalized use of rules of origin as a protectionist device in Latin America. The results of NAFTA (in industries like textiles and clothing and autos), however, illustrate the dangers involved. Moreover, the proliferation of regional arrangements and the consequent overlap of rules of origin tend to conspire against the transparency of the trade regimes in the region.

Concerning the second condition, it is not clear how open the various regional trading arrangements are toward nonmembers that want to join. Arrangements that have ambitious objectives (for example, those that want to create a common market or those with broad, deep integration objectives) are likely to foster greater cohesion among members at the cost of increasing the "entry fee" for nonmembers. The relative closeness may result in a degree of exclusivity as the natural outcome of the fact that countries that join must be willing to accept a much wider set of rules than those required in conventional free trade agreements. Nonetheless, even in the case of free trade agreements, "widening" (that is, the accession of new members to the existing arrangement) has not been a smooth process. For example, why hasn't the Group of Three been organized as a Group of Four, including Chile as part of the arrangement? After all, the four countries already have free trade agreements among them. What are the factors that preclude this outcome? The answer must be that there exist forces that oppose such a move in any or all of the countries. A better understanding of what these forces are is important in determining whether or not the series of free trade agreements that have been negotiated are indeed building blocks of hemispheric free trade. For the moment, this question remains unanswered.

The future of regional integration crucially depends on the position of the United States. Is the United States going to follow suit with its earlier promises (in the context of the EAI) and promote a free trade area in the hemisphere? Is it going to do it by extending NAFTA or through bilateral agreements? Does NAFTA qualify as an open trading bloc? The answers to these questions are not clear. NAFTA's accession clause leaves everything to the decision of each of the members' legislatures. Given the intensity of the opposition to NAFTA's approval, the prospects for a rapid widening of NAFTA do not seem very encouraging. Moreover, since the rules of eligibility for membership have not been clearly established, the entry fees can be raised arbitrarily and can, in fact, make entry impossibly expensive for even the most eager party. Protection of intellectual property rights above and beyond what has been agreed at the multilateral level in the context of the trade-related intellectual property rights (or TRIPs) agreement, for example, has become a condition for negotiations with the United States.[27] Until the U.S. government defines its position and strategy, the process of hemispheric integration will continue to be haphazard, and the potential for conflicting trends significant.

The discussion above illustrates the point that if the goal is to promote free trade in the hemisphere, the agenda has been left unfinished. As has been pointed out by several authors, one way to ensure that the regional integration arrangements do not become closed blocs is through support for a multilateral agency with monitoring powers.[28] It is unlikely that the existing candidate, the GATT (or the future World Trade Organization — WTO), will be able to monitor the process closely enough to avoid frictions among blocs and nonmembers. The Dispute Settlement Understanding of the Uruguay Round will improve the GATT's institutional capacity to discipline "GATT-illegal" behavior. Yet given the problems of punishing noncooperative behavior in a timely fashion at the multilateral level, the road to an open trading bloc encompassing the whole hemisphere will depend significantly on the future trade strategy of the United States.

To sum up, it is clear that the new outward orientation of Latin American economies is here to stay. In the years ahead, however, further trade liberalization is more likely to happen in the context of regional initiatives than as a result of unilateral reforms. This trend toward regionalism (and discrimi-nation) raises several challenges for policymakers in the region — in particular, the need to avoid the possibility of these blocs becoming inward-oriented.

Perhaps the region could use an agency dedicated to monitoring regional trading arrangements and to documenting cases of trade and investment diversion. This agency could eventually operate as a mini-GATT at the regional level, promoting convergence among the different tracks of regional preferential liberalization and paving the way for hemispheric free trade.[29] The setup of such an agency could be a topic for discussion in the upcoming hemispheric summit to be hosted by the United States.

Table 1. Tariffs and Liberalizing Reforms in Latin America and the Caribbean

COUNTRY (Pre-reform year, post-reform year)*	Average Unweighted Legal Tariff Rates (%)		Tariff Range (%)		Coverage of QRs on Imports (% of tariff, unless otherwise noted)	
	Pre-Reform	Post-Reform (2)	Pre-Reform	Post-Reform (2)	Pre-Reform	Post-Reform
Argentina (1987, 1991)	42(p)	10	15-115(p)	0-22	(of dom. prod.) 62	8
Belize 1992	NA	NA		5-45	NA	NA
Bolivia (1985, 1994)	35	7.5	0-100	5-10	NA	minimal
Brazil (1987, 1993)	51	14.2	0-105	0-35	39	10
Chile (1984, 1992)	35	11	35	11	minimal	0
Colombia (1984, 1993)	61	12	0-220	5-20	99	1.4
Costa Rica (1985, 1992)	53(p)	15(p)	0-1400(p)	5-20	NA	0
Dominican Republic (1990, 1994)	NA	NA		3-35		significant
Ecuador (1989, 1994)	53	9.3	0-290	5-37	100	0
El Salvador 1992	NA	NA		?-30		minimal
Guatemala (1985, 1993)	50(p)	15(p)	5-90	5-20	(of dom. prod.) 6	0(1)
Honduras (1985, 1992)	41(p)	15(w,p)	5-90	5-20	NA	0
Jamaica (1981, 1993)	NA	20	NA	5-30	NA	0(1)
Mexico (1985, 1994)	22.6	12.5(w)	0-100	0-20	28	1.6
Nicaragua 1992	NA	NA		0-20		NA
Panama 1991	88.2	59.8		0-90		NA
Paraguay (1988, 1991)	NA	16	NA	0-20(y)	NA	significant
Peru (1990, 1994)	66	16	0-120	15-25	100	0 (1)
Uruguay (1987, 1993)	32	18(y)	10-55	6-20	0	0
Venezuela (1989, 1992)	37	10(m)	0-135	0-20	40	10

* where applicable. (p): Including tariff surcharges. (w): production-weighted average tariff (m): import-weighted average tariff (y): for 1992

1/ Some QRs exist for health and safety reasons.

2/ In practice, several countries have higher actual tariffs than those which appear in the table. These are tariffs that have been applied to some specific goods and/or temporarily to control sudden import surges. See more in text.

Sources: Asad Alam and Sarath Rajapatirana, *Trade Policy Reform in Latin America and the Caribbean in the 1980s,* Policy Research Working Papers (World Bank, 1993); ECLAC, Social Equity and Changing Production Patterns: An Integrated Approach (Libros de la CEPAL #32, 1992); Sebastian Edwards, "Latin American Economic Integration," *The World Economy* Vol. 16 No.3 and staff reports, May 1993; GATT, *Trade Policy Review* (various issues); IDB staff reports; IMF, *Exchange Arrangements and Exchange Restrictions, Annual Report 1993;* World Bank, staff estimates and reports.

Table 2. Trade Volume as a Percentage of GDP for Selected Countries in LAC 1985, 1992

Country	GDP (million $ 1988)		Imports (million $ 1988)		Exports (million $ 1988)		((M+X)/GDP)*100		Growth
	1985	1992	1985	1992	1985	1992	1985	1992	1985-1992
Argentina	119704	143880	6347	16209	10991	12988	14.48	20.29	0.40
Belize	245	428	153	286	145	251	121.63	125.47	0.03
Bolivia	5596	6670	767	1185	602	923	24.46	31.60	0.29
Brazil	302978	331534	16082	25792	29898	40378	15.18	19.96	0.32
Chile	24765	38925	4617	11107	6523	13042	44.98	62.04	0.38
Colombia	37602	49795	5288	6882	5166	9628	27.80	33.16	0.19
Costa Rica	4135	5607	1237	2673	1204	2531	59.03	92.81	0.57
Dom. Rep.	4353	5184	1881	2628	1597	2587	79.90	100.60	0.26
Ecuador	12140	14344	2095	2891	2215	3189	35.50	42.39	0.19
El Salvador	4995	5946	1344	1520	1059	1245	48.11	46.50	-0.03
Guatemala	7250	9045	1322	2314	1318	1540	36.41	42.61	0.17
Honduras	3333	4169	926	1178	970	1160	56.89	56.08	-0.01
Jamaica	2839	3599	1393	1933	1474	2096	100.99	111.95	0.11
Mexico	171839	196434	18779	51115	23760	32555	24.76	42.59	0.72
Nicaragua	2383	2025	809	763	343	423	48.34	58.57	0.21
Panama	5153	5676	1786	2256	1495	1796	63.67	71.39	0.12
Paraguay	5499	6908	879	1842	794	1445	30.42	47.58	0.56
Peru	31220	29086	3306	4285	4769	3917	25.86	28.20	0.09
Uruguay	7224	9507	964	2141	1605	2308	35.56	46.80	0.32
Venezuela	57510	78564	12188	16363	9273	13211	37.32	37.64	0.01
All	810763	947326	82163	155363	105201	147213			
Average	40538.15	47366.3	4108.2	7768.15	5260.05	7360.65	46.57	55.91	0.24

Source: IDB, *Economic and Social Progress in Latin America* (Washington, D.C.: Johns Hopkins University Press, 1993).

Table 3. Initiations of Antidumping and Countervailing Investigations in Latin America, 1985-1992

	1985-1990	1990-1991	1991-1992
ANTIDUMPING INVESTIGATIONS			
Brazil	2	2	9
Mexico	45	14	25
COUNTERVAILING INVESTIGATIONS			
Brazil	0	0	8
Chile	11	2	5
Memorandum item:			
UNITED STATES			
Antidumping investigations	185	53	62
Countervailing investigations	82	7	15
EUROPEAN UNION			
Antidumping investigations	195	24	23
Countervailing investigations	3	0	0

Source: GATT, *Basic Instruments and Selected Documents* (GATT, Geneva, several years).

Table 4. Regional Integration Arrangements in the Americas

PREFERENTIAL ARRANGEMENTS

Membership	Date	Objective	Current Status	Memoranda (1990)
ANDEAN TRADE PREFERENCE ACT (ATPA)				
Bolivia, Colombia, Ecuador, Peru, United States	1991	Duty-free status for $324 million in imports from Andean countries to the United States	Operational	
CANADIAN-CARIBBEAN AGREEMENT (CARIBCAN)				
Angilla, Antigua and Barbuda, The Bahamas, Bermuda, Belize, British Virgin Islands, Cayman Islands, Dominica, Grenada, Guyana, Jamaica, Montserrat, St. Christopher and St. Nevis, St. Lucia, St. Vincent and the Grenadines, Trinidad & Tobago, and Turks and Caicos Islands	1986	Objective: to provide duty-free access to the Canadian market for certain imports from the Commonwealth Caribbean countries.	Operational	
CARIBBEAN BASIN INITIATIVE (CBI)				
Antigua and Barbuda, Aruba, The Bahamas, Barbados, Belize, British Virgin Islands, Costa Rica, Dominica, the Dominican Republic, El Salvador, Grenada, Guatemala, Guyana, Haiti, Honduras, Jamaica, Montserrat, the Netherlands Antilles, Nicaragua, Panama, St. Kitts and Nevis, St. Lucia, St. Vincent and the Grenadines, and Trinidad & Tobago	1983	Objective: to provide duty-free access to the U.S. market for certain imports from Central America and the Caribbean.	90 percent of CBI countries' exports to U.S. are covered under the agreement. Garments, textiles, and leather goods are excluded.	

Table 4. Regional Integration Arrangements in the Americas (Continued)

RECIPROCAL ARRANGEMENTS

Membership	Date	Objective	Current Status	Memoranda (1990)

LATIN AMERICAN INTEGRATION ASSOCIATION (LAIA)

Membership	Date	Objective	Current Status	Memoranda (1990)
All Spanish-speaking South-American countries, Mexico and Brazil **Modality:** Bilateral Agreements exchanging preferences on specific products	1980	Established as a result of the failure to achieve the objectives set by the Latin American Free Trade Association (LAFTA) in 1960. Objectives: to gradually achieve a common market. Instruments: Area of Economic Preferences constituted by Regional Tariff Preferences, Regional Agreements and Partial Agreements (economic complementation, agricultural and/or trade promoting agreements).	All member countries have signed bilateral agreements exchanging preferences for pre-determined lists of products. A number of member countries have signed economic complementation agreements. Recent Economic Complementation Agreements include those signed by Argentina-Chile (1990), Mexico-Honduras (1990), Chile-Venezuela (1990), Bolivia-Uruguay (1991), Chile-Mexico (1991), El Salvador-Honduras (1992), Guatemala-El Salvador (1992), Guatemala-Honduras (1992). The non-extension to other members of preferences granted by Mexico to imports from Canada and the U.S. under NAFTA will demand a reform, a waiver or a sanction under the terms of the Montevideo Treaty.	Aggregate GDP: US$863.5 billion Population: 380 million Total Foreign Trade: US$202.4 billion Intra-Regional Trade as % of Total Foreign Trade: 10.3

FREE TRADE AGREEMENTS

CANADA-UNITED STATES FREE TRADE AGREEMENT (CUSFTA)

Membership	Date	Objective	Current Status	Memoranda (1990)
	1988	Objective: to establish a free trade area in January 1988. Some tariffs and quotas will be eliminated immediately but most will be phased out in 5 to 10 years in annual installments. Major exceptions: agricultural quotas, price support and subsidy programs of both countries; Canadian regulations on beer, books, video and audio recording and government procurement	Signed and ratified by U.S. Congress and Canadian Parliament.	Aggregate GDP: US$5,990 billion Population: 276.5 million Total Foreign Trade: US$1,161 billion Intra-Regional Trade as % of Total Foreign Trade: 34.0

Table 4. Regional Integration Arrangements in the Americas (Continued)

FREE TRADE AGREEMENTS (CONTINUED)

Membership	Date	Objective	Current Status	Memoranda (1990)
CANADA-UNITED STATES FREE TRADE AGREEMENT (CUSFTA): (Continued)				
		not governed by GATT. The agreement phases out within 3 years most of the screening requirements to investments. U.S. banks and insurance companies will enjoy much greater market access. Almost all existing restrictions on trade in non-financial services — which are excluded from the agreement — are grandfathered.		
CHILE-COLOMBIA FTA				
	1993	Establishment of a free trade area.	Operational as of January 1994.	
CHILE-MEXICO FTA				
	1991	Objective: to establish a free trade area by 1-1-96.	Present maximum reciprocal tariff: 7.5%	Aggregate GDP: US$240.2 billion Population: 99.4 million Total Foreign Trade: US$78.8 billion Intra-Regional Trade as % of Total Foreign Trade: 0.1
CHILE-VENEZUELA FTA				
	1993	Objective: to establish a free trade area by 1999.	Maximum tariff to imports from Chile scheduled to be 20% in 1994. Chile's tariff rate remains at 11%. Tariffs scheduled to reach 0 in 1999.	Aggregate GDP: US$240.2billion Population: 32.9 million Total Foreign Trade: US$78.8 billion Intra-Regional Trade as % of Total Foreign Trade: 0.1
COLOMBIA-VENEZUELA FTA				
	1992	Objective: to establish a free trade area by 1992.	A common tariff was agreed in 1992. Conversations were initiated with Mexico (Group of 3) to establish a free trade area (see below).	Aggregate GDP: US$91.3 billion Population: 52 million Total Foreign Trade: US$34.7 billion Intra-Regional Trade as % of Total Foreign Trade: 1.4
EL SALVADOR-GUATEMALA FREE TRADE AGREEMENT				
	1991	Establishment of a free trade area.	Entered into operation in October 1991.	

Table 4. Regional Integration Arrangements in the Americas (Continued)

FREE TRADE AGREEMENTS (CONTINUED)

Membership	Date	Objective	Current Status	Memoranda (1990)

NORTH AMERICAN FREE TRADE AGREEMENT (NAFTA)

| | 1992 | Objective: to create a free trade area by 2009. Elimination of tariffs in 5, 10, or 15 years depending on the type of product. Exceptions are to Canadian agricultural and Mexican petroleum products. The agreement contains precedent-setting rights and obligations regarding intellectual property rights, services, trade and investment. NAFTA extends the U.S.-Canada Free Trade Agreement dispute settlement system to Mexico in return for trade law revisions that will align Mexico administrative practices more closely to U.S.-Canadian norms. | Agreement signed and ratified. In phase as of January 1, 1994. | Aggregate GDP: US$6,204.6 billion Population: 362.7 million Total Foreign Trade: US$1,223.8 billion Intra-Regional Trade as % of Total Foreign Trade: 18.8 |

NUEVA OCOTEPEQUE AGREEMENT

| El Salvador, Honduras, and Guatemala | 1992 | Objective: to establish a free trade area by 1993. Long-run objective: to establish a customs union. Includes recent Economic Complementation Agreements signed among these countries. | Not clear. | Aggregate GDP: US$17.1 billion Population: 19.5 million Total Foreign Trade: US$7.3 billion Intra-Regional Trade as % of Total Foreign Trade: 11.8 |

COMMON MARKETS

ANDEAN PACT

| Bolivia, Colombia, Ecuador, Peru, and Venezuela | 1969 | Objective: to promote harmonious development of member countries and the gradual formation of a Latin American common market. Instruments: harmonization | The date was not met due to internal disagreements. In 1992 Peru suspended its tariff preferences, but has since reinstated them. A new common tariff structure with 4 levels | Aggregate GDP: US$130.9 billion Population: 91.2 million Total Foreign Trade: US$47.3 billion Intra-Regional Trade as % of Total Foreign Trade: 3.8 |

Table 4. Regional Integration Arrangements
in the Americas (Continued)

COMMON MARKETS (CONTINUED)

Membership	Date	Objective	Current Status	Memoranda (1990)

ANDEAN PACT (CONTINUED)

Membership	Date	Objective	Current Status	Memoranda (1990)
		of social and economic policies, joint programs, Liberalization Program and Minimum common External Tariff. In 1991, a new date (1-1-92) was set to establish a common market.	ranging between 5% and 20% is currently being negotiated, with 95% of covered items already agreed upon. The target date of December 1993 has been postponed, but a CET should be in place by May 1994. Colombia and Venezuela negotiated a bilateral free trade agreement (see previous page).	

CARIBBEAN COMMUNITY (CARICOM)

Membership	Date	Objective	Current Status	Memoranda (1990)
Jamaica, S. Cristobal, Dominica, S. Vincent, Antigua, Barbados, Guyana, Belize, Grenada, S. Lucia, Trinidad & Tobago, Montserrat, and Bahamas	1973	Objectives: to create a common market regime in order to strengthen, coordinate, and regulate trade and economic relations among members. In 1990 member countries reformulated the objectives and set December 1991 as the deadline to establish a common external tariff.	Due to the failure to meet the calendar, a new deadline (1994) to establish a common market was agreed. Members agreed in October 1992 on reduction of the CET in phases, to reach a 5-20% range by 1996.	Aggregate GDP: US$28.2 billion Population: 9.4 million Total Foreign Trade: US$12.4 billion Intra-Regional Trade as % of Total Foreign Trade: 3.0

CENTRAL AMERICAN COMMON MARKET (CACM)

Membership	Date	Objective	Current Status	Memoranda (1990)
Costa Rica, Guatemala, Honduras, El Salvador, and Nicaragua	1960	Objective: to establish a common market in 1965.	In 1991, member countries made the commitment to establish a common external tariff (5-20%) by January 1993. Due to the failure to meet the targets, El Salvador, Honduras, and Guatemala agreed to establishment of a free-trade area by January 1993. In early 1993, a CET with four levels (5%-10%-15%-20%) was agreed upon for a number of products. Negotiations over the CET for other products are currently in negotiation or not agreed upon.	Aggregate GDP: US$25.6 billion Population: 26.2 million Total Foreign Trade: US$11.5 billion Intra-Regional Trade as % of Total Foreign Trade: 5.7

Table 4. Regional Integration Arrangements in the Americas (Continued)

COMMON MARKETS (CONTINUED)

Membership	Date	Objective	Current Status	Memoranda (1990)
MERCOSUR (SOUTHERN COMMON MARKET)				
Argentina, Brazil, Uruguay, and Paraguay	1991	Objective: to establish a common market by 1-1-95. Instruments: commercial liberalization program, macroeconomic policy coordination, common external tariff, sectoral agreements.	Present tariff preferences: 68% Dispute Resolution Agreement signed. Products are being gradually removed from national lists of exclusion as planned. Common external tariff negotiations hung up on differences over capital goods, electronics, and telecommunications, especially between Brazil and Argentina. Observers disagree over the likelihood of attaining customs union by 1995, but most concur that the process of trade liberalization is well under way.	Aggregate GDP: US$492.3 billion

FREE TRADE AGREEMENTS IN PROGRESS

CARICOM-COLOMBIA FTA				
Belize, Antigua and Barbuda, Bahamas, Barbados, Colombia, Dominica, Grenada, Jamaica, Montserrat, St. Kitts and Nevis, St. Lucia, St. Vincent and Gren., Trinidad and Tobago	1991	Provides for a non-reciprocal transition period in which unilateral tariff cuts will be made by Colombia, with the eventual goal of a free trade agreement.	Negotiations are proceeding slowly due to CARICOM demands for unilateral tariff reduction.	
CARICOM-VENEZUELA FTA				
Belize, Antigua and Barbuda, Bahamas, Barbados, Dominica, Grenada, Jamaica, Montserrat, St. Kitts and Nevis, St. Lucia, St. Vincent and Gren., Trinidad and Tobago, Venezuela	1991	Provides for duty-free imports from CARICOM nations into Venezuela to be phased in over a five-year period. After five years, negotiations are to begin to eliminate tariffs on Venezuelan exports to signatory countries.	Negotiations are proceeding slowly due to CARICOM demands for unilateral tariff reduction.	

Table 4. Regional Integration Arrangements in the Americas (Continued)

FREE TRADE AGREEMENTS IN PROGRESS (CONTINUED)

Membership	Date	Objective	Current Status	Memoranda (1990)
COLOMBIA-CENTRAL AMERICA FTA				
Costa Rica, El Salvador, Guatemala, Honduras, Nicaragua, Panama, Venezuela	1993	Provides for a non-reciprocal transition period in which unilateral tariff cuts will be made by Colombia, with the eventual goal of a free trade agreement.	Negotiations gained impetus after G-3 Presidential summit in 1993, but have proceeded slowly since.	
GROUP OF 3: COLOMBIA-VENEZUELA-MEXICO FREE TRADE AGREEMENT				
	1993	Objective: economic cooperation. In April 1993, the three countries agreed to establish a free trade area by 1994.	Agreements in the energy sector signed. Negotiation underway. Draft agreement of November 1993 provides for an immediate 0 tariff for some items and a 10-year transition for others, excepting automobiles and agricultural goods. Mexico is to cut tariffs faster than Colombia or Venezuela. Signing date of January 1994 postponed at request of Mexican government due to rebellion in Chiapas. Agreement ratified by Venezuelan government February 1994.	Aggregate GDP: US$305.8 billion Population: 138.2 million Total Foreign Trade: US$94.4 billion Intra-Regional Trade as % of Total Foreign Trade: 0.8
MEXICO-COSTA RICA FTA				
	1994	Establishment of a free trade area.	Negotiations in progress.	
MEXICO-COSTA RICA-EL SALVADOR-GUATEMALA-HONDURAS-NICARAGUA FTA				
	1992	Objective: to establish a free trade area by 31-12-96. Agreements under negotiation. Framework Agreement for Trade Cooperation signed 8/92. Costa Rica currently engaged in bilateral negotiations with Mexico.	Safeguard regime, Technical rules, and Dispute Resolution. Population: 112.4 million Total Foreign Trade: US$74.2 billion Intra-Regional Trade as % of Total Foreign Trade: 1.6	

Table 4. Regional Integration Arrangements
in the Americas (Concluded)

FREE TRADE AGREEMENTS IN PROGRESS (CONTINUED)

Membership	Date	Objective	Current Status	Memoranda (1990)
VENEZUELA-CENTRAL AMERICA FTA				
Costa Rica, El Salvador, Guatemala, Honduras, Nicaragua, Panama, Venezuela	1992	Provides for a non-reciprocal transition period in which unilateral tariff cuts will be made by Venezuela, with the eventual goal of a free trade agreement.	Negotiations gained impetus after G-3 Presidential summit in 1993, but have proceeded slowly since.	

Note: The "Modality" refers to the stated objective, not necessarily what has actually been achieved.

Sources: "Americas embrace 'open regionalism,'" *Financial Times* 22 March 1994, p. 4; Geoffrey Bannister, Joe Petry and C. A. Primo Braga, "Transnational Corporations, the Neo-Liberal Agenda, and Regional Integration: Establishing a Policy Framework", *Quarterly Review of Economics and Finance*, forthcoming; Richard Bernal, "Regional Trade Arrangements in the Western Hemisphere", *The American University Journal of International Law and Policy*, vol. 8 no. 4 (Summer 1993); Roberto Bouzas and Jaime Ros, "The North-South Variety of Economic Integration: Issues and Prospects for Latin America", unpublished paper, March 1993; "Colombia Finds Friends in Drive to Open Up", *Financial Times*, Jan. 5, 1994, p. 4; Winston Fritsch and Alexandre A. Tombini, "The Mercosul: An Overview",in Roberto Bouzas and Jaime Ros, eds. *Economic Integration in the Western Hemisphere: Issues and Prospects for Latin America* (Notre Dame Univ. Press, forthcoming); IDB staff information; Maria Beatriz Nofal, "Mercosur and Free Trade in the Americas", unpublished draft paper to be presented at conference "Future of Western Hemisphere Economic Integration", Washington, D.C., Mar. 1994; José Antonio Ocampo and Pilar Esquerra, "Colombia and Latin American Integration", in Roberto Bouzas and Jaime Ros, eds. *Economic Integration in the Western Hemisphere: Issues and Prospects for Latin America* (Notre Dame Univ. Press, forthcoming); Sylvia Saborio and contributors, *The Premise and the Promise: Free Trade in the Americas* (Transaction Publishers, 1993); Saborio, Note on progress of CA trade arrangements; "Venezuela: G-3 Presidential Summit Postponed at Request of Mexico", AFP News Agency Feb. 22, 1994; "Venezuela: New Venezuelan Gov't Ratifies Integration Accords", Reuter Newswire Feb. 22, 1994.

Notes

1   Nontariff barriers include quantitative restrictions (e.g., import prohibitions, quotas, nonautomatic licensing, "voluntary" export restraints, and restraints under the Multifiber Arrangement), price control measures (e.g., official reference prices), and variable levies. For a discussion of alternative definitions of NTBs, see Sam Laird and Alexander Yeats, 1990, *Quantitative Methods for Trade-Barrier Analysis* (London: Macmillan Press).

2   For a survey of trade policy reform in Latin America, see Asad Alam and Sarath Rajapatirana, 1993, *Trade Policy Reform in Latin America and the Caribbean in the 1980s* (Washington, D.C.: World Bank), and World Bank, 1993, *Latin America and the Caribbean: A Decade After the Debt Crisis* (Washington, D.C.: World Bank), both World Bank Working Papers.

3   For example, Mexico joined the GATT on August 24, 1986, immediately before the beginning of the Uruguay Round negotiations. Since then, the following Latin American and Caribbean countries have acceded to the GATT: Antigua and Barbuda (1987), Bolivia (1990), Costa Rica (1990), Venezuela (1990), El Salvador (1991), Guatemala (1991), Dominica (1993), St. Lucia (1993), St. Vincent and the Grenadines (1993), Grenada (1994), Paraguay (1994), and St. Kitts and Nevis (1994).

4   Sebastian Edwards, 1993, "Openness, Trade Liberalization, and Growth in Developing Countries," *Journal of Economic Literature* 31 (September): 1358-1393.

5   Anne O. Krueger, 1978, *Foreign Trade Regimes and Economic Development: Liberalization Attempts and Consequences* (Cambridge: Ballinger Publishing Co. for NBER).

6   These exceptions exist in Colombia, Costa Rica, Guatemala, Honduras, Ecuador, and Uruguay.

7   Jose Tavares, 1994, "A Note on Ecuador's Current Trade Policy," unpublished Inter-American Development Bank document.

8   Other sectors where quantitative restrictions are still significant are petroleum, gas, and petroleum derivatives (100 percent); tobacco (100 percent); and agriculture (47.6 percent).

9   See GATT, 1993, *Trade Policy Review - Brazil*, vol. 1 (Geneva: GATT), 110.

10   Michael Finger, ed., 1993, *Anti-Dumping: How It's Used and Who It Hurts* (Ann Arbor: University of Michigan Press).

11   Jose Tavares, 1992, "Latin American Trade Policies: Issues and Options," IDB-ECLAC Working Papers on Trade in the Western Hemisphere, no. 12. (September), 2.

12   There is further discussion on this topic in Manuel R. Agosín and Diana Tussie, 1993, "Globalización, regionalización y nuevos dilemas en la política de comercio exterior para el desarrollo," *El Trimestre Economico* LX, 239 (July-September): 559-600, and in Asad Alam and Sarath Rajapatirana 1993.

13 GATT, 1992, *Trade Policy Review: Argentina*, vol. 1 (Geneva: GATT) 5. Editions, volumes, and page numbers in *Trade Policy Review* for other countries are *Bolivia* 1992, vol. 1, 8; *Brazil* 1992, vol. 2, 7; *Mexico* 1992, vol. 2, 48; and *Uruguay* 1992, vol. 1, 8.

14 See Guillermo Calvo, Leonardo Leiderman, and Carmen Reinhardt, 1992, "Capital Inflows and Real Exchange Rate Appreciation," IMF Working Paper no. 62. (Washington, D.C.: International Monetary Fund).

15 The "old" structuralist argument against devaluations was that since imports and exports were inelastic with respect to changes in relative prices, a devaluation would restore equilibrium only through quantity adjustments (i.e., a contraction in the level of activity). Instead, the use of import controls could restore the balance of payments equilibrium at a lower cost in terms of output loss.

16 The new regional arrangements are Chile-Mexico FTA (1991); Chile-Venezuela FTA (1993); Chile-Colombia (1993); Colombia-Venezuela FTA (1992); El Salvador-Guatemala-Honduras FTA (1991); MERCOSUR (1991); Mexico-Central America FTA (1992); and Nueva Ocotepeque FTA (1992). A Mexico-Costa Rica FTA was signed in March 1994 and is expected to go into effect on January 1, 1995. Moreover, there are several agreements being negotiated: the Group of Three FTA (Colombia, Mexico, and Venezuela), a Caribbean Community and Common Market (CARICOM)-Colombia FTA and a CARICOM-Venezuela FTA. For more details on the history and characteristics of these initiatives, see Richard Bernal, 1993, "Regional Trade Arrangements in the Western Hemisphere," *The American University Journal of International Law and Policy* 8, 4 (Summer); Roberto Bouzas and Nora Lustig, eds., 1992, *Liberalización Comercial e Integración Regional: De Nafta a Mercosur* (FLACSO Grupo Editor Latinoamericano); Roberto Bouzas and Jaime Ros, 1993, "The North-South Variety of Economic Integration: Issues and Prospects for Latin America," unpublished paper (March); Sebastian Edwards, 1993, "Latin American Economic Integration," *The World Economy* 16, 3 (May); and Joseph Grunwald, 1993, "El escabroso camino hacia la integración económica hemisférica. Análisis regional de antecedentes orientado al futuro," *El Trimestre Económico* LX, 239 (July-September).

17 Transnational corporations, for example, are eager to pursue further rationalization of their structures of production in Latin America. Open regional integration arrangements can foster this process by enhancing the credibility of liberalization efforts and by addressing not only trade but also regulatory barriers (e.g., differences in standards, competition laws, intellectual property, and investment regimes). On this theme, see Geoffrey Bannister, Joe Petry, and C.A. Primo Braga, "Transnational Corporations, the Neo-liberal Agenda," and "Regional Integration: Establishing a Policy Framework," *Quarterly Review of Economics and Finance*, forthcoming.

18 Analyses of the Latin American and Caribbean countries' position vis-à-vis negotiating free trade agreements with the United States and free trade in the Western Hemisphere can be found in Roberto Bouzas and Nora Lustig, eds. 1992; Roberto Bouzas and Jaime Ros 1993; Peter Hakim, 1993, "Western Hemisphere Free Trade: Why Should Latin America Be Interested?" ANNALS, AAPSS, (March) 526; and Sylvia Saborio, ed. 1993, *The Premise and the Promise: Free Trade in the Americas* (New Brunswick, N.J.: Transaction Publishers).

19 See Andrew Hughes Hallett and C.A. Primo Braga, "The New Regionalism and the Threat of Protectionism," IECIT Working Paper (Washington, D.C.: World Bank), processed, and the bibliographical references cited in it.

20 See Robert Lawrence, "Emerging Regional Arrangements: Building Blocks or Stumbling Blocks?" in Richard O'Brien, ed., 1991, *Finance and the International Economy: 5, The Amex Bank Review Prize Essays* (Oxford: Oxford University Press).

21 See more on the preconditions for "open regionalism" in Anne O. Krueger, 1992,"Conditions for Maximizing the Gains from a Western Hemisphere Free Trade Agreement," unpublished draft IDB/ECLAC Working Papers on Trade in the Western Hemisphere, no. 6 (July); W. Max Corden, 1992, "A Western Hemisphere Free Trade Area: Possible Implications for Latin America," IDB/ECLAC Working Papers on Trade in the Western Hemisphere, no. 3 (May); Sidney Weintraub, 1992, "Western Hemisphere Free Trade: Getting from Here to There," IDB/ECLAC Working Papers on Trade in the Western Hemisphere, no. 13 (November); and the United Nations Economic Commission for Latin America and the Caribbean, 1994, "Open Regionalism in Latin America and the Caribbean," LC/l.808(CEG. 19/3) (January).

22 Curiously, this phenomenon has not occurred with members of MERCOSUR. It is not fully apparent why, for example, Argentina has not tried to put pressure on Brazil. The costs of breaking away must be higher than the perceived benefits so far.

23 See José Antonio Ocampo and Pilar Esquerra, "Colombia and Latin American Integration," in Roberto Bouzas and Jaime Ros, eds., *Economic Integration in the Western Hemisphere: Issues and Prospects for Latin America* (Notre Dame, Ind.: Notre Dame University Press), forthcoming.

24 For a detailed description of the difficulties involved in determining the common external tariff, see Winston Fritsch, 1990, "Domestic Trade Reform and Policies Towards the Trade System: Is There a Common Latin American Agenda?" unpublished paper, Inter-American Dialogue (May); María Beatriz Nofal, "MERCOSUR and Free Trade in the Americas," unpublished draft presented at CSIS/IAD/North-South Center conference, "Future of Western Hemisphere Economic Integration," Washington, D.C. (February 1994); and José Antonio Ocampo and Pilar Esquerra, forthcoming.

25 See GATT, 1993, *Final Act Embodying the Results of the Uruguay Round of Multilateral Negotiations*, MTN/FA (Geneva: GATT), December.

26 For example, a producer of finished garments in country A may find it profitable to buy fabric woven from country B's yarn rather than from cheaper imported yarn from outside the FTA in order to qualify for free access to country B's market. See Anne O. Krueger, 1993, "Free Trade Agreements as Protectionist Devices: Rules of Origin," NBER Working Paper No. 4352 (Cambridge: NBER).

27 For a comparison of the NAFTA and TRIPs standards of protection, see C.A. Primo Braga, "Intellectual Property Rights in NAFTA: Implications for International Trade," in A.R. Riggs and Tom Velk, eds., 1993, *Beyond NAFTA: An economic, political and sociological perspective* (Vancouver: Fraser Institute).

28 See Hughes Hallett and Primo Braga, "The New Regionalism and the Threat of Protectionism."

29 Needless to say, recent experiments in regional integration suggest that there is a clear preference for less formal institutional arrangements, as exemplified by the architectural structures of NAFTA, MERCOSUR, and the new FTAs. Accordingly, any attempt to create a strong central institution at the hemispheric level is unlikely to succeed.

References

Agosín, Manuel R., and Diana Tussie. 1993. "Globalización, regionalización y nuevos dilemas en la política de comercio exterior para el desarrollo." *El Trimestre Economico* 60(239).

Alam, Asad, and Sarath Rajapatirana. 1993. *Trade Policy Reform in Latin America and the Caribbean in the 1980s*. World Bank Working Paper. Washington, D.C.: World Bank.

Bannister, Geoffrey, Joe Petry, and C.A. Primo Braga. "Transnational Corporation, the Neo-liberal Agenda, and Regional Integration: Establishing a Policy Framework." *Quarterly Review of Economics and Finance*. Forthcoming.

Bernal, Richard. 1993. "Regional Trade Arrangements in the Western Hemisphere." *The American University Journal of International Law and Policy* 8(4).

Bouzas, Roberto, and Nora Lustig, eds. 1992. *Liberalización Comercial e Integración Regional: De Nafta a Mercosur*. Buenos Aires: FLACSO Grupo Editor Latinoamericano.

Bouzas, Roberto, and Jaime Ros. 1993. "The North-South Variety of Economic Integration: Issues and Prospects for Latin America." Unpublished.

Calvo, Guillermo, Leonardo Leiderman, and Carmen Reinhardt. 1992. "Capital Inflows and Real Exchange Rate Appreciation." IMF Working Paper No. 62. Washington, D.C.: International Monetary Fund.

Corden, W. Max. 1992. "A Western Hemisphere Free Trade Area: Possible Implications for Latin America." IDB/ECLAC Working Paper on Trade in the Western Hemisphere, No. 3. May.

Edwards, Sebastian. 1993a. "Openness, Trade Liberalization, and Growth in Developing Countries." *Journal of Economic Literature* 31(September).

Edwards, Sebastian. 1993b. "Latin American Economic Integration." *The World Economy* 16(3).

Finger, Michael, ed. 1993. *Anti-Dumping: How It's Used and Who It Hurts*. Ann Arbor: University of Michigan Press.

Fritsch, Winston. 1990. "Domestic Trade Reform and Policies Towards the Trade System: Is There a Common Latin American Agenda?" Unpublished paper. Washington, D.C.: Inter-American Dialogue. May.

General Agreement on Tariffs and Trade. 1993a. *Final Act Embodying the Results of the Uruguay Round of Multilateral Negotiations*. MTN/FA Geneva.

General Agreement on Tariffs and Trade. 1993b. *Trade Policy Review: Brazil*, Vol. 1. Geneva.

General Agreement on Tariffs and Trade. 1992. *Trade Policy Review: Argentina*, Vol. 1. Geneva.

Grunwald, Joseph. 1993. "El excabroso camino hacia la integración económica hemisférica. Análisis regional de antecedentes orientado al futuro." *El Trimestre Económico* 60(239).

Hakim, Peter. 1993. "Western Hemisphere Free Trade: Why Should Latin America Be Interested?" ANNALS, AAPSS, 526. March.

Hallett, Hughes, and C.A. Primo Braga. "The New Regionalism and the Threat of Protectionism." IECIT Working Paper. Washington, D.C.: World Bank.

Krueger, Anne O. 1993. "Free Trade Agreements as Protectionist Devices: Rules of Origin." NBER Working Paper, No. 4352. Cambridge.

Krueger, Anne O. 1992. "Conditions for Maximizing the Gains from a Western Hemisphere Free Trade Agreement." Unpublished draft. IDB/ECLAC WP-TWH, No. 6.

Krueger, Anne O. 1978. *Foreign Trade Regimes and Economic Development: Liberalization Attempts and Consequences*. Ballinger Publishing Co. for NBER.

Laird, Sam, and Alexander Yeats. 1990. *Quantitative Methods for Trade-Barrier Analysis*. London: Macmillan Press.

Lawrence, Robert. 1991. "Emerging Regional Arrangements: Building Blocks or Stumbling Blocks?" ed. Richard O'Brien. New York: Oxford University Press.

Nofal, María Beatriz. 1994. "MERCOSUR and Free Trade in the Americas." In *Integrating the Americas: Shaping Future Trade Policy,* ed. Sidney Weintraub. Coral Gables, Fla.: North-South Center, University of Miami.

Ocampo, José Antonio, and Pilar Esquerra. "Colombia and Latin American Integration." In *Economic Integration in the Western Hemisphere: Issues and Prospects for Latin America,* eds. Roberto Bouzas and Jaime Ros. South Bend, Ind.: Notre Dame University Press. Forthcoming.

Primo Braga, C.A. 1993. "Intellectual Property Rights in NAFTA: Implications for International Trade." In *Beyond NAFTA: An Economic, Political and Sociological Perspective,* eds. A.R. Riggs and Tom Velk. Vancouver: Fraser Institute.

Saborio, Sylvia. 1993. *The Premise and the Promise: Free Trade in the Americas.* New Brunswick, N.J.: Transaction Publishers.

Tavares, Jose. 1994. "A Note on Ecuador's Current Trade Policy." Unpublished IDB document.

Tavares, Jose. 1992. "Latin American Trade Policies: Issues and Options." IDB/ECLAC Working Paper on Trade in the Western Hemisphere, No. 12. September.

United Nations Economic Commission for Latin America and the Caribbean (ECLAC). 1994. "Open Regionalism in Latin America and the Caribbean." LC/1.808(CEG. 19/3). January.

Weintraub, Sidney. 1992. "Western Hemisphere Free Trade: Getting from Here to There." IDB/ECLAC Working Paper on Trade in the Western Hemisphere, No. 13. November.

Chapter 3

Toward Free Trade in the Americas: Building Blocks, Stumbling Blocks, and Entry Fees

Moisés Naím

Currently, prospects for free trade in the Americas are better than ever. Yet not surprisingly, confusion about trade relationships in the hemisphere is at a new high. After all, it was only a few years ago that Latin American countries figured among the most consummate protectionists in the world, and the United States' main economic concern in the region was to help commercial banks collect bad loans.

The economic situation was unhealthy, but clearer: Protectionism and statism reigned in the South, while liberalism and markets dominated thought and policies in the North. In the 1990s, political and economic transitions have enormously improved Latin America's prospects, but rapid and complex changes make clarity harder to come by.[1] Most recently, democratized countries throughout Latin America are becoming more economically stable and unexpectedly open to imports and foreign investment. Adjacent countries, like Colombia and Venezuela or Argentina and Brazil, which spent decades talking about the need to integrate their economies while adopting economic policies that stifled integration, discovered that true liberalization propelled trade and investment among them to previously unknown levels.

This paper was prepared for the Conference on the Future of Western Hemisphere Economic Integration, sponsored by The Center for Strategic and International Studies, the Inter-American Dialogue, and The North-South Center of the University of Miami, and held in Washington, D.C. on March 2-4, 1994. Zan Northrip's invaluable research assistance and Martin Stein's help with the trade statistics are gratefully acknowledged. Ricardo Hausmann provided many useful insights about trade negotiations in Latin America. Thanks to Morton Abramowitz, Delal Baer, Jonathan Coles, Uri Dadush, Jorge Dominguez, Luigi Einaudi, Larry Fabian, Peter Hakim, Charles William Maynes, Joseph Tulchin, Sidney Weintraub, and Carol Wise for their comments on earlier drafts. All the usual disclaimers apply.

Presidents seized the political opportunity, first by signing free trade agreements that formalized the realities created by their unilateral trade liberalization and then by pushing for further deregulation of trade and investment. Inward-looking import substitution policies were replaced by new export-oriented strategies, thus making access to export markets a top priority. Indeed, market access became so important that the political costs of abandoning centuries of economic nationalism were tolerable. A bewildered world saw Mexico, traditionally known for its rancorous denunciations of U.S. imperialism, suddenly commence to be willing to go to any length to join the 1992 North American Free Trade Agreement (NAFTA). At the same time, speeches in the United States Congress opposing free trade with Mexico bore a striking resemblance to the manifestos of the Latin intelligentsia during the 1960s.

NAFTA has been passed; expectations in Latin America and the Caribbean (LAC) have soared; and an unprecedented hemispheric presidential summit has been planned for December 1994. What is next? What *can* be next? Can President Bill Clinton's statement that his administration would "... reach out to the other market-oriented democracies of Latin America to ask them to join in this great American pact" be easily reconciled with the priority that he is giving to the Asia-Pacific economic community and with the need to deal with the chronic trade deficits that the United States maintains with Japan and China? Will the countries in Latin America and the Caribbean be willing and able to satisfy the precedents set in the negotiations with Mexico? Will these "entry fees" prove to be prohibitively high? Does paying them help or hinder the cause of market reform in Latin America? Countries in Latin America are creating an ever-growing web of bilateral and multilateral free trade agreements among themselves. Will these agreements be building blocks or stumbling blocks toward freer trade in the region?

In seeking answers to these questions, some commonly held beliefs about the expansion of free trade to other countries in Latin America are assessed, and then recent economic integration efforts and trade patterns and barriers within the Americas are examined. Next, the origins of Latin America's recent conversion to economic liberalization are discussed, and some of the forces operating for and against the extension of NAFTA to other countries are reviewed. A running theme throughout the argument is the narrowness of Latin America's commitment to free trade. Absent a broad ideological consensus capable of sustaining the short- and medium-term costs of adjusting to a market orientation, popular support for economic reforms will be determined by their ability to deliver quickly visible benefits. The economic crises that provided initial justification for radical reform measures are now on the wane, and governments will be challenged to maintain the momentum of these measures. Additional adjustment costs may not be sustainable unless the political position of Latin America's economic reformers is shored up first.

Common Misconceptions

Shifts in the hemisphere's trade arena have been so quick, drastic, and unexpected that common perceptions and assumptions have lagged behind the rapid pace of change. Future debates and negotiations over free trade may suffer as a result.

1. *Latin America has embraced free trade.* Not really. During the late 1980s and early 1990s, some Latin American *governments* embraced free trade. The power of traditional protectionist coalitions ebbed for a while as a consequence of major economic crises. Some pro-free trade actors have emerged. But Latin America is far from converted to a free trade ideology, and as trade deficits soar, further trade liberalization will become more difficult. Also, it is hard to argue that Latin America has turned toward free trade when Brazil, which accounts for over one-third of the region's total output, continues to resist the kind of liberalization that Chile, Mexico, or even Peru has adopted. Trade statistics and horror stories from exporters indicate that — notwithstanding a recent lowering of tariffs — Brazil's economy continues to be the most protected in the hemisphere.

2. *Free trade agreements with the United States will dramatically increase Latin exports to it.* Not in the short run. Most sectors of the U.S. economy in which Latin exports compete are already close to tariff free, and all past evidence suggests that those with significant barriers will be liberalized only slowly. Latin companies that can compete in U.S. markets are already doing so.

3. *Free trade agreements are about free trade.* No. For Latin countries, the agreements are much more about foreign investment and the need not to be left out of the economic blocs into which the world is organizing. Since most Latin exports already enter the United States untaxed, the goal of reaching free trade agreements is most clearly seen as the outward manifestation of the more profound imperative to minimize the risks of being excluded from the emerging world economic order. Countries that have recently adopted an export-oriented strategy and that are critically dependent on foreign investment flows cannot afford the risk of not being part of an economic alliance with large industrialized markets. In the international competition for capital, market access, and technology, countries that are part of such alliances will have clear competitive advantages over those that are not. Additionally, the international treaties that formalize free trade agreements serve the important domestic political function of making it more difficult for new governments in Latin America to backslide on the reforms adopted by the market-oriented governments of the late 1980s and early 1990s.

4. *Latin America is desperate to sign free trade agreements with the United States.* Wrong. Only small, though influential, groups now in government are eager to do so. The threat of being excluded from the new trading blocs toward which the world economy seems to be drifting is certainly a powerful incentive to join hemispheric agreements. Behind this reasoning, however, is a geopolitical sophistication that is far from universal in Latin America, even among political and business leaders. The reality is that skepticism about neoliberal reforms still lingers. A tradition of mistrust concerning the functioning of the international economy has been bred by decades of dependency theory; this mistrust continues to inform much of the local political culture and gives cover to private sector groups hurt by trade liberalization. These groups continue to lobby for the recovery of their lost privileges and tariff protection. For Latin America, free trade with the United States means opening domestic markets even more and accepting costly and unpopular conditions in exchange for critical but largely long-term or indirect benefits. While free trade will not mean increased exports from Latin America to the United States in the short run, it will mean an almost immediate increase of U.S. exports to Latin America and a probable deterioration of the region's trade balance.

5. *NAFTA and the negotiations with Mexico are a model.* Precedents were set, but the model built seems unworkable. Negotiations with Mexico gave rise to "NAFTA standards" that will guide future free trade negotiations with the rest of Latin America. Unfortunately, such standards assume many conditions and possibilities that, in fact, are unique to Mexico. Meeting these precedents will be very difficult for most democratic governments in the region. Mexico's ability to deliver on the demands imposed by the United States was the result of powerful economic incentives and an unusual political system. This system gave the administration of Carlos Salinas de Gortari an autonomy vis-à-vis the Mexican Congress, organized labor, the private sector, farmers, the media, and other political parties that few other governments in the region have. Furthermore, existing levels of economic integration between Mexico and the United States created strong incentives in both countries to formalize the "special" relationship between them.

6. *The carrot of free trade with the United States is enough to motivate countries to move ahead with other costly reforms.* Not so. Enforcing intellectual property rights, labor laws, environmental standards, and other conditions required by NAFTA or the United States will have high short-term costs. Countries will have to balance the long-term hypothetical benefits of a free trade agreement with the United States with the short-term and very tangible impact of higher medicine prices and

added fiscal pressures. They will also have to consider the political impact of adopting public investment and spending priorities driven more by U.S. interest groups than by their own constituencies. In Latin America, political support for market reforms was never widespread and is beginning to suffer from the population's impatience with dire economic conditions and the easing of the economic crises that justified the emergency reforms taken by newly elected governments. Market-oriented governments convinced of the importance of free trade agreements with the United States will be put in the difficult position of exposing their reforms to even greater political risks as they undertake to satisfy the entry fees imposed by the NAFTA precedent.

7. *Subregional free trade agreements are the building blocks of a hemispheric free trade zone.* They are more likely to be stumbling blocks. Once such agreements are in place, the private sector interests that have been able to secure market niches in neighboring countries will fiercely oppose the advent of new competition from nonmember states. Why should Brazilian exporters to Argentina welcome the extension of their privileged Southern Common Market (Mercado Común del Sur — MERCOSUR) access to competitors from Chile or Mexico, not to mention the United States? Subregional agreements may also hinder a more accelerated evolution toward free trade in the hemisphere through the added need for coordination and convergence among their constituent countries, always a burdensome task. In fact, Argentina's commitment to MERCOSUR — where Brazil's economic instability and protectionism is slowing down its consolidation — offers an example. In the near future, Argentina, realizing that it is no longer in its interest to wait for MERCOSUR to be ready to expand beyond its current members, may be forced to abandon that agreement in favor of bilateral trade agreements with the United States. While subregional agreements may well serve as positive intermediate-stage arrangements toward the goal of hemispheric free trade, the danger that they will end up being yet another obstacle to overcome still exists.

8. *NAFTA has been achieved.* Too soon to tell. NAFTA has been ratified but is far from fully implemented. Many trilateral institutions have yet to be created, and extremely complex enforcement and monitoring mechanisms have to be put in place. Also, the consequences of NAFTA have so far not been digested by the economies and polities of Mexico, Canada, and the United States.[2] While "docking" provisions may be built into the new institutions to facilitate the incorporation of new members, the first order of business is to create the institutions and to make them fully functional, not to expand them. It will take some time for NAFTA to be ready to accept new members — perhaps even more

time than what it would take to complete the negotiations with other interested countries. This institutional lag may well result in longer negotiations than would be the case were only trade issues on the table.

9. *U.S. conditions on access to free trade help economic reforms and those who support them.* Perhaps not. While most of the U.S. prerequisites aim to hasten desirable — even inevitable — reforms, an inflexible approach may threaten liberalization's chances by alienating powerful constituents. Reformist governments bent on signing free trade agreements with the United States may be forced to accept a sequence and pace of reforms that is different from what their purely domestic economic priorities would indicate or from what political calculations would recommend in order to strengthen political support for the cause of economic liberalization. Latin American presidents are well aware of these risks. They saw the extremely vulnerable position in which President Salinas was left when, after having satisfied politically difficult conditions designed to mollify the U.S. Congress, his administration and his country became the target of a barrage of scathing denunciations. The prospect of paying free trade's steep entry fees and then not being allowed to enter is a nightmare political scenario that Latin presidents will certainly try to avoid.

10. *Integration can be achieved without community institutions.* Experience shows that many will be needed. Unfortunately, free trade in the Western Hemisphere will have to proceed without them. Latin America may well need a mechanism to smooth free trade's costs for losers, much as has been done for Greece and Portugal through the European Community's "super funds." While their impact might be limited, such institutions would be politically useful as governments strain to construct supporting coalitions. The need to have multilateral coordinating institutions seems to be another central lesson of the European experience. Building effective community institutions, however, would be a major challenge, given the devastation of state capacity experienced by most of Latin America during the 1980s. But the key problem, of course, is that the fiscal situation in the United States, Canada, and Latin America makes paying adjustment compensation to countries, sectors, and regions that may suffer from the impact of free trade agreements an impossible proposition. Channeling scarce fiscal resources to pay for a new hemispheric bureaucracy does not seem to be a winning proposition, either. The NAFTA debate in the United States and Canada clearly showed that free trade per se had substantial opposition. Adding an explicit price tag for taxpayers may be the kiss of death for new agreements. At this point, it seems that free trade and integration in the Western Hemisphere will have to proceed without relying on new multilateral institutions, regardless of how necessary they may be.

How Much Integration Has Occurred?

Since the late 1980s, an ever-growing number of new and relaunched subregional integration groups, as well as a mushrooming array of bilateral free trade agreements, has reshaped the institutional setting for trade in the Western Hemisphere (see Table 1). Bold integration goals make headlines every day.

To some observers, the current attention may seem puzzling because Western Hemisphere economic integration is, in fact, old news. The now-defunct Latin American Free Trade Association (LAFTA) was launched in 1960, and Central Americans signed an Economic Integration Treaty the same year. But by the measure of openness to the outside world, those agreements of three decades ago bear greater similarities to the "integration" experience of the 1930s than they do to the subregional groupings that have emerged in the last five years.[3]

Thirty years ago, open markets were not truly on the table. Instead, the objective of the interwar years — to divert trade and to spur domestic production through the formation of blocs — was shared in practice by most of the integration groups in Latin America and the Caribbean that emerged in the 1960s.[4] While the rhetoric of economic integration among Latin American countries flourished, intraregional trade sank under the weight of protectionism and statism. The import substitution policies of the region's economies made trade liberalization almost impossible, and decades passed with scant opening to either neighbors or extraregional trading partners.

The new and resurrected integration efforts of the 1990s are fundamentally different. Defensive, inward-looking economic integration dependent on government planning is out. Competitive, market-based, export-oriented integration is in.

Previous attempts were inspired by the need to shield the regional economy from exchanges with industrialized countries, which were generally viewed as unfair and exploitative. In contrast, the new integration efforts are driven by the need to bolster the global competitiveness of the region and to promote private investment. Most important, they take place against a background of widespread unilateral economic liberalization and unprecedented hope and reliance on markets. By 1992, average unweighted tariffs had been cut by 50 percent in Venezuela, by 64 percent in Argentina, and by more than 80 percent in Colombia (see Table 2). Domestic economies were liberalized as well, through privatization, scaled-down subsidies, and the wholesale deregulation of foreign investment, stock markets, manufacturing, agriculture, and many other areas of economic activity.

Thanks to this new environment, subregional integration in the 1990s has progressed at a rate unthinkable to the earlier integration architects. With barriers already lowered unilaterally, it has been relatively easy to commit to their near elimination within select groups like the Caribbean Community

(CARICOM), the Central American Common Market (CACM), and MERCO-SUR. Unilateral opening also paved the way for totally new initiatives like NAFTA, the Group of Three (G-3, comprising Colombia, Mexico, and Venezuela), and numerous bilateral accords. Many of the groups envision integration beyond the liberalization of trade, most frequently attempting to establish common external tariffs. Some have gone further, making commitments to institutionalize labor mobility and other more ambitious features of common markets. Integration in the 1990s is both faster and deeper than was the case in earlier experiments.

Free Trade Prospects

For all these reasons, the prospects for a hemispheric free trade zone are better than they have been at any time. Economic, political, and geopolitical calculations have motivated an unprecedented commitment by governments to free trade agreements.

First, the economic benefits of freer trade in the hemisphere are well known and have been thoroughly argued and documented.[5] More important, small but influential policy circles in Latin America now accept these arguments in favor of open trading systems. In the long run, hemispheric free trade is bound to expand exports from Latin America and the Caribbean in a few key sectors. Free trade's dynamic benefits will be even greater, especially as competitive pressures — always dormant in Latin America — are spurred by a more open, market-based environment. Foreign investment is also stimulated by free trade, and when trade treaties are broadened to include provisions that guarantee market access, institutionalized dispute settlement mechanisms, and the protection of intellectual property rights, the stimulus to foreign investment is accelerated. Furthermore, a more open trading regime is viewed as an indispensable complement to the market-based reforms undertaken throughout Latin America and as an ally in the fight to restore economic growth and control inflation.

Second, free trade agreements have important political consequences. They normally engender a web of international treaties and give rise to a wide array of interlocking constraints within the domains of domestic economic policy. As a result, these international treaties act as a deterrent to new governments wishing to reverse the market-oriented policies adopted by their predecessors. In turn, such constraints on governmental actions reduce the investment risk derived from the traditional volatility of the "rules of the game" imposed by governments on the private sector.

The third and perhaps most essential factor driving the interest of Latin governments toward free trade agreements stems from the risks of exclusion from the trading blocs that are being formed both inside and outside the hemisphere.[6] Latin countries liberalized their trade regimes unilaterally, not as a result of negotiations leading to reciprocal liberalization from their trading partners. They have done so at the same time that a major reorganization of the world economy seems in the making. The recent General Agreement on Tariffs and Trade (GATT) negotiations showed how vigorous and sophisticated are the forces of protectionism in industrialized countries. The intense drive toward the formation of trading blocs is also, in some ways, an expression of this "state of the art" protectionism. In fact, most industrialized countries are entering into special trading alliances, blocs, and understandings that, in effect, are facilitating trade with their neighbors and in their regions and locking in many of the existing patterns and trends. Naturally, all this is very threatening for new entrants.[7] Latin countries recently began to bet their future on an export-based strategy and on their capacity to attract substantial flows of private international capital. Hence, for them, being left out of new global, or even regional, arrangements that may result in exclusionary trading and investment regimes would be nothing short of catastrophic.

On the other hand, the same geopolitical factors are also likely to drive the interest of the United States in furthering free trade in the hemisphere. NAFTA provides North America with a low-cost manufacturing base that generates considerable competitive advantages for some sectors. Such North American competitive advantages will surely encourage the European Community to develop more aggressively its trading links with Eastern Europe and parts of North Africa in order to have similar access to the pool of low-wage labor that is necessary to insure European competitiveness. Furthermore, the same migration pressures that were so instrumental in moving NAFTA forward exist now in Europe and are very likely to increase over time. Europe's move toward closer integration with its neighboring regions will certainly have some effects in motivating the United States to renew its efforts toward hemispheric free trade.

Trade Patterns and Trends

But arguments in favor of free trade have seldom been enough to make liberalization easy. Political and institutional hurdles to free trade and hemispheric integration remain in the United States and in Latin America. Before they are discussed, it is useful to review both fundamental trade patterns and the determinants of Latin America's recent moves toward trade liberalization. Table 3 provides a summary of export flows in the hemisphere.

Flows

The first point to be made is that Latin America's intraregional trade is booming and has much room to grow. Latin American exports to other LAC destinations increased in value over 135 percent between 1986 and 1992. Intra-Latin American and Caribbean exports now account for 18 percent of the region's total exports, still recovering from a 40 percent drop in the 1980s.

Second, intra-LAC trade growth is impressive but uneven. As shown in Figure 1, it has increased most rapidly within the subregional agreements. Andean Pact exports to other pact members (exports involving Bolivia, Colombia, Ecuador, Peru, and Venezuela), for example, grew at an average annual rate of 20 percent between 1986 and 1992, while the group's exports to all LAC countries grew at a rate of 15 percent per year. Andean Pact exports to the United States increased more slowly; growth was 10 percent per year during the same period. The Colombia-Venezuela aggregate demonstrates the identical trend more starkly. After liberalization, the two countries' exports increased at annual rates of 25 percent to the G-3, 18 percent to the rest of the region, and 12 percent to the United States. In U.S. dollar terms, trade between the two countries jumped from less than $300 million per year in the late 1980s to almost $2 billion in 1993.[8]

Within the subregions, individual country exports have shifted in a similar manner. The case of Brazil is a good example. Figure 2 shows the changing destination of Brazilian exports in response to LAC's widespread unilateral liberalization and the MERCOSUR agreement. While the United States was the main market for Brazilian exports as recently as 1986, by 1992, it had been eclipsed by sales to Latin America. Exports to the region climbed from 12 percent to 23 percent of total Brazilian exports during the period, with neighboring countries — particularly Argentina — being the primary destinations.

Third, Latin American exports to the United States are also growing, though not as fast as trade within the region. The value of LAC exports to the United States increased 89 percent between 1986 and 1992 — a compounded annual average of 11 percent — while the share of LAC exports sold to this country climbed two points to 42 percent.

Fourth, over half of LAC's exports to the United States originate in Mexico. Figure 3 illustrates Mexico's rapid climb to its current 52 percent share of the total exports from Latin America to the United States. In fact, as evidenced by Figure 4, Mexico accounted for over 75 percent of the growth of LAC exports to the United States that occurred between 1986 and 1992. Of LAC's US$29 billion increase in exports to the United States, fully US$22 billion accrued to Mexico. The significance of the U.S. market to Latin America is clearly skewed by Mexico's unique trading relationship.

Removing Mexico from the aggregate data for LAC allows for some interesting comparisons. Figure 5 shows that while LAC sends 42 percent of its exports to the United States, the figure for LAC excluding Mexico drops to 28 percent, with a corresponding rise in importance of the intra-LAC market. That this pattern has been accelerating rapidly is revealed by Figure 6. The exports of LAC excluding Mexico to the United States grew at a compounded annual rate of 4.7 percent between 1986 and 1992, while those to other LAC countries grew at a compounded annual rate of 15.7 percent. If these trends continue into the mid-1990s, Latin America will become a more important market than the United States for all Latin exporters except Mexico.

Fifth, between 1987 and 1992, Latin America was the fastest growing market for U.S. exports. In fact, the United States runs sizable trade surpluses with both Mexico and the rest of Latin America. As a percentage of exports to each, however, the U.S. surplus with LAC is growing much faster than is the surplus with Mexico. The 1992 U.S. surplus with Mexico stood at US$8 billion on exports of US$41 billion, or 20 percent (up from 16 percent in 1986). The U.S. trade surplus with the rest of Latin America and the Caribbean in 1992 was US$5.4 billion on exports of US$35 billion, or 15 percent. Though somewhat smaller than the surplus with Mexico, the surplus with the rest of Latin America has grown rapidly from a 1986 deficit of US$4 billion, a shortfall equivalent to 21 percent of that year's U.S. exports. As discussed next, this general pattern would be very slow to change in any foreseeable Western Hemisphere Free Trade Agreement (WHFTA).

Sixth, Latin America is accumulating substantial trade deficits. The year 1992 saw Latin America's first trade deficit in many years, and the gap has been growing ever since. The deficit reached about US$14 billion in 1993. Its causes are fairly clear. Unilateral trade liberalization, coupled with depressed prices for Latin American exports and large capital inflows that tend to drive up local currency values (thus stimulating imports and inhibiting exports), has created a problem throughout the region. Also at fault is an anti-export bias rooted in institutions, laws, and industrial structures engendered by decades of import substitution industrialization. While countries throughout the world export an average of around 13 percent of their output, Latin America exports only 7 percent of its total regional product.[9] Most Latin countries have been able to offset their trade deficits with substantial inflows of foreign — mostly portfolio — investment, but chronic trade imbalances compensated by inflows of volatile portfolio investments do not provide for a solid macroeconomic foundation. If higher interest rates and better yields in other regions slow the capital inflows now entering Latin America or if world prices of Latin exports — primarily cotton, oil, coffee, sugar, copper, and soybeans — do not recover and no major strides in export performance are made, Latin America will face renewed pressures on its balance of payments. Under such circumstances, further trade opening may be hard to achieve.

Composition and Barriers

Latin America's exports are dominated by natural resources and agricultural products. In fact, sales of crude and refined petroleum account for over 22 percent of all Latin American exports to the United States.[10] While sales of manufactured goods are considerable in a few countries — notably Mexico and Brazil — it is the prominence of raw material and agricultural trade that is most striking. Latin America accounts for 13 percent of the world's exports of metals, 11 percent of food, and 10 percent of fuel, but only about 1 percent of machinery and transportation equipment.[11]

This trait is important because U.S. tariff and nontariff barriers tend to escalate with the production ladder. As value is added, so too are trade taxes. Therefore, current LAC export patterns mean that only a minority of Latin products encounter significant barriers in the U.S. market. In fact, only 18 percent of LAC exports encounter tariffs of 5 percent or higher. Only 8 percent of LAC exports encounter such tariffs coupled with nontariff barriers.[12]

As a result, LAC countries specializing in low tariff primary commodity trade (Bolivia, Chile, Ecuador, Peru, and Venezuela) initially would experience only marginal export expansion on entering a free trade agreement with the United States. Most of the benefits would accrue to countries that export manufactures more intensively. It has been projected that free trade in the hemisphere would boost export values by about 8 percent. But more than half of that increase accrues to Mexico. Mexico and Brazil together account for almost 90 percent of the gains.[13]

Even those potential gains might be overestimated. Where substantial tariff and nontariff liberalization has occurred, the world trading system has witnessed a roughly parallel rise of antidumping and countervailing duties. The United States is one of the leading practitioners of this thinly veiled protectionism. From 1988 to 1993, U.S. companies petitioned that antidumping or countervailing duties be imposed on fifty-four manufactured products exported from Latin American countries.[14]

Firms attempting to defend themselves against the charges lodged by U.S. companies normally face long, complex, and costly procedures. For example, the legal actions of U.S. firms seeking to protect their domestic markets cost Venezuelan exporters an estimated US$400 million per year in lost potential earnings.[15] In many instances, the exporters charged are just beginning to sell to the United States and have yet to operate on a meaningful scale. Faced with legal fees and other costs that cannot be justified by their low export volumes, they are unlikely to take up expensive and uncertain international legal battles. Instead, they "voluntarily" limit their export drive into the United States.

These nontariff barriers constitute a major deterrent to the expansion of exports from Latin America to the United States, given that companies in the region generally face much less competition at home than in the United States. To penetrate the U.S. market, firms are often forced to charge less for their exports than they charge in domestic markets. While unfair trading practices may sometimes drive these pricing policies, asymmetric competitive pressures make nearly all Latin exporters extremely vulnerable to charges of dumping lodged by U.S. companies. This vulnerability tends to be higher for exporters of manufactured goods than for exporters of raw materials.[16]

Therefore, the export benefits of liberalizing trade with the United States will be both small and slow to emerge in LAC except for Mexico. As far as imports are concerned, larger Latin trade deficits with the North should be expected.

For most countries in Latin America, signing a free trade agreement with the United States is more analogous to furthering their unilateral trade liberalization than it is to gaining access to new markets. As noted, in the long run, a free trade agreement is bound to stimulate exports from LAC to the U.S. market, and their composition will reflect more closely the countries' competitive advantages. In the short run, however, Latin companies that are competitive enough to export to the United States are already doing so. With few exceptions, a free trade agreement with the United States is not likely to improve their access. In contrast, a free trade agreement does lower the average tariffs that U.S. exporters now face in most of Latin America and the Caribbean.

Further, if current trends continue, Latin America's export performance soon will be as dependent on intraregional trade as it will be on its exports outside the region. In fact, in the short run, Latin American countries could increase their export performance more readily through freer access to the Brazilian market than they could by signing a free trade agreement with the United States. Competitive Latin exporters that have been able to secure market niches in the United States and that are successfully exporting all over the world have not yet been able to gain access to the large and much closer Brazilian market.[17]

The Determinants of Recent Trade Liberalization in Latin America

Much recent thinking and writing about the extension of free trade in the hemisphere is based on the assumption that Latin America has undergone an ideological conversion that saw country after country dump its protectionist past for a free trade future. But despite sweeping economic liberalization, the "conversion" to free trade in Latin America is incipient and is still concentrated in small circles with substantial influence over public policies.[18] Latin America picked up free trade on the rebound of a disastrous affair with foreign-financed import substitution. With some exceptions, grass roots political support for open markets, deregulation, and privatization remains tentative and superficial. In many countries, "conversion" is actually resignation.

This may seem illogical. If the commitment to free trade is only superficial, how is it that reformist governments throughout the hemisphere have been able to muster the power to impose pro-liberalization measures? For most countries, the answer is that the need for a common front in a severe economic emergency enabled reformist governments to secure the authority to adopt radical policy changes in a variety of areas, including trade. In general, trade reform in Latin America was not adopted by the political system, but rather smuggled through it inside macroeconomic stabilization packages by reformist governments. Weakened by crisis, the opposition was caught by surprise. Indeed, the debt crisis helped reformers break long-standing protectionist coalitions formed by government officials, political groups, organized labor, and industrialists.

A recent study analyzing conditions immediately preceding trade liberalization episodes in Latin America found that out of 16 surveyed countries, 12 were experiencing negative or decreasing real gross domestic product (GDP) growth rates, 7 had inflation rates exceeding 50 percent per annum, 16 either had been forced to reschedule or had fallen behind on debt payments, 10 were suffering declining foreign exchange reserves, and all 16 had growing or consistently large balance of payments deficits.[19] Economic debacle seems to have been more consequential in creating the conditions leading to trade reform than was the widespread adoption of free market ideas.

While no ideological commitment is required to follow a path that seems the only alternative, such a commitment is necessary to maintain or deepen the recent reforms. This is especially so now that inflation is no longer so fearsome and export-led growth is running into problems caused by overvalued currencies, LAC's general lack of export-oriented infrastructure and institutions, and the continuing protectionism of the Organization for Economic Cooperation and Development (OECD) in key export sectors. Governmental goals to achieve further liberalization will be almost impossible to achieve under these circumstances. While Latin American industries are now more competitive than ever, they are not very competitive by world standards.[20] Many sectors remain protected and regulated, and much industrial conversion and privatization is still pending. To cope with these additional adjustments as the specter of a common enemy retreats, market-oriented governments will need to find a different rationale with which to sustain their market reforms. Progress toward further trade opening will be an even bigger political challenge, especially since the immediate gains that resulted from the bold initial reforms will be harder to obtain in this second, more burdensome phase.

The majority of the population in most Latin countries has yet to abandon hope for a benevolent welfare state and the protectionism bred by decades of rhetoric that extolled nationalism and blamed industrialized countries for poverty at home. In the absence of widespread ideological commitment to free markets, support for the reforms will critically hinge on their short-term ability to improve living conditions and on the political capacity of governments to stay the course in the face of strong attacks from the opposition. While the political conditions required to launch radical policy reforms are by now relatively well understood, the politics of sustaining such reforms once the sense of acute crisis has dissipated is still terra incognita for both practitioners and academics.

With the exception of Chile and possibly Mexico, most of the governments implementing market reforms in Latin America are still facing onerous battles to consolidate the reforms and build stable political coalitions in their support. The Chilean embrace of free trade ideology is not representative of any country south (and probably north) of the Rio Grande, and Mexico's "embrace" of free trade with the United States was driven by special economic and political circumstances that will be absent in future negotiations with potential NAFTA entrants.

Another crucial point that should be kept in mind is that the economic costs of trade liberalization in Latin America have been greatly lowered by the inflows of private capital that have dampened the consequences of the region's trade imbalances. Absent such capital inflows, balance of payments equilibriums would have been much more costly to obtain. Slower growth and, in some cases, an even harder battle to control inflation would have ensued. The region's vulnerability to a reduction of these flows of private capital to Latin America is substantial.[21] Open trade regimes are often the first victims of balance of payments crises.

The Rocky Road Toward Free Trade in the Americas

The bitterness of the internal debate in the United States over NAFTA shocked most observers. Four decades of postwar international economic relations suggested that Mexico should be the footdragger, fending off pressure from the hemispheric free trade giant as best it could. While fundamental changes in Mexico can account for its change of heart, what of the unexpected resistance to free trade in the United States? Additionally, what does that resistance mean for the likelihood of broadening NAFTA to become a hemispheric treaty?

In fact, it is possible that the U.S. debate actually bodes well for future liberalization in the Americas. To begin with, it put Latin America back on the U.S. nonmilitary radar for the first time in decades. More important, as harsh as it was, the battle ultimately forced the adoption and the staunch defense of the *principle* of hemispheric free trade. If the Clinton administration had not explicitly embraced the concept of free trade and the *long-run* benefits that greater competition would bring to the U.S. economy, NAFTA's fate would have been different. Rejected by Congress, the agreement (if not killed outright) would have been returned in emasculated form so as to avoid any pain from short-term adjustments.

The debate catapulted free trade in the Americas to the forefront of U.S. public awareness and explicitly set the stage for the extension to other countries of the principles on which NAFTA was argued. As Vice President Albert Gore has noted, "The NAFTA debate demonstrated the importance of dispelling myths and stereotypes concerning Latin America. It is clear to us that we must rethink the way we deal with the new Latin America that has emerged."[22]

Support of free trade as an ideological commitment was less necessary when (as in the early days of the GATT) U.S. industries were unquestionably the world's most efficient or when (as in the free trade agreement with Israel) predominantly noneconomic goals held sway. By approving NAFTA, the United States adopted a free trade policy with the expectation that the most valuable benefits were several years down the road and that there may even be some small but very noticeable losses before the realization of a net gain. That this could be accomplished with Mexico suggests that the path has been cleared for future agreements with other Latin American states, whose impact on the U.S. economy is much less and that have, in turn, made significant unilateral strides toward freer trade.

But while the prospects for achieving hemispheric free trade are better than ever, stumbling blocks remain. These must be borne in mind as strategies are crafted to realize and lock in the current potential.

In the United States, for example, NAFTA may be difficult to widen in substantial ways without the passage of a new fast-track negotiating authority. Securing it may be problematic, but without it, members of Congress can be relied upon to vote for narrow rather than national interests. One has only to recall the legislative process leading to the Caribbean Basin Initiative (CBI) to appraise the ease with which targeted amendments can riddle a trade package with protectionist loopholes. The lack of U.S. lobbies taking an interest in Central America and South America raises another issue now that NAFTA's extension must be pushed onto the 1995 congressional calendar. It is hard to imagine that the governors, Nobel prize winners, think tanks, chambers of commerce, media, and other interest groups that systematically rallied to Mexico's support during the legislative battle over NAFTA will be as active in support of free trade with Argentina or Venezuela. The same, of course, may be true for the forces that opposed NAFTA. While organized labor, environ- mental groups, and other members of the anti-NAFTA lobby have already stressed that they intend to be as active in discussions about new free trade agreements as they were with NAFTA, it is unlikely that their opposition will be as fierce or effective.

Another area of problems for the expansion of hemispheric free trade lies in the institutional constraints of the U.S. policy-making machinery. What opportunity costs will be faced by the Clinton administration in expending executive effort on negotiations with, say, Chile or Argentina, instead of with the larger economies of Asia?

There may also be opposition to widening NAFTA before it is deepened. Most of the institutions NAFTA is supposed to create have yet to be born, much less consolidated. As several of them were designed to mollify the treaty's opponents — the North American Development Bank, the Border Environ- ment Cooperation Commission, the Oversight Commission on Labor Matters, for example — progress on NAFTA's extension may be blocked so long as the agreement's institutional foundation is weak.

Finally, the relative ease of the negotiations with Mexico has set precedents and created expectations in the United States that other LAC countries will be hard-pressed to meet. Mexico already had a level of economic integration with the United States matched by no other country except Canada. Nonetheless, it seems commonly ignored that Mexico had the economic, political, and institutional incentives to make concessions to the United States that other Latin governments are less likely to have. Concluding NAFTA was made much easier by Mexico's unique dependence on the U.S. market and U.S. foreign investment, by Mexico's large constituency in the United States, and by the Mexican government's political, organizational, and financial capacity to mobilize that constituency. Even when major last-minute concessions were sought by the Clinton administration, Mexico's executive grip over the legislature, the unions, the private sector, and television gave it the autonomy to overcome domestic opposition and close the deal (see Box 1).

While other Latin American *governments* tend to have the same intense motivation exhibited by the Salinas administration to enter into a free trade agreement with the United States, they may very well lack the political autonomy to push a NAFTA-like agreement through their political system successfully. This will be especially so if, as was the case with Mexico, the United States expects to exempt future entrants' most competitive products from tariff-free treatment or if the agreement implies increases in the price of medicines as a result of changes in intellectual property laws or the redeployment of scarce public funds out of needed domestic investments into environmental projects.

In any event, putting Latin American governments that are already under severe political pressures in the position of having to pay the same entry fees imposed on Mexico will surely add to the already substantial burdens that reformers in Latin America are having to bear.

Moreover, when Canada is considered, the picture becomes even more complex. Relationships between Canada and Latin America are very distant. The frequent calls for a different NAFTA — a North *Atlantic* Free Trade Agreement with Europe — that were heard during the political debate in Canada are not likely to abate in the future. For many Canadians, furthering the ties to regions that are culturally and economically closer may be more seductive than deeper integration with Latin America. Canada's closest relationship with Latin America has been with Mexico. Yet in 1990, only three hundred Canadian business executives even visited the country.[23] Canadian exports to Latin America excluding Mexico have grown only anemically, while total trade levels between Canada and MERCOSUR actually declined between 1986 and 1992. Many of the trade expansion hurdles confronting the United States apply with even greater intensity to Canada.

On the other hand, Latin America has hurdles of its own, the most obvious of which is the perceived lack of short-term *trade* benefits stemming from free trade with the United States. Export growth will not be appreciable in the short term, while the trade deficit with the United States is likely to grow. Long-run dynamic gains are too hypothetical and too vague to compensate for the immediate costs faced by local business sectors that are struggling to penetrate protected export markets as their local customers abandon them in favor of cheaper imports. Denunciation of the "naive trade opening" under-taken by romantic government technocrats is rapidly becoming part of daily debate throughout Latin America. Coupling this with the sorry example of continued U.S. protection in sensitive sectors leaves important Latin constituencies with little tangible to cheer for in "free" trade with the United States.

Even if free trade's dynamic impacts were credible in LAC, they would not be embraced by a number of influential constituencies. Major institutional changes will cause certain sectors even more adjustment pain than did unilateral tariff liberalization. In fact, the explicit prerequisites the United States has made for NAFTA accession imply significant short- and medium-term resource transfers from South to North. Stringent enforcement of intellectual property rights will drive up the costs of pharmaceuticals, software, and other such knowledge-based products. The elimination of trade-related investment measures — like local content requirements or export performance targets — will impose heavy adjustment costs on those sectors that now benefit from these policies. Enforcement of higher environmental standards will shift resources from underfunded areas of higher domestic priority, and LAC governments will be challenged to explain why public choices made in North America should be adopted by their own countries.

Finally, what is needed in Latin America is that existing labor laws be revamped before they are enforced. Most countries provide very generous labor regulations, but do so exclusively for workers in the formal sector and mostly for public workers. Because of this formal sector focus, many regulations — especially those surrounding dismissal — are so costly and so divorced from actual conditions that compliance is limited, irregular, and often impossible. Assessing the impact of a labor conditionality in a WHFTA is greatly complicated by this gap between law and actual practice. The United States should bear in mind that labor market liberalization is one of the largest pending reforms throughout the region. Locking in the status quo would be counterproductive. In this respect, it is worth citing a comment of the Venezuelan Minister of Planning at the time NAFTA was being negotiated:

> As a Latin American economist, I cannot but poke some fun at the insistence to include in free trade negotiations a side agreement to insure "appropriate attention to workers rights." In Latin America, it is common to have 150 days of paid postnatal leave, large severance payments, heavy taxes on the wage bill, substantial union powers, closed-shop legislation, and many other worker benefits of this nature. Do you really want to create a level playing field along these lines...?[24]

The main point is that at this time few countries other than Chile can satisfy the set of conditions that were incorporated into the NAFTA treaty. This reality is being increasingly recognized by officials in the Clinton administration. As the Under Secretary of Commerce for International Trade has noted:

The fact is that few nations are at this time likely to be far enough in their reform efforts, or in their labor and environmental policies, to meet the NAFTA standard. Moreover, few are willing to expose their industries to the full brunt of competition from abroad that a NAFTA-type arrangement would entail.[25]

Nonetheless, fear of exclusion makes many governments in the region very committed to joining a free trade treaty with the hemisphere's industrialized North, either through NAFTA or through a bilateral agreement with the United States. Unfortunately, many other significant political actors are not so committed. Governments in the process of liberalization and their negotiating partners must both be mindful of these differences, but the primary challenge is internal. Demanding that countries pay NAFTA-like entry fees will require LAC governments to carry out skillful coalition building among a skeptical polity. The prospects for free trade may look bright, but it won't be achieved on the cheap.

Conclusions

One of the central messages of this chapter is that overloading trade negotiations with conditions that impose added political burdens on reformist governments may be a mistake. Most countries' economic reforms are incipient, and their political foundations are weak. Reformist coalitions are having to struggle to push their economic reforms beyond macroeconomic stabilization, deregulation, and the "easier" privatizations into the much more complex stage of institutional reform. Free trade agreements can certainly support these difficult transitions. The risk, however, is that domestic dynamics in the United States and Canada may create entry conditions with political costs that will burden even Latin America's most reform-minded governments — precisely those that can least afford to be left out of the new international economic arrangements. Many Latin governments understand the costs of exclusion from free trade agreements with industrialized countries, but they will have a hard time rallying political support for international treaties that give tangible and immediate benefits to the industrialized North in exchange for future payoffs viewed with skepticism by powerful Latin American constituencies.

Enlightened statecraft would pay as much attention to the goal of long-term stabilization of market reforms as it does to the immediate opening of markets for U.S. firms or to insuring their rights to intellectual property. In fact, the conditions required to enter a free trade agreement designed to achieve such narrow goals may well end up undermining the political standing of constituencies pushing for overall economic liberalization in Latin America. Concern for these internal constituencies and their political dynamics should replace notions generated by negotiations with Mexico, which had the economic incentives and executive autonomy to be both willing and able to accommodate demands that flowed from U.S. domestic politics and unilateral interests.

In summary, efforts at expanding free trade in the hemisphere will have major impacts on the future of economic liberalization in Latin America. And while reform's fate will be played out on domestic stages unique to each country, negotiating positions taken by industrialized trading partners will have a profound influence on the turn of events. The United States can increase the perceived benefits of opening to the U.S. market by committing to an accelerated timetable for the liberalization of those "sensitive" sectors in which Latin America might expect to boost its export performance significantly. The United States and Canada should also be mindful of the political challenges that long-haul liberalization will face in each reforming country and should strive to remain flexible as trade agreement timetables are hammered out. Hemispheric free trade can be achieved. It will be accomplished both faster and more durably if negotiating partners are willing to shed many of the assumptions that have guided their recent thought and action in this area.

Box 1

Trade and investment dependence on the United States gave Mexico the economic, political, and institutional incentives to make significant concessions during NAFTA's negotiation. Equally important, strong executive control gave Mexico the political capacity to deliver on the promise it made, thus ensuring that both the necessary and sufficient conditions for treaty conclusion were in place. The United States will find that neither situation is prevalent in the rest of Latin America.

Conditions	Mexico	Rest of L.A.
INCENTIVES		
Exports to the United States/ Total Exports	76%	28%
Imports from the United States/ Total Imports	69%	31%
U.S. Net Foreign Direct Investment	$13B	$76B
Legal Migration to the United States	5.1M	5.4M
EXECUTIVE BRANCH AUTONOMY		
Executive Influence Over Congress	Very High	Med – Low
Executive Influence Over the Judiciary	Higher	Lower
Executive Influence Over the Unions	Higher	Lower
Executive Influence Over the Media	Higher	Lower
Strength of Political Opposition	Low	Higher

Source: The International Monetary Fund and the U.S. Departments of Commerce and Justice.

Table 1. Subregional Trade Pacts in the Americas

Name	Date Signed	Member States
TRI- AND MULTILATERAL PACTS		
Andean Pact	1969	Bolivia, Colombia, Ecuador, Peru, Venezuela
CACM (Central American Common Market)	1960	Costa Rica, El Salvador, Guatemala, Honduras, Nicaragua
CARICOM	1973	Antigua-Barbuda, Bahamas, Barbados, Belize, Dominica, Grenada, Guyana, Jamaica, Montserrat, St. Kitts-Nevis, St. Lucia, St. Vincent-Grenadines, Trinidad and Tobago
G-3	1991	Colombia, Mexico, Venezuela
MERCOSUR	1991	Argentina, Brazil, Paraguay, Uruguay
NAFTA	1993	Canada, Mexico, United States
LAIA (Latin American Integration Association. LAIA replaced LAFTA, the Latin American Free Trade Association, formed in 1960)	1980	Mexico and all South American countries except French Guiana, Guyana, and Suriname
Mexico-Central America	1991	
Venezuela-CARICOM	1992	Venezuela with CARICOM members
El Salvador-Honduras-Guatemala	1992	
BILATERAL PACTS		
Mexico-Chile	1991	
Colombia-Venezuela	1991	
Colombia-Chile	1993	
Chile-Venezuela	1993	
PREFERENTIAL PACTS		
Andean Trade Preference Act	1991	United States with Bolivia, Colombia, Ecuador, and Peru
CBI (Caribbean Basin Initiative)	1983	United States with CARICOM and CACM members plus Aruba, British Virgin Islands, Dominican Republic, Haiti, Netherlands Antilles, and Panama
CARIBCAN (Canadian-Caribbean Agreement)	1986	Canada and Caribbean members of the Commonwealth, including Belize and Guyana

Source: *U.S.-Latin Trade,* January 1994; Governments of Venezuela and the United States.

Table 2. Latin American Tariffs
Before and After Reform

	Average Unweighted Tariffs (%)	
	Pre-Reform	Post-Reform
Argentina (1987 vs. 1991)	42	15
Bolivia (1985 vs. 1991)	12	8
Brazil (1987 vs. 1992)	51	21
Chile (1984 vs. 1991)	35	11
Colombia (1984 vs. 1992)	61	12
Costa Rica (1985 vs. 1992)	53	15
Ecuador (1989 vs. 1992)	37	18
Guatemala (1985 vs. 1992)	50	15
Honduras (1985 vs. 1992)	41	15
Jamaica (1981 vs. 1991)	N.A.	20
Mexico (1985 vs. 1990)	24	13
Paraguay (1988 vs. 1991)	N.A.	16
Peru (1988 vs. 1992)	N.A.	17
Trinidad (1989 vs. 1991)	N.A.	41
Uruguay (1987 vs. 1992)	32	18
Venezuela (1989 vs. 1991)	37	19

Source: Asad Alam and Sarath Rajapatirana, "Trade Policy Reform in Latin America and the Caribbean in the 1980s," World Bank, WPS 1104, 1993.

Table 3. Hemispheric Export Patterns:
1986 to 1992

				Exporting Region					
United States					Mexico				
1986			1992		1986			1992	
US$ M	% Tot X	Average Annual Growth Rate	US$ M	% Tot X	US$ M	% Tot X	Average Annual Growth Rate	US$ M	% Tot X
—	—	—	—	—	10,424	65%	**20.9%**	32,624	76%
12,392	6%	**21.9%**	40,598	9%	—	—	—	—	—
31,071	14%	**16.0%**	75,739	17%	1,073	7%	**10.7%**	1,971	5%
18,679	9%	**11.1%**	35,141	8%	1,073	7%	**10.7%**	1,971	5%
3,885	2%	**6.7%**	5,740	1%	167	1%	**9.5%**	288	1%
5,099	2%	**11.1%**	9,608	2%	318	2%	**7.9%**	503	1%
5,866	3%	**11.0%**	10,943	2%	236	1%	**10.9%**	438	1%
4,460	2%	**11.8%**	8,720	2%	157	1%	**11.4%**	300	1%
16,852	8%	**19.6%**	49,318	11%	157	1%	**11.4%**	300	1%
217,292	100%	**12.8%**	447,400	100%	16,120	100%	**17.6%**	42,700	100%

Continued next page

Table 3. Hemispheric Export Patterns:
1986 to 1992 (Continued)

					Exporting Region				
	LAC					**LAC – Mexico**			
1986			**1992**		**1986**			**1992**	
US$ M	% Tot X	Average Annual Growth Rate	US$ M	% Tot X	US$ M	% Tot X	Average Annual Growth Rate	US$ M	% Tot X
33,026	40%	11.2%	62,409	42%	22,602	34%	4.7%	29,785	28%
393	0%	32.2%	2,094	1%	393	1%	32.2%	2,094	2%
11,629	14%	15.3%	27,277	18%	10,556	16%	15.7%	25,306	24%
11,236	14%	14.4%	25,183	17%	10,163	15%	14.8%	23,212	22%
1,795	2%	13.4%	3,826	3%	1,628	2%	13.8%	3,538	3%
4,146	5%	15.5%	9,835	7%	3,828	6%	16.0%	9,332	9%
2,533	3%	13.2%	5,316	4%	2,297	3%	13.4%	4,878	5%
1,293	2%	13.7%	2,796	2%	1,136	2%	14.0%	2,496	2%
1,686	2%	19.4%	4,890	3%	1,529	2%	20.1%	4,590	4%
82,444	100%	10.4%	149,357	100%	66,324	100%	8.2%	106,657	100%

Continued next page

Table 3. Hemispheric Export Patterns:
1986 to 1992 (Continued)

Exporting Region									
Brazil					MERCOSUR				
1986			1992		1986			1992	
US$ M	% Tot X	Average Annual Growth Rate	US$ M	% Tot X	US$ M	% Tot X	Average Annual Growth Rate	US$ M	% Tot X
6,315	28%	2.1%	7,143	20%	7,161	23%	3.1%	8,595	17%
156	1%	38.7%	1,111	3%	321	1%	28.0%	1,413	3%
2,774	12%	19.7%	8,166	23%	4,996	16%	17.4%	13,101	26%
2,618	12%	18.0%	7,055	19%	4,675	15%	16.5%	11,688	23%
—	—	—	—	—	1,086	4%	11.2%	2,050	4%
1,176	5%	23.3%	4,128	11%	2,593	8%	18.0%	7,007	14%
952	4%	7.4%	1,458	4%	1,342	4%	8.7%	2,220	4%
457	2%	9.6%	791	2%	570	2%	12.0%	1,124	2%
613	3%	20.8%	1,902	5%	891	3%	19.0%	2,537	5%
22,405	100%	8.3%	36,207	100%	30,578	100%	8.8%	50,786	100%

Continued next page

Table 3. Hemispheric Export Patterns:
1986 to 1992 (Concluded)

Exporting Region									
Andean Pact					Colombia + Venezuela				
1986			1992		1986			1992	
US$ M	% Tot X	Average Annual Growth Rate	US$ M	% Tot X	US$ M	% Tot X	Average Annual Growth Rate	US$ M	% Tot X
7,468	40%	9.5%	12,853	42%	5,295	39%	12.3%	10,637	46%
29	0%	53.9%	386	1%	17	0%	57.9%	263	1%
3,292	17%	14.5%	7,436	24%	2,267	17%	17.7%	6,042	26%
3,263	17%	13.7%	7,050	23%	2,250	17%	17.0%	5,779	25%
200	1%	25.9%	798	3%	77	1%	41.2%	609	3%
701	4%	7.6%	1,089	4%	153	1%	28.7%	696	3%
641	3%	19.7%	1,883	6%	422	3%	22.6%	1,431	6%
402	2%	17.3%	1,047	3%	255	2%	20.5%	779	3%
431	2%	22.2%	1,433	5%	272	2%	25.1%	1,042	3%
18,836	100%	8.3%	30,362	100%	13,520	100%	9.2%	22,936	100%

Hemispheric Export Patterns: 1986 to 1992

	Exporting Region														
	United States					Canada					Mexico				
	1986		Average Annual Growth	1992		1986		Average Annual Growth	1992		1986		Average Annual Growth	1992	
To:	US$ M	% Tot X	Rate	US$ M	% Tot X	US$ M	% Tot X	Rate	US$ M	% Tot X	US$ M	% Tot X	Rate	US$ M	% Tot X
United States	–	–	–	–	–	67,183	75%	7.5%	103,860	78%	10,424	65%	20.9%	32,624	76%
Canada	45,333	21%	12.1%	90,156	20%	–	–	–	–	–	224	1%	46.4%	2,207	5%
Mexico	12,392	6%	21.9%	40,598	9%	288	0%	13.4%	613	0%	–	–	–	–	–
LAC	31,071	14%	16.0%	75,739	17%	1,979	2%	4.0%	2,501	2%	1,073	7%	10.7%	1,971	5%
World	217,292	100%	12.8%	447,400	100%	89,706	100%	6.8%	133,447	100%	16,120	100%	17.6%	42,700	100%
Argentina	943	0%	22.7%	3,222	1%	49	0%	8.5%	80	0%	96	1%	11.1%	1812	0%
Bolivia	112	0%	12.1%	222	0%	7	0%	7.8%	11	0%	1	0%	38.3%	7	0%
Brazil	3,885	2%	6.7%	5,740	1%	566	1%	-1.9%	506	0%	167	1%	9.5%	288	1%
Chile	824	0%	20.0%	2,455	1%	63	0%	12.5%	128	0%	23	0%	43.3%	199	0%
Colombia	1,319	1%	16.4%	3,282	1%	134	0%	6.5%	195	0%	107	1%	5.0%	151	0%
Ecuador	601	0%	8.8%	999	0%	61	0%	-1.4%	56	0%	50	0%	-2.5%	43	0%
Paraguay	171	0%	15.9%	415	0%	2	0%	12.2%	4	0%	1	0%	–	0	0%
Peru	693	0%	6.3%	1,002	0%	79	0%	-1.1%	74	0%	28	0%	21.0%	88	0%
Uruguay	100	0%	15.0%	231	0%	9	0%	1.8%	10	0%	54	0%	-7.4%	34	0%
Venezuela	3,141	1%	9.6%	5,438	1%	291	0%	4.8%	386	0%	50	0%	20.0%	149	0%
G-3	16,852	8%	19.6%	49,318	11%	713	1%	9.0%	1,194	1%	157	1%	11.4%	300	1%
Mercosur	5,099	2%	11.1%	9,608	2%	626	1%	-0.7%	600	0%	318	2%	7.9%		
Andean Pact	5,866	3%	11.0%	10,943	2%	572	1%	4.0%	722	1%	236	1%	10.9%	438	1%
NAFTA	57,725	27%	14.6%	130,754	29%	67,471	75%	7.6%	104,473	78%	10,648	66%	21.8%	34,831	82%
Colomb+Ven	4,460	2%	11.8%	8720	2%	425	0%	5.3%	581	0%	157	1%	11.4%	300	1%
LAC - Mex	18679	9%	11.1%	35141	8%	1691	2%	1.9%	1,888	1%	1,073	7%	10.7%	1,971	5%

Page 1 of 7

N.B. Paraguay data are from 1991 and 1990. All yearly trade figures under $500,000 are recorded as zero.
Source: Country export values from IMP, Direction of Trade Statistics Yearbook, 1993. Aggregates and analysis by author.

Hemispheric Export Patterns: 1986 to 1992 (Continued)

	Exporting Region														
	LAC					Argentina					Bolivia				
	1986		Average Annual Growth	1992		1986		Average Annual Growth	1992		1986		Average Annual Growth	1992	
To:	US$ M	% Tot X	Rate	US$ M	% Tot X	US$ M	% Tot X	Rate	US$ M	% Tot X	US$ M	% Tot X	Rate	US$ M	% Tot X
United States	33,026	40%	11.2%	62,409	42%	706	10%	9.9%	1,245	10%	97	15%	2.6%	113	16%
Canada	1,449	2%	17.3%	3,782	3%	54	1%	9.5%	93	1%	0	0%	—	0	0%
Mexico	393	0%	32.2%	2,094	1%	158	2%	8.6%	259	2%	0	0%	—	7	1%
LAC	11,629	14%	15.3%	27,277	18%	1,639	24%	16.2%	4,035	33%	413	65%	-5.9%	287	41%
World	82,444	100%	10.4%	149,357	100%	6,852	100%	10.3%	12,366	100%	640	100%	1.6%	705	100%
Argentina	1,570	2%	18.2%	4,275	3%	—	—	—	—	—	341	53%	-12.6%	152	22%
Bolivia	309	0%	12.3%	621	0%	61	1%	5.1%	82	1%	—	—	—	—	—
Brazil	1,795	2%	13.4%	3,826	3%	698	10%	14.8%	1,598	13%	26	4%	-12.1%	12	2%
Chile	718	1%	22.0%	2,373	2%	137	2%	30.9%	688	6%	20	3%	-1.7%	18	3%
Colombia	563	1%	14.3%	1,258	1%	61	1%	5.9%	86	1%	2	0%	52.3%	25	4%
Ecuador	336	0%	11.0%	627	0%	11	0%	41.2%	87	1%	0	0%	—	3	0%
Paraguay	370	0%	13.6%	797	1%	67	1%	20.1%	201	2%	0	0%	—	1	0%
Peru	595	1%	13.5%	1,272	1%	189	3%	3.4%	231	2%	22	3%	17.5%	58	8%
Uruguay	411	0%	14.7%	937	1%	129	2%	16.0%	314	3%	0	0%	—	1	0%
Venezuela	730	1%	13.2%	1,538	1%	45	1%	30.4%	221	2%	0	0%	—	5	1%
G-3	1,686	2%	19.4%	4,890	3%	264	4%	13.6%	566	5%	2	0%	62.3%	37	5%
Mercosur	4,146	5%	15.5%	9,835	7%	894	13%	15.4%	2,113	17%	367	57%	-12.4%	166	24%
Andean Pact	2,533	3%	13.2%	5,316	4%	367	5%	11.5%	707	6%	24	4%	24.9%	91	13%
NAFTA	34,868	42%	11.9%	68,285	46%	918	13%	9.7%	1,597	13%	97	15%	3.6%	120	17%
Colomb + Ven	1,293	2%	13.7%	2,796	2%	106	2%	19.4%	307	2%	2	0%	57.0%	30	4%
LAC - Mex	11,236	14%	14.4%	25,183	17%	1,481	22%	16.9%	3,776	31%	413	65%	-6.2%	280.4	40%

Page 2 of 7

N.B. Paraguay data are from 1991 and 1990. All yearly trade figures under $500,000 are recorded as zero.
Source: Country export values from IMP, Direction of Trade Statistics Yearbook, 1993. Aggregates and analysis by author.

Hemispheric Export Patterns: 1986 to 1992 (Continued)

Exporting Region

To:	Brazil 1986 US$ M	% Tot X	Avg Annual Growth Rate	1992 US$ M	% Tot X	Chile 1986 US$ M	% Tot X	Avg Annual Growth Rate	1992 US$ M	% Tot X	Colombia 1986 US$ M	% Tot X	Avg Annual Growth Rate	1992 US$ M	% Tot X
United States	6,315	28%	2.1%	7,143	20%	915	22%	10.3%	1,650	17%	1,531	30%	10.5%	2,786	39%
Canada	437	2%	-1.4%	402	1%	58	1%	4.5%	75	1%	73	1%	6.7%	108	1%
Mexico	156	1%	38.7%	1,111	3%	10	0%	45.0%	93	1%	11	0%	33.0%	61	1%
LAC	2,774	12%	19.7%	8,166	23%	720	17%	15.7%	1,726	17%	581	11%	19.2%	1,670	23%
World	22,405	100%	8.3%	36,207	100%	4,226	100%	15.4%	9,956	100%	5,108	100%	6.0%	7,226	100%
Argentina	682	3%	28.5%	3,070	8%	161	4%	19.2%	462	5%	67	1%	-8.6%	39	1%
Bolivia	204	1%	8.5%	333	1%	31	1%	30.3%	152	2%	1	0%	38.3%	7	0%
Brazil	—	—	—	—	—	293	7%	7.5%	451	5%	8	0%	41.1%	63	1%
Chile	247	1%	24.7%	930	3%	—	—	—	—	—	32	1%	24.1%	117	2%
Colombia	108	0%	21.5%	347	1%	41	1%	10.3%	74	1%	—	—	—	—	—
Ecuador	134	1%	0.1%	135	0%	28	1%	14.8%	64	1%	59	1%	14.5%	133	2%
Paraguay	291	1%	10.9%	541	1%	5	0%	43.1%	43	0%	0	0%	—	1	0%
Peru	157	1%	4.0%	199	1%	66	2%	17.4%	173	2%	71	1%	27.4%	304	4%
Uruguay	203	1%	16.9%	517	1%	11	0%	21.3%	35	0%	1	0%	0.0%	1	0%
Venezuela	349	2%	4.1%	444	1%	41	1%	10.6%	75	1%	150	3%	21.1%	473	7%
G-3	613	3%	20.8%	1,902	5%	92	2%	17.5%	242	2%	161	3%	22.1%	534	7%
Mercosur	1,176	5%	23.3%	4,128	11%	470	11%	13.2%	991	10%	76	1%	5.4%	104	1%
Andean Pact	952	4%	7.4%	1,458	4%	207	5%	17.3%	538	5%	281	6%	21.8%	917	13%
NAFTA	6,908	31%	3.8%	8,656	24%	983	23%	10.8%	1,818	18%	1,615	32%	10.6%	2,955	41%
Colomb+Ven	457	2%	9.6%	791	2%	82	2%	10.5%	149	1%	150	3%	21.1%	473	7%
LAC-Mex	2,618	12%	18.0%	7,055	19%	710	17%	14.9%	1,633	16%	570	11%	18.9%	1,609	22%

N.B. Paraguay data are from 1991 and 1990. All yearly trade figures under $500,000 are recorded as zero.
Source: Country export values from IMP, Direction of Trade Statistics Yearbook, 1993. Aggregates and analysis by author.

Page 3 of 7

Hemispheric Export Patterns: 1986 to 1992 (Continued)

Exporting Region

To:	Ecuador 1986 US$ M	% Tot X	Ecuador Avg Annual Growth Rate	Ecuador 1992 US$ M	% Tot X	Paraguay 1986 US$ M	% Tot X	Paraguay Avg Annual Growth Rate	Paraguay 1992 US$ M	% Tot X	Peru 1986 US$ M	% Tot X	Peru Avg Annual Growth Rate	Peru 1992 US$ M	% Tot X
United States	1,322	61%	0.4%	1,358	42%	9	4%	24.8%	34	6%	754	30%	-0.2%	745	21%
Canada	5	0%	40.2%	38	1%	0	0%	—	0	0%	18	1%	35.6%	112	3%
Mexico	9	0%	15.2%	21	1%	0	0%	—	1	0%	3	0%	77.9%	95	3%
LAC	250	12%	11.4%	477	15%	156	67%	6.1%	222	37%	362	14%	9.7%	630	18%
World	2,171	100%	6.9%	3,237	100%	233	100%	16.8%	593	100%	2,505	100%	5.7%	3,484	100%
Argentina	21	1%	-1.7%	19	1%	35	15%	4.3%	45	8%	57	2%	-11.2%	28	1%
Bolivia	0	0%	—	1	0%	0	0%	—	2	0%	11	0%	20.7%	34	1%
Brazil	23	1%	-10.3%	12	0%	92	39%	10.6%	168	28%	74	3%	14.3%	165	5%
Chile	47	2%	20.8%	146	5%	14	6%	22.8%	48	8%	49	2%	-2.2%	43	1%
Colombia	30	1%	2.4%	35	1%	0	0%	—	1	0%	66	3%	4.9%	88	3%
Ecuador	—	—	—	—	—	0	0%	—	0	0%	29	1%	5.5%	40	1%
Paraguay	0	0%	—	0	0%	—	—	—	—	—	0	0%	—	1	0%
Peru	10	0%	29.9%	48	1%	4	2%	0.0%	4	1%	—	—	—	—	—
Uruguay	4	0%	—	0	0%	6	3%	7.0%	9	2%	2	0%	0.0%	2	0%
Venezuela	3	0%	20.1%	9	0%	0	0%	—	12	2%	46	2%	15.1%	107	3%
G-3	42	2%	7.4%	65	2%	0	0%	—	14	2%	115	5%	16.7%	290	8%
Mercosur	48	2%	-7.0%	31	1%	133	57%	8.9%	222	37%	133	5%	6.7%	196	6%
Andean Pact	43	2%	13.6%	93	3%	4	2%	29.2%	19	3%	152	6%	10.0%	269	8%
NAFTA	1,336	62%	1.0%	1,417	44%	9	4%	25.4%	35	6%	775	31%	3.5%	952	27%
Colomb+Ven	33	2%	4.7%	44	1%	0	0%	—	12.58	2%	112	4%	9.7%	195	6%
LAC - Mex	241	11%	11.2%	456	14%	156	67%	6.0%	221	37%	359	14%	6.9%	535	15%

N.B. Paraguay data are from 1991 and 1990. All yearly trade figures under $500,000 are recorded as zero.
Source: Country export values from IMP, Direction of Trade Statistics Yearbook, 1993. Aggregates and analysis by author.

Hemispheric Export Patterns: 1986 to 1992 (Continued)

Exporting Region

To:	Uruguay 1986 US$ M	% Tot X	Average Annual Growth Rate	1992 US$ M	% Tot X	Venezuela 1986 US$ M	% Tot X	Average Annual Growth Rate	1992 US$ M	% Tot X	G-3 1986 US$ M	% Tot X	Average Annual Growth Rate	1992 US$ M	% Tot X
United States	131	12%	4.7%	173	11%	3,764	45%	13.0%	7,851	50%	15,719	53%	18.4%	43,261	66%
Canada	7	1%	12.2%	14	1%	272	3%	0.6%	282	2%	569	2%	28.8%	2,597	4%
Mexico	7	1%	34.8%	42	3%	6	0%	79.7%	202	1%	17	0%	57.9%	263	0%
LAC	427	39%	8.0%	678	42%	1,686	20%	17.2%	4,372	28%	3,340	11%	15.7%	8,013	12%
World	1,088	100%	6.9%	1,620	100%	8,412	100%	11.0%	15,710	100%	29,640	100%	14.2%	65,636	100%
Argentina	89	8%	18.8%	250	15%	8	0%	20.1%	24	0%	171	1%	6.1%	244	0%
Bolivia	1	0%	20.1%	3	0%	0	0%	—	1	0%	2	0%	39.9%	15	0%
Brazil	296	27%	-0.7%	284	18%	69	1%	41.2%	546	3%	244	1%	24.2%	897	1%
Chile	7	1%	38.7%	50	3%	116	1%	3.5%	143	1%	171	1%	17.9%	459	1%
Colombia	4	0%	12.2%	8	0%	105	1%	19.5%	306	2%	212	1%	13.7%	457	1%
Ecuador	1	0%	12.2%	2	0%	5	0%	58.4%	79	1%	114	0%	14.4%	255	0%
Paraguay	5	0%	12.2%	10	1%	0	0%	—	0	0%	1	0%	0.0%	1	0%
Peru	10	1%	10.3%	18	1%	31	0%	26.7%	128	1%	130	0%	26.0%	520	1%
Uruguay	—	—		—	—	0	0%	—	22	0%	55	0%	0.6%	57	0%
Venezuela	3	0%	8.9%	5	0%	—	—	—	—	—	200	1%	20.8%	622	1%
G-3	14	1%	25.6%	55	3%	111	1%	28.9%	508	3%	429	1%	20.9%	1,342	2%
Mercosur	390	36%	5.7%	544	34%	77	1%	40.5%	592	4%	471	2%	16.9%	1,199	2%
Andean Pact	19	2%	11.2%	36	2%	141	2%	24.1%	514	3%	658	2%	19.0%	1,869	3%
NAFTA	145	13%	7.9%	229	14%	4,042	48%	12.8%	8,335	53%	16,305	55%	18.9%	46,121	70%
Colomb+Ven	7	1%	10.9%	13	1%	105	1%	19.5%	306	2%	412	1%	17.4%	1,079	2%
LAC - Mex	420	39%	7.2%	636	39%	1,680	20%	16.4%	4,170	27%	3323	11%	15.2%	7,750	12%

N.B. Paraguay data are from 1991 and 1990. All yearly trade figures under $500,000 are recorded as zero.
Source: Country export values from IMP, Direction of Trade Statistics Yearbook, 1993. Aggregates and analysis by author.

Hemispheric Export Patterns: 1986 to 1992 (Continued)

	MERCOSUR					Andean Pact					NAFTA				
	1986		Average Annual Growth	1992		1986		Average Annual Growth	1992		1986		Average Annual Growth	1992	
To:	US$ M	% Tot X	Rate	US$ M	% Tot X	US$ M	% Tot X	Rate	US$ M	% Tot X	US$ M	% Tot X	Rate	US$ M	% Tot X
United States	7,161	23%	3.1%	8,595	17%	7,468	40%	9.5%	12,853	42%	77,607	24%	9.9%	136,484	22%
Canada	498	2%	0.4%	509	1%	368	2%	6.6%	540	2%	45,557	14%	12.5%	92,363	15%
Mexico	321	1%	28.0%	1,413	3%	29	0%	53.9%	386	1%	12,680	4%	21.7%	41,211	7%
LAC	4,996	16%	17.4%	13,101	26%	3,292	17%	14.5%	7,436	24%	34,123	11%	15.3%	80,211	13%
World	30,578	100%	8.8%	50,786	100%	18,836	100%	8.3%	30,362	100%	323,118	100%	11.6%	623,547	100%
Argentina	806	3%	26.9%	3,365	7%	494	3%	-10.0%	262	1%	1,088	0%	21.4%	3,483	1%
Bolivia	266	1%	7.9%	420	1%	12	0%	23.7%	43	0%	120	0%	12.2%	240	0%
Brazil	1,086	4%	11.2%	2,050	4%	200	1%	25.9%	798	3%	4,618	1%	6.0%	6,534	1%
Chile	405	1%	27.2%	1,716	3%	264	1%	10.0%	467	2%	910	0%	20.5%	2,782	0%
Colombia	173	1%	16.9%	442	1%	203	1%	14.3%	454	1%	1,560	0%	15.1%	3,628	1%
Ecuador	146	0%	7.4%	224	0%	93	0%	18.3%	255	1%	712	0%	7.5%	1,098	0%
Paraguay	363	1%	12.9%	752	1%	0	0%	ERR	3	0%	174	0%	15.8%	419	0%
Peru	360	1%	3.9%	452	1%	134	1%	26.1%	538	2%	800	0%	6.4%	1,164	0%
Uruguay	338	1%	16.4%	840	2%	7	0%	24.8%	26	0%	163	0%	9.1%	275	0%
Venezuela	397	1%	9.4%	682	1%	199	1%	20.0%	594	2%	3,482	1%	9.4%	5,973	1%
G-3	891	3%	19.0%	2,537	5%	431	2%	22.2%	1,433	5%	17,722	5%	19.2%	50,812	8%
Mercosur	2,593	8%	18.0%	7,007	14%	701	4%	7.6%	1,089	4%	6,043	2%	10.0%	10,711	2%
Andean Pact	1,342	4%	8.7%	2,220	4%	641	3%	19.7%	1,883	6%	6,674	2%	10.4%	12,103	2%
NAFTA	7,980	26%	4.7%	10,517	21%	7,865	42%	9.8%	13,779	45%	135,844	42%	12.1%	270,058	43%
Colomb+Ven	570	2%	12.0%	1,124	2%	402	2%	17.3%	1,047	3%	5,042	2%	11.3%	9,601	2%
LAC - Mex	4,675	15%	16.5%	11,688	23%	3,263	17%	13.7%	7050.4	23%	21,443	7%	10.5%	39,000	6%

Page 6 of 7

N.B. Paraguay data are from 1991 and 1990. All yearly trade figures under $500,000 are recorded as zero.
Source: Country export values from IMP, Direction of Trade Statistics Yearbook, 1993. Aggregates and analysis by author.

Hemispheric Export Patterns: 1986 to 1992 (Concluded)

	Exporting Region									
	Colombia – Venezuela					LAC - Mexico				
	1986		Average Annual % Growth	1992		1986		Average Annual % Growth	1992	
To:	US$ M	% Tot X	Rate	US$ M	% Tot X	US$ M	% Tot X	Rate	US$ M	% Tot X
United States	5,295	39%	12.3%	10,637	46%	22,602	34%	4.7%	29,785	28%
Canada	345	3%	2.1%	390	2%	1,225	2%	4.3%	1,575	1%
Mexico	17	0%	57.9%	263	1%	393	1%	32.2%	2,094	2%
LAC	2,267	17%	17.7%	6,042	26%	10,556	16%	15.7%	25,306	24%
World	13,520	100%	9.2%	22,936	100%	66,324	100%	8.2%	106,657	100%
Argentina	75	1%	-2.9%	63	0%	1,474	2%	18.6%	4,094	4%
Bolivia	1	0%	41.4%	8	0%	308	0%	12.2%	614	1%
Brazil	77	1%	41.2%	609	3%	1,628	2%	13.8%	3,538	3%
Chile	148	1%	9.8%	260	1%	695	1%	20.9%	2,174	2%
Colombia	105	1%	19.5%	306	1%	456	1%	15.9%	1,107	1%
Ecuador	64	0%	22.1%	212	1%	286	0%	12.6%	584	1%
Paraguay	0	0%	ERR	1	0%	369	1%	13.7%	797	1%
Peru	102	1%	27.2%	432	2%	567	1%	13.1%	1,184	1%
Uruguay	1	0%	68.6%	23	0%	357	1%	16.7%	903	1%
Venezuela	150	1%	21.1%	473	2%	680	1%	12.6%	1,389	1%
G-3	272	2%	25.1%	1,042	5%	1,529	2%	20.1%	4,590	4%
Mercosur	153	1%	28.7%	696	3%	3,828	6%	16.0%	9,332	9%
Andean Pact	422	3%	22.6%	1,431	6%	2,297	3%	13.4%	4,878	5%
NAFTA	5,657	42%	12.2%	11,290	49%	24,220	37%	5.5%	33,454	31%
Colomb + Ven	255	2%	20.5%	779	3%	1,136	2%	14.0%	2,495	2%
LAC - Mex	2,250	17%	17.0%	5,779	25%	10,163	15%	14.8%	23,212	22%

N.B. Paraguay data are from 1991 and 1990. All yearly trade figures under $500,000 are recorded as zero.
Source: Country export values from IMP, Direction of Trade Statistics Yearbook, 1993. Aggregates and analysis by author.

Figure 1. Average Annual Export Growth Rates
1986–1992

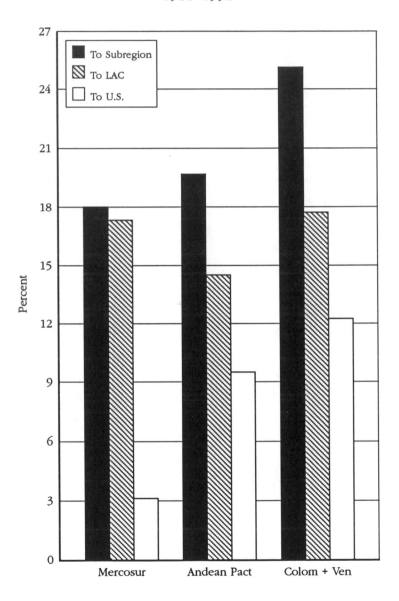

Figure 2. Destination of Brazilian Exports

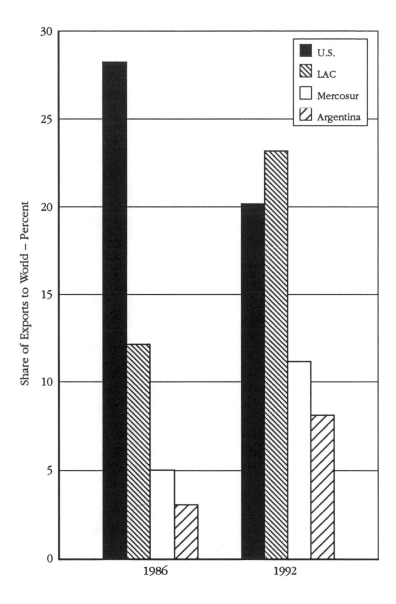

Figure 3. Origin of LAC Exports to the U.S.

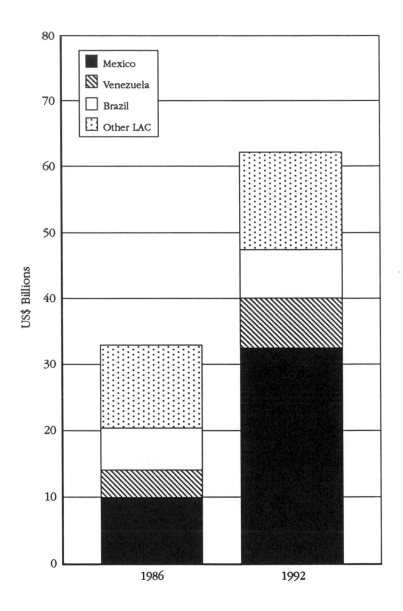

Figure 4. Distribution of LAC's 1986–1992
Growth in Exports to the U.S.

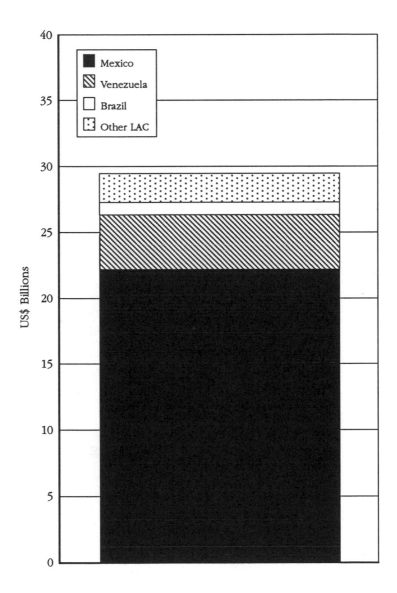

Figure 5. 1992 Export Destinations
LAC vs. LAC Excluding Mexico

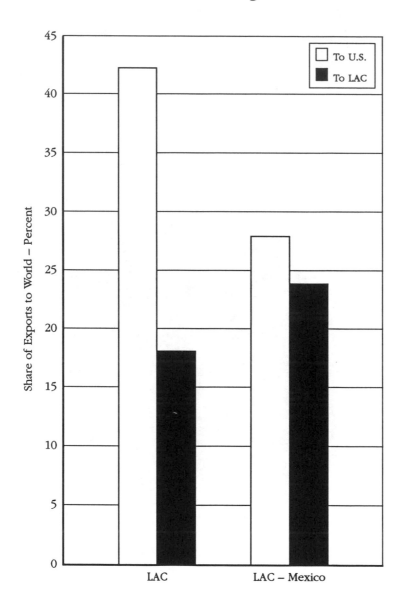

Figure 6. Trade Within the U.S. vs. Trade Within LAC
Projecting Historical Compound Growth Rates for
LAC Excluding Mexico

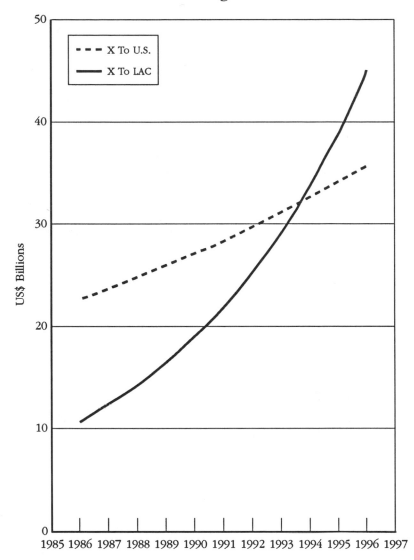

Notes

1   The terms "Latin America" and "Latin America and the Caribbean" (as well as the latter's acronym, LAC) are used interchangeably throughout the text to include all countries in the Western Hemisphere except Canada, Cuba, and the United States.

2   An illustration of the lingering effects of the NAFTA debate in the United States was provided by the congressional hearings on the recent events in Chiapas, Mexico, and the inquiry about the potential link between NAFTA and the human rights issues made prominent by the uprising and its suppression.

3   See Sistema Económico Latinoamericano (SELA), 1993, *Evolución del Proceso de Integración Regional*, XIX Reunión Ordinaria del Consejo Latinoamericano, October, Doc. SP/CL/XIX O/DI, No. 11, Caracas, Venezuela.

4   For more on the historical phases of twentieth-century economic integration, see Robert Z. Lawrence, 1993, "Regionalism, Multilateralism and Deeper Integration," monograph prepared for The Brookings Institution project "Integrating the World Economy." See also Sebastian Edwards, 1993, "Latin American Economic Integration: A New Perspective on an Old Dream," *The World Economy* 16 (3, May): 317-338.

5   Rudiger Dornbusch, 1993, "The Case for Free Trade in the Hemisphere," paper presented at the IDB/ECLAC conference on Trade Liberalization in the Western Hemisphere, Washington, D.C., November and Sebastian Edwards, 1993, *Latin America: A Decade after the Debt Crisis*, (Washington, D.C.: World Bank).

6   Roberto Bouzas and Jaime Ros, 1993, "The North-South Variety of Economic Integration: Issues and Prospects for Latin America," paper presented at the workshop on Economic Integration in the Western Hemisphere, Kellogg Institute for International Studies, University of Notre Dame, April.

7   The remarks of Chile's Finance Minister Alejandro Foxley are representative of the dilemmas faced by policymakers in Latin America with respect to their respective country's and the region's positioning in the international economy. See Alejandro Foxley, 1993, "Toward an Era of Hemispheric Cooperation," A Special Report of the Inter-American Dialogue and The Brookings Institution, (Washington, D.C.: Inter-American Dialogue) May.

8   Trade liberalization between Colombia and Venezuela has also led to an important expansion of cross-border investments. A study conducted by Arthur D. Little, a consulting firm, found that within 10 months of signing the agreement, 161 Colombian firms had established operations in Venezuela and 39 Venezuelan companies had begun operating in Colombia. Also, for the first time in history, the Venezuelan government floated its bonds in the Colombian financial market and Colombian firms raised funds in the Venezuelan market.

9   *Oxford Analytica Daily Brief*, 1993, "Latin America: Trade Performance," December 14. Calculated using purchasing power parity instead of average dollar exchange rates.

10 Refik Erzan and Alexander Yeats, 1992, *Free Trade Agreements with the United States: What's in It for Latin America*, Policy Research Working Paper Series, No. 827, (Washington, D.C.: World Bank) 13.

11 *Oxford Analytica Daily Brief* 1993.

12 Erzan and Yeats 1992, 18.

13 Erzan and Yeats 1992, 31. It should also be noted that Erzan and Yeats' simulation assumes that U.S. nontariff barriers would be significantly liberalized. Actual agreements (NAFTA, Uruguay Round) indicate that progress in nontariff-barriers-covered sectors is likely to be slow or left out altogether.

14 The breakdown of the 54 petitions by country is as follows: Brazil 22, Argentina 12, Mexico 11, Venezuela 6, and one each for Chile, Costa Rica, and Trinidad and Tobago. Forty percent of the petitions resulted in the imposition of countervailing or antidumping duties; 30 percent resulted in the investigation being terminated by the International Trade Commission or the Department of Commerce; 24 percent are still pending; and the rest were either withdrawn or privately settled. Source: Rogers and Wells, private communication.

15 Moisés Naím, 1993, *Paper Tigers and Minotaurs: The Politics of Venezuela's Economic Reforms* (Washington, D.C.: Carnegie Endowment for International Peace) 89.

16 The definition of dumping does not recognize a well-known fact about trade in branded goods: they are marked to market. Since the American market is more competitive than many home markets, prices in the United States will have to be lower. This counts as dumping. I thank Ricardo Hausmann for pointing this out.

17 See Moisés Naím, 1992, "Instead of NAFTA, Shooting for SAFTA," *CEO/ International Strategies* (December).

18 A more elaborate presentation of this point is made in Moisés Naím, 1993, "Latin America: Post-Adjustment Blues," *Foreign Policy* (Fall). For an economic interpretation of the turn toward trade liberalization, see Dani Rodrik, "The Rush Towards Free Trade in the Developing World: Why So Late? Why Now? Will It Last?" in *Voting for Reform: The Politics of Adjustment in New Democracies*, eds. Stephen Haggard and Stephen Webb (New York: Oxford University Press) forthcoming, and for the politics of trade opening, see Carol Wise, 1993, "Trading Outward: The Politics of Commercial Policy Reform in Latin America," Research Proposal.

19 Asad Alam and Sarath Rajapatirana, 1993, *Trade Policy Reform in Latin America and the Caribbean in the 1980s*, Policy Research Working Paper Series, No. 1104 (Washington, D.C.: World Bank).

20 See *The World Competitiveness Report*, 1993 (Geneva: IMI\WEF).

21 For a discussion of the size, composition, and macroeconomic consequences of the recent inflow of private capital to Latin America, as well as the analysis of its risks, see G. Calvo, L. Leiderman, and C. Reinhart, 1992, *Capital Inflows and Exchange Rate Appreciation in Latin America: The Role of External Factors*, IMF Working Paper (Washington, D.C.: International Monetary Fund).

22 Vice President Albert Gore, 1993, "Toward a Western Hemisphere Community of Democracies," address to Mexican, American, and Latin American Chambers of Commerce, Mexico City, December 1. Text distributed by the White House.

23 Juan Gallardo, 1994, briefing session, "NAFTA and the EC: What Future for Their Relations?" Annual Meeting, World Economic Forum, Davos, Switzerland. By 1993, the number of Canadian business executives had risen to four thousand.

24 Ricardo Hausmann, 1993, comments on *Convergence and Community: The Americas in 1993*, a Report of the Inter-American Dialogue, Panel Discussion, Carnegie Endowment for International Peace, Washington, D.C., March.

25 Jeffrey Garten, 1994, "United States-Latin American Relations in the New Global Economy." Speech delivered at the World Trade Center, Miami, February 1. Mimeo distributed by the U.S. Department of Commerce.

References

Alam, Asad, and Sarath Rajapatirana. 1993. *Trade Policy Reform in Latin America and the Caribbean in the 1980s.* Policy Research Working Paper Series, No. 1104. Washington, D.C.: World Bank.

Bouzas, Roberto, and Jaime Ros. 1993. "The North-South Variety of Economic Integration: Issues and Prospects for Latin America." Paper presented at the workshop on "Economic Integration in the Western Hemisphere," Kellogg Institute for International Studies, University of Notre Dame. April.

Calvo, G., L. Leiderman, and C. Reinhart. 1992. *Capital Inflows and Exchange Rate Appreciation in Latin America: The Role of External Factors.* IMF Working Paper. Washington, D.C.: International Monetary Fund.

Dornbusch, Rudiger. 1993. "The Case for Free Trade in the Hemisphere." Paper presented at the IDB/ECLAC conference on "Trade Liberalization in the Western Hemisphere," Washington, D.C. November.

Edwards, Sebastian. 1993a. "Latin American Economic Integration: A New Perspective on an Old Dream." *The World Economy* 16 (3, May): 317-338.

Edwards, Sebastian. 1993b. *Latin America: A Decade after the Debt Crisis.* Washington, D.C.: World Bank.

Erzan, Refik, and Alexander Yeats. 1992. *Free Trade Agreements with the United States: What's in It for Latin America.* Policy Research Working Paper Series, No. 827. Washington, D.C.: World Bank.

Foxley, Alejandro. 1993. *Toward an Era of Hemispheric Cooperation.* A Special Report of the Inter-American Dialogue and The Brookings Institution. Washington, D.C.: Inter-American Dialogue. May.

Gallardo, Juan. 1994. "NAFTA and the EC: What Future for Their Relations?" Briefing session at the 1994 World Economic Forum, Davos, Switzerland.

Garten, Jeffrey. 1994. "United States-Latin American Relations in the New Global Economy." Speech delivered at the World Trade Center, Miami. December 1. Mimeo distributed by the U.S. Department of Commerce.

Gore, Vice President Albert. 1993. "Toward a Western Hemisphere Community of Democracies." Address to Mexican, American, and Latin American Chambers of Commerce. December 1. Text distributed by the White House.

Hausmann, Ricardo. 1993. Comments in *Convergence and Community: The Americas in 1993.* A Report of the Inter-American Dialogue. Washington, D.C.: Inter-American Dialogue.

Lawrence, Robert Z. 1993. "Regionalism, Multilateralism and Deeper Integration." Monograph prepared for The Brookings Institution project, "Integrating the World Economy."

Naím, Moisés. 1992. "Instead of NAFTA, Shooting for SAFTA." *CEO/International Strategies* (December).

Naím, Moisés. 1993a. "Latin America: Post-Adjustment Blues." *Foreign Policy* (Fall).

Naím, Moisés. 1993b. *Paper Tigers and Minotaurs: The Politics of Venezuela's Economic Reforms.* Washington, D.C.: Carnegie Endowment for International Peace.

Oxford Analytica Daily Brief. 1993. "Latin America: Trade Performance." December 14.

Rodrick, Dani. "The Rush Towards Free Trade in the Developing World: Why So Late? Why Now? Will It Last?" In *Voting for Reform: The Politics of Adjustment in New Democracies,* eds. Stephen Haggard and Stephen Webb. New York: Oxford University Press. Forthcoming.

Sistema Económico Latinoamericano (SELA). 1993. *Evolución del Proceso de Integración Regional.* XIX Reunión Ordinaria del Consejo Latinoamericano, October. Doc. SP/CL/XIX O/DI, No. 11. Caracas, Venezuela.

Wise, Carol. 1993. "Trading Outward: The Politics of Commercial Policy Reform in Latin America." Research proposal.

World Economic Forum. 1993. *World Competitiveness Report.* Geneva: IMI/WEF.

Chapter 4

Post-NAFTA: Can the United States, Canada, and Mexico Deepen Their Economic Relationships?

Leonard Waverman

Introduction

Now that the North American Free Trade Agreement (NAFTA) has been established and the Uruguay Round of the General Agreement on Tariffs and Trade (GATT) has ended successfully, many will assume that the mechanisms are in operation to ensure a deepening of the economic relationships between the United States, Canada, and Mexico.[1] This chapter will extend the hypothesis that the present NAFTA agreement is an unstable equilibrium and that events will occur either to unravel NAFTA or to expand it to a more formal community model. It will not prophesy which way the agreement will turn, but the potential to unravel the agreement in North America is real. The changes induced by NAFTA (and GATT) on trade and investment flows will bring new pressures to bear, and many of these pressures will be protectionist. In one crucial way, NAFTA is incomplete, as it leaves domestic policies in place, policies that can be equivalent to nontariff barriers (NTBs).[2] The survival of NAFTA will depend on the ultimate desires of the three national governments to respond to growing nontariff barriers.

It is evident that cross-border antidumping (AD) actions between the United States and Canada have increased substantially in the last two years. It is also evident that the costs of the process have risen due to almost unanimous appeals of domestic antidumping orders to binational panels and

This paper was written for the Inter-American Dialogue, Center for Strategic and International Studies, and North-South Center Symposium, held in Washington, D.C., on March 2, 1994. Helpful comments were received from Alan Alexandroff, Sidney Weintraub, Sylvia Ostry, and John Curtis. All errors and views are my own.

the growing use or threat in the United States of extraordinary challenges to binational panel decisions. Mexico has been vigorous in its use of antidumping even prior to NAFTA, perhaps to set a "good" example. Antidumping and countervailing duty actions (CVD) have no place in a free trade agreement (FTA). Yet it is most difficult to see how the domestic sovereignty embedded in domestic AD (and CVD) laws can be changed. The next part of this chapter deals with antidumping issues and examines steps to reduce their use.

NAFTA cannot be compared with the European Union (EU) (although several writers have tried to do so) as they are totally different ventures. Yet by examining the nontariff barriers that became major issues within the community, the issues, besides AD, that could become the unsettling issues of NAFTA can be predicted. The Cecchini Report, which provided the empirical base for the movement in Europe to the Single Market, identified technical barriers — border controls, standards, rules of origin, and technical requirements — as the main costs of a "non-Europe." While NAFTA does attempt to come to grips with these issues, it cannot do so adequately for the same reason that antidumping actions are still so prevalent — the inability to relinquish domestic sovereignty in a number of critical areas.[3] Minimizing the protectionist side of technical issues requires one of three principles: a political vision of North America, an overarching court similar to the Court of Justice in the EU that could implement a North American vision, or a Single North American Act. None of these three principles seems feasible in North America. This chapter examines how these issues could become important irritants to trade.

There is one area where some Canadian economists wish immediate deepening. A small but growing group appears to be suggesting either a fixed exchange rate vis-à-vis the U.S. dollar or even a currency common to North America.[4] These issues are discussed below. Here the lessons of Europe are instructive. It is most unlikely that a fixed exchange rate would be of any value to Canada. Only two countries in the EU12 and North America currently meet the criteria for convergence to monetary union as set out in the Maastricht Treaty — Luxembourg and Mexico!

The tensions that may become evident in NAFTA will determine the agreement's future. The new Liberal government in Canada was unable to proclaim NAFTA until an agreement was reached with the United States to appoint a working group substitute for antidumping as well as to develop a strengthened subsidies code by the end of 1995. This working group does not seem to be a token to placate an uneasy Canadian electorate but rather an essential continuing Canadian demand for "secure access." Antidumping, countervailing duties, border disputes over content, and differences in technical standards all mean that the present NAFTA is an incomplete agreement. The committee structure set up in NAFTA is one means of reducing frictions, and means of improving those committee workings are suggested below. In addition, Article 2006 of NAFTA may prove meaningful. In this article, any party may request consultation regarding "...any matter that it considers might affect the operation of the Agreement." This consultative process could become a constructive means of change to the agreement reducing trade frictions if countries utilize the process in an aggressive but positive manner.

Recent data show that Canadian exports to the United States and U.S. exports to Canada have grown substantially in those areas liberalized in the Canada-U.S. Free Trade Agreement (CUSFTA).[5] NAFTA can make all economies prosper. However, for it to do so in the long run requires the ceding of sovereignty in areas of domestic policy where most countries (especially the United States) may be unwilling to go. Thus, while Europe wonders whether to widen before or after deepening, North America will likely widen (into Latin America) long before it deepens. Yet the process of widening now under way, first to Mexico, makes the process of deepening between Canada and the United States even more distant. If Canada and the United States could not jointly agree on convergence of some of their domestic policies, Canada, the United States, and a host of Latin American countries have even less ability to come to a common policy on antidumping, standards, and border issues.

The NAFTA Agreement

It is important to remember what NAFTA does and does not do.

1. NAFTA and CUSFTA lower tariffs for most manufactured products flowing across the three borders while working toward elimination of tariffs over a 15-year period.

   Tariffs between the United States and Canada fall over the ten-year period 1989 to 1999. All Mexican tariffs fall to zero by the year 2004; half became zero on January 1, 1994. U.S. and Canadian tariffs against Mexican products are scheduled to fall to zero over fifteen years, most over five years but with long adjustment periods for "sensitive" sectors (household glassware, footwear, and ceramic tile — the definition of "sensitive" appears to be how crucial the sector was to congressional votes). "Snapback" provisions allow tariffs to revert to previous levels for a limited period if an import surge occurs. CUSFTA has been in place for five years. In 1988, the year before CUSFTA was established, the average trade-weighted Canadian tariff was 9.9 percent and the U.S. tariff was 3.3 percent, while in 1993, "most Mexican tariffs were currently between 10 and 20 percent."[6] Producers have requested speedier reductions than were contained in the agreement on a considerable number of the products subject to Canadian and U.S. tariffs. This fact suggests that tariffs between

Mexico and its northern neighbors will also come down faster than the negotiated minimum path. As tariffs fall, sectors facing new competition from producers in the other NAFTA countries could increasingly turn to other protectionist measures.

2. For a number of key manufactured goods, elaborate rules of origin determine the ability to cross borders duty free. Since U.S. tariffs are already low, quotas exist for some commodities (textiles and apparel), while customs interpretation can remain significant. (One earlier example dealt with the percentage of costs that are incurred in North America, namely, the 1992 dispute between U.S. and Canadian customs over the degree of regional content in Honda automobiles produced in Canada.) Generally, a good crosses one of the two borders as a regional good if it is processed in North America so that a change in tariff classification occurs.[7]

For chemicals, footwear, machinery, electronics, and autos, a change in tariff classification is insufficient to acquire regional status. These five categories must meet *cost* tests — 50 percent to 62.5 percent (autos) of costs must be regional.[8] In 1991, these five categories accounted for 46.6 percent of Canadian exports to the United States, 50 percent of Mexican exports to the United States, and 58.2 percent of U.S. exports to its two neighbors. In other words, cost tests are utilized for just over half of North American trade.

For apparel and textiles, 50 percent of costs incurred in North America is insufficient to make the good regional. Most cotton and manmade goods must meet a "triple transformation" test; that is, fibers, textiles, and apparel must be North American in origin.

3. For agricultural products, there are three bilateral agreements: between Canada and the United States, between Canada and Mexico, and between Mexico and the United States. Agriculture does not come close to free trade for Canada; U.S.-Mexico agricultural trade is closer.

4. Mexico, because of constraints in its constitution, opted out of the clauses ensuring national treatment for its energy exports in U.S. markets and those ensuring nondiscrimination for energy exports in times of domestic Mexican energy shortages.[9]

5. Border disputes of the type that have arisen between the United States and Canada under CUSFTA are still prevalent in the European Union and could become serious problems in NAFTA. Many disputes are based on implicit nontariff barriers. For example, there will be differing interpretations of the elaborate language ruling product eligibility for free trade. If the three countries cannot agree on the data

measuring the size of past exports and imports, how will they agree on the measurement of the percentage of costs of a particular commodity that is undertaken in North America?

NAFTA is a clear improvement over CUSFTA. However, NAFTA leaves AD powers largely for each of the three countries to determine. AD decisions of a national agency are, as in CUSFTA, appealable to a binational appeal mechanism. While this mechanism is important and does remove the most egregious kinds of protectionism, data indicate an expansion of AD cases between Canada and the United States since 1991. These trade disputes are critical barriers, and their escalation shows that new remedies to reduce their impact are required.

An area that could emerge as a major source of disputes is the vast area of differing technical requirements. Significant disputes will likely arise over technical standards. A major concern, the lack of a "mutual recognition" clause in NAFTA, is identified below.

6. NAFTA, in effect, is a pact on investment. Five basic principles are in play: a) national and/or most-favored-nation (MFN) treatment (whichever is better for the foreigner); b) elimination of most performance requirements (except research and development, production, training and employment, construction, and, for Canada, technology transfer); c) free transfer of funds; d) expropriation protection; and e) dispute resolution. However, as Michael Gestrin and Alan Rugman point out, most existing impediments to foreign direct investment (FDI) are grandfathered.[10] The existing restrictions are substantial. In the United States, these include broadcasting, telecommunications, airlines, shipping, and banking.[11] In addition, specific exemptions are allowed. Canada kept the Investment Canada review of transactions above C$150 million and an exemption for "cultural industries."[12] Mexico imposes a review mechanism starting at $25 million in 1994 but increasing to the Canadian threshold (but in U.S. dollars) by the year 2004 (as well as being indexed to inflation and economic growth).[13]

7. Over time, NAFTA liberalizes trade and investment in a wide variety of services, including banking, finance, insurance, enhanced telecommunications services, and some land transportation. Mexico exempts oil and gas drilling and gasoline retailing; Canada exempts culture, as well as airlines, telecommunications, and broadcasting.

Antidumping and Countervailing Duty Actions — Will They Wreck NAFTA?[14]

The U.S. Agenda

In discussing deepening new trading relationships in North America, it is important to begin with U.S. desires and the U.S. agenda. In the electoral politics of 1992, President Bill Clinton supported the demands for more aggressive actions against nations in Europe and Asia, many former Cold War allies, that had failed to play "fairly" in the global economy. In *Putting People First*, Clinton urged that these nations abandon unfair trade subsidies in order to build a more "level playing field." (The United States uses sports or military analogies to refer to trade issues.)[15] To that end, Clinton suggested, among other things, that his administration would propose passage of a stronger and sharper "Super 301" trade bill provision.[16] As was stated in Clinton's campaign document, "if other nations refuse to play by our trade rules, we'll play by theirs."[17]

In focusing on the unfair practices of other nations, Clinton was adopting a well-developed position that the failure of American competitiveness pointed in the direction of others as opposed to being a result of internal failures. The debate had grown increasingly loud and accusatory in the latter half of the 1980s as the United States' trade imbalance exploded.[18]

Aggressive U.S. trade policy employs a number of policy instruments. First, there has been encouragement or tacit support for the use of U.S. trade remedy laws (including AD and CVD) by the private sector. This reliance on national trade remedy laws has been most evident in the U.S.-Canada relationship and was central in stimulating the actions taken by Canada's new Liberal government over the proclamation of NAFTA in Canada. Next, the immediate past administrations had employed an array of managed trade instruments including Voluntary Exports Restraints (VERs) and Orderly Market Arrangements (OMAs). When the steel VER ended in 1991, Canadian steel producers, despite the existence of free trade, were swept up in a broad U.S. industry attack on steel imports. Finally, and most troubling, has been the willingness of U.S. administrations to extract unilateral concessions from others and to threaten trade retaliation on the failure to achieve a satisfactory resolution. The abandonment of reciprocity or MFN treatment and the turn to unilateral demands for concessions has been labeled "aggressive unilateralism."[19] Such unilateralism has included the use of Section 301[20] actions against the practices of various states as well as actions described as Voluntary Import Expansion agreements (VIEs) to open the markets of "offending" states. A revised Super 301 could be used against Canada were the United States to determine that certain Canadian practices did not leave the playing field level. NAFTA limits the kinds of retaliation the United States might take against Canada (or Mexico) but does not leave unilateralism on the sidelines. The same is obviously true for Canada and Mexico. They can undertake trade sanctions against the United States.

The Clinton administration's trade policy appears to build on the belief that there is no contradiction between aggressive trade policy and free trade.[21] This is not to suggest that the United States is the evil party in the agreement and that Canada and Mexico are saintly. Each party is maximizing its own self-interest. Canada has been an aggressive user of antidumping and in a number of sectors, such as marketing boards, beer, and wine, particularly protectionist. Mexico is quickly moving to become the hub of NAFTA by signing FTAs with several Latin American countries.[22] It was expected that parties to NAFTA would have considered expanding the agreement before undertaking new FTAs themselves. However, the United States has the power and an aggressive trade agenda. NAFTA does not fully protect Mexico and Canada against a number of present and potential U.S. protectionist policies. Neither does NAFTA fully protect the United States against such policies from its two neighbors. However, with 70 percent of Canadian and Mexican exports going to the United States and only 30 percent of U.S. exports flowing to Mexico and Canada, the power asymmetry parallels a trade asymmetry. That is why, in 1985, Canada wanted secure access to the U.S. market. It is in this context of continued protectionism that the widening and deepening of economic relations in North America will take place.

Antidumping

Article VI of GATT (pre-Uruguay Round) allows a country to use its national laws to levy an antidumping duty "on imports that cause or threaten to cause material injury."[23] While exporting nations to the United States tried to wrest significant concessions on the use of antidumping law from U.S. negotiators in the Uruguay Round, these attempts were largely unsuccessful and, some suggest, may allow a greater exercise of domestic AD: "...this would permit U.S. Uruguay Round implementing legislation [which is yet to be seen] to include antidumping rules that are even more trade restrictive than the current rules."[24]

Table 1 provides data on the extent of AD cases launched by Canada and the United States against each other over the period from 1986 to 1993. A quick perusal of the table shows a number of interesting facts:

- The number of AD cases, both those initiated and those with affirmative findings, has fallen since CAFTA began if the three-year periods 1986 to 1988 and 1989 to 1991 are compared, although the number of cases rises in 1992 and again in 1993.

- In any time period examined in Table 1, Canada initiates and brings to successful conclusion *more* AD cases than does the United States, although the ratio of Canadian to U.S. cases launched falls over the period. Thus, while it is the United States that is relatively increasing its use of AD, Canada remains an aggressive user of AD.[25]

- The number of AD cases brought rises sharply in 1992-1993 (doubling in the United States over the previous two-year period); more AD cases have been initiated in 1992 and 1993 than in any previous two-year period in Canada-U.S. trade.

- The set of cross-border steel AD cases in 1993 signals a new strategy of retaliation.

- The timing of cases shows substantial differences in Canada and the United States. Canadian cases have been more or less evenly spread over the years, while U.S. cases are increasing in the more recent period.

- Eighty percent of all AD decisions have been put before binational panels since CUSFTA began. In the last two years, all but two AD trade disputes have been appealed.

- One expert on AD has recently written "...the Chapter 19 binational review process under the FTA has little or no chilling effect on the invocation of anti-dumping laws on either side of the border."[26]

There is, then, a recent increase in trade disputes and a now near-inevitable appeal of decisions in the world's latest and largest bilateral free trade area. These disputes exist despite free trade and despite a dispute resolution process that was introduced on the insistence of Canada as a means of limiting the exercise of AD. It is fair to say that the basic Canadian reason for negotiating free trade — unconstrained access to the U.S. market — still has unacceptable impediments.

Antidumping actions within a free trade area are purely protectionist, are contrary to good sense, and are obvious barriers to free trade.[27] AD is a trade barrier; it is the opposite of national treatment and is discriminatory. AD cases, expected AD cases, and threatened AD cases are equivalent to tariffs. Firms threatened by those actions face not only the possibility of tariffs but also the high fixed and sunk costs of defending themselves in lengthy court hearings in Washington, Ottawa, or Mexico City. Even if the case is without merit, the exporter challenged has no recourse for the costs of defense. AD fits into the classic economic actions of "raising rival costs" and is a strategy designed to force rivals to raise prices through threats, or through costs of defense, or through actual penalties. A recent work by Robert Staiger and Frank Wolak demonstrates that simply initiating an AD case provides half of the gains (restriction of imports) that result from a positive finding of dumping.[28]

The recent sets of steel actions launched in the United States as the VER program in steel ended and the retaliatory responses in Canada to these actions are obvious examples of the protectionist, trade-distorting nature of AD in a free trade area. The actions launched by Armco Steel and others on June 30, 1992, against imports of steel plates and of hot-rolled, cold-rolled, and galvanized steel from a number of countries alleged dumping in the United States that caused injury to U.S. producers. A number of articles and books examine and condemn the processes by which the U.S. Department of Commerce determines dumping and the U.S. International Trade Commission (ITC) determines injury.[29] Canadian antidumping processes are marginally superior. However, there is widespread if not unanimous agreement among economists that the process is stacked in favor of domestic producers and that the costing rules and the determination of costs are biased toward the finding of dumping.[30]

These arguments do not need to be repeated here. Instead, it will be shown how AD cases are discriminatory against foreign producers, are inconsistent with national treatment, and, thus, are inconsistent with the basic premise of a free trade agreement. Take as an example U.S. domestic Firm USA, which produces cold-rolled steel. Firm USA competes with three other U.S. producers and two Canadian producers. Competition in the market reduces prices below the "costs" of Firm USA, which considers this competition unfair and decides to launch actions against domestic competitor USB for predatory behavior and against foreign competitor CAN for dumping.[31] In order for Firm USA to win a private antitrust suit for predation against domestic competitor USB, it must prove two things: first, that prices were below variable costs, and second, that Firm USB intended to drive Firm USA out of the market in order to recoup the losses from its rival's pricing below cost.[32]

Predation cases are rare since the proof is difficult and the onus is on the firm alleging predation to demonstrate that its rival priced below average variable cost.

Contrast the case between Firm USA and Firm USB with the much easier requirements for Firm USA to show that foreign Firm CAN dumped its products in the United States. The plaintiff can utilize costs constructed from accounting data including all overhead and a reasonable profit margin. Here the proof of dumping is not difficult, and the burden of proof is on the firm alleged to have engaged in dumping to demonstrate that, in fact, it did not do so.[33]

In order for foreign Firm CAN to avoid a dumping charge in a free trade area, it has to price in the United States at production costs that are defined as fully allocated costs, plus an 8 percent notional return on capital. U.S. domestic Firm USB, however, has to price below cost (defined as below incremental cost) with the "dangerous probability" of recouping its investment by driving Firm USA out of the market before being liable for a charge of predation. In the U.S. market, Firm CAN then faces a much more stringent pricing rule than does Firm USB. However, in a free trade area there should be no "U.S." or "Canadian" or "Mexican" market. The existence of AD creates artificial markets by raising entry barriers against foreign competitors. In the above example, if Firm CAN were located in the United States instead of in Canada and had the identical costs in the United States as its Canadian counterpart, it could not be accused of dumping. Since dumping laws discriminate against foreigners, they affect investment decisions.

The only reason for accusing Firm CAN of dumping rather than of the more difficult test of predation is its foreign identity. The continued existence of AD cases across borders in an FTA is contrary to national treatment. Foreign firm CAN is not treated in the U.S. market in the same way as is domestic Firm USB. Firm CAN is treated differently and worse.

These arguments are not news in Ottawa, Washington, or Mexico City. The February 1994 Economic Report to Congress of the Council of Economic Advisors states: "Both in the United States and elsewhere, antidumping laws go beyond preventing anticompetitive practices — which should be their rationale — and often have the effect of protecting domestic industries from foreign competition."[34] But the possibility for the current U.S., Mexican, and Canadian administrations coming to a new understanding to reduce or replace AD (and CVD) actions by other schemes (such as the use of antitrust law) is low. The U.S. administration did pull out all stops to have NAFTA passed; now, new trade accords with Latin America are being floated.[35]

However, given the Clinton administration's aggressive trade stance, there is likely little desire or ability in the United States to reduce or remove the U.S. ITC's and Department of Commerce's oversight for AD, which would require revising or removing significant pieces of legislation. There is zero probability post-NAFTA to persuade a hostile Congress of the benefits of removing U.S. protectionist measures against Canada and Mexico. Adding Mexico to the FTA has clearly complicated the process. The fear of Mexican low wages will heighten the attention paid to the prices of Mexican goods entering the United States. Thus, dumping will be examined more closely.[36] The U.S. desire to implement the Enterprise of the Americas Initiative also works to put AD revisions outside the realm of near-term possibility. How could Congress be convinced to open borders to Chile, Colombia, and Peru and simultaneously to remove the safety valve of AD cases?

North American markets will become more integrated as tariffs are reduced. Domestic firms threatened by low tariffs can increasingly rely on AD remedies. These remedies will either be through "visible" cases or through the use of threats to launch actions unless the exporter "understands" the domestic pressures and agrees to raise its price. Thus, it is possible to predict an expansion of trade disputes within NAFTA. It is this expansion of disputes within a free trade area that creates political problems, as it has in Canada and as it could in Mexico. The exports involved may be a small share of North American trade, but the visibility of the disputes is a continuing source of political instability for the agreements.

As indicated above, a wholesale removal of AD is unlikely. To remove AD in North America or at least to prevent this practice from escalating, the following steps are suggested:

- Under pressure from the new Canadian Liberal government, the United States and Mexico agreed to resurrect the Working Group in CUSFTA (Article 1907), which is "to conclude a report on the unfair trade codes by the end of 1995, but ... neither the United States nor Canada would be bound to comply with the report."[37]

  This group should 1) be made up of high-level officials as well as business representatives; 2) meet regularly, at a minimum of six times per year; 3) operate under the NAFTA Free Trade Commission (FRTC) and its Secretariat (see the section "Institutions and NAFTA" of this chapter); 4) report to each legislature in 1994 as to the progress made toward the goal; and 5) report in 1995 as to whether an agreement has been reached and what reasons any party may have not to be bound by the new agreement.

  This 1995 report is only part of the solution.

  The United States and Canada did establish such a working group under CUSFTA. The group met several times to discuss replacing AD law with competition law, but "...little progress was made before it was agreed in 1991 to defer the process pending the outcome of the GATT Uruguay Round."[38] Therefore, other actions are necessary.

- An amendment of domestic laws on AD to require reimbursement of all an exporter's legal costs if the action fails could be incorporated into each country's laws. This step raises the costs to domestic firms of frivolous cases and should act to reduce the number of cases. Raising the price of launching cases should also reduce their number.

- An education process for industry and labor demonstrating that AD is not clearly beneficial to domestic producers and workers because it limits "unfair" imports should be launched. AD actions are two-way tools, also used by foreign governments to reduce exports, and, thus, these measures harm domestic producers and labor.

- The introduction by three countries of the principle of *stare decisis* for trinational panel decisions. Under CUSFTA and NAFTA, Chapter 19 dispute resolution panels do not now draw on other panel decisions as precedents. Inconsistencies can arise, and no "codified" law necessarily develops. The legal principle of *stare decisis* would require panels to use precedents and to distinguish decisions if the precedents were not followed. This principle would prevent affirmative dumping decisions from being taken where the authority knew that a similar decision had been overturned.

- There could be merit in having the relevant administrative agencies of each country meet regularly to discuss and potentially to harmonize procedures, technical requirements, and information requests. This concept of process harmonization could help reduce the costs of meeting an AD challenge.

- Perhaps a joint committee of the three legislatures could examine the total impact of AD on all three economies and discuss convergence (or the elimination of these laws).

- Finally, each country should over time move to the replacement of AD by domestic competition law.

New Barriers to Trade: Border Controls and Product and Technical Standards

NAFTA is a free trade agreement, but as the European Union has found, free trade in goods involves many issues beyond the removal of tariffs. While NAFTA and the EU are not directly comparable, it is interesting to examine several of the issues that the European Community (EC) and the Court of Justice have dealt with in order to ensure "a free flow of imports and exports." Article 3 of the February 7, 1992, Treaty on European Union calls for "the elimination, as between Members States, of customs duties and quantitative restrictions on the import and export of goods, *and of all other measures having equivalent effect;* ...and *an internal market* characterized by *the abolition,* as between Member States, of *obstacles to the free movement* of goods, persons, services, and capital"(emphasis added).

The surveys of European business undertaken in 1987 preceding the Cecchini Report listed technical barriers as *the* major impediment to the completion of the internal market. It is instructive to examine the technical barriers that the EC considered removing and to compare these with the methods of dealing with technical barriers in North America.

Border Issues

Clearly, for imports to be equivalent to domestically produced goods, especially in a world of "just-in-time" production, timely and low-cost delivery are crucial. The EU has attempted to minimize delays and paperwork at border crossings, but real problems exist today, thirty-six years after the Treaty of Rome.

The European Commission attempted to reduce the impact of border controls (the physical inspection and administrative formalities involved when goods cross borders) by adopting directives that provided broad-based principles that member states were to follow. The directives did not have the expected effect, however; "it seemed that some member states purposely applied [them on the] narrowest definition."[39] Since 1990, under the Single Market Act, the Commission has moved to eliminate border controls on intra-Community flights, sea crossings, and train movements, but with little real effects due to the worries that illegal goods (such as drugs) could slip across unguarded frontiers. Movement to a borderless Community appears halted at this point.[40]

The Commission has proposed a Common Community Customs Code. Although the EU is a customs union (unlike North America) with common tariffs against third countries, there is, as yet, no common basis of handling third-country imports. "The objective of the proposal [Community Customs Code] is to establish one coherent text replacing a multiplicity of different instruments and therefore ensuring greater legal transparency."[41] The EU is grappling with setting up a common computerized information system at borders, systems to detect fraud, and even EU rather than national training of border officials.

NAFTA is far behind the EU on these issues. NAFTA has set up a Working Committee on Trade in Goods that annually brings together officials concerned with border issues. This committee is probably an insufficient mechanism to deal with the complex issues that will arise on a day-to-day basis. The NAFTA negotiators have announced a trilingual one-page common certificate of origin.[42] However, it is much more than the origin of a commodity that is checked at a border. Phytosanitary standards, fraud detection, immigration, and detection of counterfeit and gray market goods are among the many potential roadblocks at borders. "U.S. customs also has the responsibility of enforcing the laws and regulations of about 40 agencies at the border."[43] Thus, the possibility of borders becoming costly impediments to increased cross-border trade is real. The issues are fourfold: first, the need for common agreement on the interpretation of the thousands of pages of detail in NAFTA; second, the need to train thousands of customs officials as to this common interpretation; third, the need for some mechanism to resolve disputes; and fourth, the problem of bottleneck infrastructure investments.[44]

With regard to the third issue, NAFTA does contain a dispute resolution process — the binational panels. However, this process is costly and long — it can take up to a year.[45] In 1992, the U.S. Customs Service interpreted the CUSFTA agreement to the detriment of Honda Canada (and to the detriment of Canada), and no process other than a binational panel could resolve differing interpretations. The U.S. interpretation involved a trade barrier increasing the costs of Honda Canada cars in the United States. The NAFTA agreement ended that dispute. However, new agreements or costly binational panels cannot be relied upon to resolve border disputes, especially those involving minor issues. Neither can "good faith" be relied upon to establish convergence of customs issues. One possible avenue for minimizing the number of disputes is to have the working group meet monthly, to provide it with a staff, and to have informal discussions of differing interpretations and potential conflicts before they become official disputes. Here the Free Trade Commission Secretariat (see below) can play a crucial role by utilizing its staff and its power under the agreement to set the agenda for the working group.

Standards

Differing standards are potentially significant nontariff barriers; their significance rises as the share of high-tech goods increases in intra-NAFTA trade. Differing technical specifications also raise barriers against imports. Within the EC, until the 1970s, technical standards were classic means of maintaining national barriers to Community trade. The Court of Justice in two benchmark cases (Casis de Dijon being the most famous) greatly reduced the ability of EC member countries to protect domestic producers on the basis of differing technical requirements. The EU has utilized several regimes in an attempt to reduce these barriers. Technical regulations cannot now be used to keep imports out if the other country's technical requirements are "equivalent."[46] "Mutual recognition" and the "harmonization of national standards" are two other approaches (besides equivalence) that the EU has introduced over the years to reduce the trade-distorting elements of technical regulations.

During the 1970s and 1980s, Community-wide standards replaced national standards for 185 products and services. The typical cases concerned safety (as with cosmetics and foodstuffs) and some industrial products. Beginning in 1985, the Commission began to realize that uniform Community-wide standards did not maximize product choice or diversity. Now, where standards do not involve risks to health, safety, or the environment, the rule of "mutual recognition" holds. A country cannot prevent the importation of a product from another member country simply because that product meets a different but qualified standard. Instead of harmonizing standards in these other areas, the Community relies on labeling and consumer choice.

In recent years, there has been a substantial increase in complaints by firms that national governments still maintain technical regulations as NTBs. The European Commission has begun to hold meetings to inform countries of all the cases where its rules are effective barriers,[47] and it has implemented exchanges of customs officials among countries and an EC training system for customs officials. It is instructive to contemplate the range of cases the Commission has dealt with recently and to consider their North American analogies and the daunting task ahead.

- Are member countries allowed to restrict the export of antiques?
- Should all motor vehicles adapt to local requirements of each country in order to be sold there?

- What common labeling criteria should be established?
- Should there be both EU and local regulations for autos?
- What are the "essential requirements" for health and safety of foodstuffs?
- What additives can be used in foods that cross borders?
- What are the common marketing requirements for pharmaceuticals?
- Should generic pharmaceuticals meet an "equivalent standards" test only?
- What are the impediments to trade if differing patent regimes and patent lifetimes exist?
- What impact do domestic health care price controls have on pharmaceutical trade?
- Does a published list of reimbursable drugs constitute a trade barrier?
- How can it be ensured that requirements on new products do not generate NTBs?
- What is the "essential requirements" minimum standard for toys?
- Are sector-level or all-purpose standards organizations more efficacious?
- Should national conformity assessment be replaced by Community-wide testing?[48]

Chapter Nine of NAFTA deals with "Standards-Related Measures." Article 904 affirms the right of each party to set "any standards-related measures," although goods of another NAFTA country receive national and MFN treatment. Article 906.1 requires "to the greatest extent practicable" the compatibility of standards-related measures. Articles 906.4 and 906.6 are key to the effective withdrawal of standards as trade barriers. In these two subsections, parties agree that a standard of an "exporting party" is equivalent where the exporting party demonstrates "to the satisfaction of the *importing* party that its technical regulation adequately fulfills the importing party's legitimate objectives" (Article 906.4, emphasis added) and that parties accept "wherever possible" the "results of a conformity assessment procedure" conducted in the other country. Article 908.2 requires mutual accreditation of conformity assessment bodies. Procedures are set out (Articles 908.33, 909, and 910) to ensure nondiscriminatory access to these bodies. Article 913 establishes the joint Committee on Standards—Related Measures, which monitors implementation and administration of the chapter, provides a forum for consultation, and can establish subcommittees (four have already been detailed).

It is easy to see the differences between the EU's mutual recognition process and Chapter Nine of NAFTA. NAFTA is a *host* country standard regime as compared with the *home* country standard regime in the EU. Canada, for example, could require that Mexico prove that Mexican standards in some area, X, meet Canada's legitimate objectives. In the EU, France can require that Portuguese firms demonstrate that their standards in some area, X, meet Portugal's objectives. NAFTA does not involve mutual recognition; that would require a home country regime. NAFTA does remove the obvious uses of standards as trade barriers and does provide for processes that lower the costs of standards setting. Each country will accept results of tests in the other two countries "whenever possible."

However, there are three ways in which standards setting in NAFTA is below the "standard" set in the EU. First, Article 904 of NAFTA allows individual country standards; for a number of goods, the EU has Community-wide standards. Second, in the EU, one cannot prevent the import of goods that meet different EU standards (except for safety, health, and the environment); in NAFTA, it appears that imported goods of differing standards can be kept out. Finally, it is open to an individual country's interpretation as to what the "legitimate objective" of a standard is and what "practicable" means for comparability across countries.[49] Early and numerous trinational problems, discussions, and panels on these definitions are likely.

There are substantial pressures from firms to harmonize standards across North America. Whereas the EU relies on a "top down" process mandating mutual recognition, within North America, there is a "bottom up" process whereby voluntary mutual recognition occurs for voluntary standards (that is, not involving health, safety, and the environment). CUSFTA certainly speeded up this process. But voluntary standards setting procedures differ across the three countries, with a Crown Corporation established in Canada in 1970 (the Canadian Standards Council — CSC) with the responsibility to manage (not regulate) the voluntary standard system in Canada.[50] In the United States, the process is much more fragmented since there are a number of standards institutes and associations. This fact raises the costs of harmonization because there are multiple and competitive accreditation organizations in the United States. As countries move to worldwide, principally International Standards Organization (ISO) standards, mutual recognition of standards is moot; the issue becomes one of judging the viability of conformity assessment. The likely future hurdle will be the evidence that the standard is met in the NAFTA country.

Monetary Union in North America?

An agreement on exchange rate stability in North America would imply some mechanism to limit relative changes in the three currencies, for example, the pre-August 1992 European Exchange Rate Mechanism (ERM), whereby the Canadian dollar and Mexican peso would be kept in narrow (3.5

percent) bands around the U.S. dollar. In order for exchange rates to remain fixed within these narrow bands, investors would expect to earn identical returns on government bonds denominated in the country currency since substantial exchange rate appreciation (or depreciation) would not exist. Thus, the "interest parity" equilibrium would require nominal and real interest rates to be nearly identical across the three countries (within narrow bands).

Domestic interest rates are determined by domestic real money supply and real domestic money demand. The real demand for money is itself a function of income, the exchange rate, and the price level (and domestic interest rates). Therefore, a rise in income (gross domestic product — GDP) or the price level will affect money demand and, consequently, interest rates. To maintain fixed exchange rates requires the government to intervene in the domestic market via the money supply. "By fixing the exchange rate, then, the central bank loses its ability to use monetary policy for the purpose of macroeconomic stabilization."[51] A common currency in North America would require Canada and Mexico to forgo monetary policy, for it is obvious that the U.S. Federal Reserve Board would be the Bundesbank of North America.

Economic theory demonstrates that there is an optimal currency area involving more than one country. However, the exact theoretical and empirical conditions which mean that two or more countries should have a common currency have never been agreed upon. Guillermo de la Dehesa and Paul Krugman survey these theoretical and empirical elements and conclude "...there is no simple test one can readily apply...."[52]

Exchange rate movements can be barriers to trade and do involve costs to exporters, importers, and investors. In the three years before CUSFTA (1986 to 1989), the Canadian dollar appreciated 21.1 percent. Since CUSFTA came into effect, the Canadian dollar has fallen 17 percent. It depreciated 12.3 percent in 1992 and again in 1993. A fall in the Canadian dollar of this magnitude appreciably increases the price of U.S. goods in Canadian markets and reduces the price of Canadian goods in U.S. markets. Variance in exchange rates is a cost of the border. While futures contracts and other hedging instruments can reduce these costs, these instruments are not costless, require staff and expertise, cannot eliminate longer-term risk, and may be out of reach for many small- and medium-size enterprises.

Table 3 shows the real exchange rate variability for a number of Central American and Latin American countries in the 1986-1990 period. Only Costa Rica and Chile had changes in the real exchange rate that were as low as the changes experienced in Canada and the United States. However, the inflation rates in this period for Chile and Costa Rica were four to six times those in Canada and the United States. Adding Latin American and Central American countries to NAFTA makes thoughts of a common currency recede into the distant future.

Should Canada unilaterally fix its exchange rate to that of the United States as Richard Harris suggests? Harris states that the purchasing power parity value of the Canadian dollar in the late 1980s was US$.78 or $.79.[53] As of April 1994, the inability of the Canadian government measurably to reduce deficits and public debt has the Canadian dollar near US$.72. Had the Canadian dollar been pegged at US$.79 over the last two years, the speculative pressure to devalue would have been intense unless policy convergence had occurred. The swings of vast resources in the capital market can undo most fixed rates, as the Europeans have learned.[54] The Canadian dollar could not withstand attacks on the exchange rate, especially those based on fundamental disequilibria. There is, of course, one way to "fix" the exchange rate, which is to adopt the U.S. dollar as legal tender in Canada (as has been done in Israel and Bermuda), a most unlikely scenario.

How close is North America to "policy convergence"? First, what policies need "converge" for a fixed exchange rate to be effective?

The Maastricht Treaty sets out the following principles for the move to a single currency in the European Union: 1) criteria for macroeconomic convergence — public deficit to GDP rates of 3.0 percent or less and gross public debt to GDP ratio of 60 percent; 2) capital mobility, with free convertibility; 3) unifying fiscal and monetary policies; 4) convergence of regulatory and institutional frameworks; 5) single currency; and 6) single central bank.

In Table 2 and Figures 1 to 4, data are provided for the United States, Canada, and Mexico on the two key indicators of macroeconomic convergence in the Maastricht Treaty and on a set of other crucial variables indicating the potential for convergence. It is fascinating to note that of the fifteen countries in the EU and North America, only Mexico and Luxembourg meet the deficit and debt targets of the Maastricht Treaty.[55] Today, the United States and Canada do not meet the EU's criteria for macroeconomic convergence.

Moreover, in terms of the ability to coordinate monetary policies with the other two countries or other prerequisites for macroeconomic policy convergence, Mexico is not an immediate candidate. Nor are Canada and the United States clear partners. Examine the data for the three North American countries presented in Table 2 and the accompanying four figures. There is "a lack of full convergence of inflation" (see note 48) in North America, with Mexican inflation rates in the years shown at least five times U.S. and Canadian inflation rates. Current account deficits in Canada and Mexico are widening. Domestic monetary policy is now significantly different in the United States as compared with Canada and Mexico. The Fed's move on February, 4, 1994, to signal tighter money supply caused the Toronto stock market to lose 2.4 percent of its value and the Canadian Minister of Finance to predict lower short-term rates in Canada than in the United States. Continued weakness in the Mexican economy also suggests a divergence, not a convergence, in monetary policy with the United States. Unemployment rates are moving in opposite directions in Canada and the United States.[56]

Adding Mexico and potentially other Latin American countries makes a common North American currency or a North American central bank even more remote. An important issue in the discussion of currency policy in North America is the rudimentary nature of the Mexican banking system. Until 1988, capital markets in Mexico were singularly undeveloped. "The lack of an established bond market and the existence of an informal credit market impeded the conduit of monetary policy...."[57] Prior to 1988, one of the major purposes of the Mexican banking system was to fund government deficits. Banks were then government-owned, not private; deposit rates were regulated; reserve requirements were 50 percent; and banks were required to invest in Mexican government paper. Restrictions on lending to the private sector were removed only in April 1989. A bond market did not exist prior to 1989 since the government could rely on forced lending from the nationalized banks.[58]

The peso does not float freely today. However, its fixed ratio relative to the U.S. dollar, a fixture of Mexican policy, is not a signal that a move to a common currency in the short run is feasible in North America. There are a number of reasons for this. First, the fixed rate of the peso is not due to the convergence of fundamental factors but to Mexican government policy.[59] Thus, the ability of the Mexican government to control exchange rates is itself evidence that a common currency is far away.[60] Second, since the Mexican banking system is not fully evolved, free flows of capital between the three NAFTA countries are not totally feasible. Third, financial markets in Mexico are mostly undeveloped. There is no futures market; there is exchange hedging, "only big treasuries and bank participants and operations are inter-bank not stock-market."[61]

Institutions and NAFTA

NAFTA sets out a number of committees, subcommittees, and working groups (see Table 4). Overall, there is a NAFTA Free Trade Commission comprised of trade ministers from the member countries that has a permanent home and a staff. But many of the committees are ill-defined;[62] none have staffs or permanent secretariats; and the linkages between committees are not spelled out (they are under the direction of the Free Trade Commission). The impact of these committees on the future of NAFTA is uncertain; several paths of development are possible.

One possible path is for the committees to meet occasionally (most committees must meet once a year to discuss critical issues). However, without staff, budgets, or the ability to generate and pass on information, their impact will likely be modest.

The Free Trade Commission supervises the implementation of the agreement and can delegate work to the committees and working groups. The FTC has a secretariat with each country establishing a permanent office for the Commission. Therefore, a second possible path is for the FTC to become a major instrument of change, a Commission that pursues its goal of implementing the agreement in terms of the spirit of free trade and realizes that there is far more to free trade than tariff reductions. The FTC could become one of the engines that will reduce the ability of domestic protectionist forces to utilize AD, CVD, border controls, and standards as trade barriers. This is more of an EU model than currently envisioned in North America. The FTC as structured is not a policy body; with secretariats in each country, it is not structured to be a Brussels-type oversight committee. However, the FTC in supervising the committee substructure can set agendas and show the determination to make free trade happen. To deepen and widen economic relationships in North America may well require a Free Trade Commission with a mandate for real free trade.

Another potential force for harmonization lies in Article 2006 under the rubric "consultations." Article 2006(1) allows any party to request a consultation "regarding any actual or proposed measure or any other matter that it considers might affect the operation of this Agreement." Take as a possible example a case in which Mexico requests a consultation with the United States over the U.S. technical standards for generic pharmaceuticals. Article 2006(2) permits Canada to join the consultation if Canada considers "it has a substantial interest in the matter." If there is no resolution of the dispute in thirty to forty-five days or such other period as the parties agree to, a meeting of the Commission can be requested (2007(1)). The Commission must meet within ten days, and if no resolution occurs, Mexico can request an arbitral panel (2008). A panel is selected from a roster of panelists; experts or scientific review boards can be called (Article 2014, 2015) and must provide an initial report within ninety days.

Parties can comment (within fourteen days), and a final report is issued within another thirty days. The final report is to be published (Article 2017[4]). If the report finds that the United States (for its technical requirements on generic pharmaceuticals) is at fault and if the two parties cannot agree to a resolution of the dispute, Mexico can retaliate by "suspending benefits of equivalent effect until such time as they have reached agreement on a resolution of the dispute" (Article 2019[1]).

It is clear from this example that an aggressive use of "consultations" could prove to be a means of policy harmonization.

This last section may be criticized for searching within the tea leaves of NAFTA for something that is not there. NAFTA is a free trade agreement, it can be argued; thus, "harmonization" issues are purposely left out. NAFTA is not a design for a community. The point of this chapter is that the divide between issues that are within and outside an FTA is no longer visible. Trade in goods is affected by a host of domestic policies. In NAFTA, tariffs have been dealt with, but some of the most visible of other impediments to trade, such as antidumping measures or standards that can be effective NTBs, have not been dealt with effectively. Thus, the hypothesis of this chapter: the agreement is unstable, and its future will require serious efforts to examine and deal with the remaining barriers to trade.

Table 1. Canada-United States Crossborder Antidumping Cases

	1986-1988	1989-1991	1990-1991	1992-1993
1. INVESTIGATIONS INITIATED				
Canada Against U.S.	15	1	7	13*
U.S. Against Canada	9	0	4	8
2. ANTIDUMPING AFFIRMATIVE FINDINGS (Dumping and Injury)				
Canada Against U.S.	7	5	4	6*
U.S. Against Canada	5	6	1	4
*3. BINATIONAL PANELS***				
Canada Against U.S.	-	18	8	11
U.S. Against Canada	-	3	3	15

* Two investigations are in progress.
** There are more binational panels than cases with affirmative findings for two reasons. First, some appeals are launched after a temporary finding of injury on dumping is made. Second, appeals to both injury and dumping determinations are made.

Table 2a

CANADA	1986	1987	1988	1989	1990	1991	1992
Government Deficit*/GDP	3.91	2.47	2.18	2.52	4.25	4.62	4.00
Public Debt/GDP	48.80	52.30	53.10	53.40	57.30	61.50	NA
M1 Rate of Growth	21.40	14.20	3.60	4.30	1.70	5.80	5.40
M2 Rate of Growth	6.10	9.50	9.80	11.40	9.80	7.20	6.90
Percent Change in GDP Deflator	2.40	4.60	4.70	4.80	3.30	2.70	1.00
Percent Change in CPI	4.20	4.40	4.00	5.00	4.80	5.60	1.50
90-Day Treasury Bill Rate	8.97	8.15	9.48	12.05	12.81	8.73	6.59
Long-term Government Bond Rate	9.52	9.95	10.22	9.92	10.85	9.76	8.77
Exchange Rate (Canadian dollar/US$)**	1.39	1.33	1.23	1.18	1.17	1.15	1.21

Sources: International Monetary Fund, *International Financial Statistics*, EIU Country Profile, Statistics Canada.
* All levels of government.
** Exchange rates are for period averages.

Table 2b

MEXICO	1986	1987	1988	1989	1990	1991	1992
Government Deficit/GDP*	16.00	16.00	12.40	5.50	4.00	1.50	NA
Public Debt/GDP	76.30	79.30	59.40	47.00	39.70	35.30	NA
M1 Rate of Growth	51.30	106.50	110.10	30.60	47.90	91.60	70.20
M2 Rate of Growth	57.50	126.50	77.80	-10.20	104.10	72.40	34.80
Percent Change in GDP Deflator	73.60	139.60	99.50	25.80	29.40	21.60	NA
Percent Change in CPI	86.20	131.80	114.20	20.00	26.70	22.70	15.50
CETES 28-Day Treasury Bill Rate	NA	103.07	69.15	44.99	34.76	19.28	15.62
Long-term Government Bond Rate	NA	NA	NA	NA	NA	NA	NA
Exchange Rate (New Mexican pesos/US$)**	0.60	1.40	2.30	2.50	2.80	3.00	3.10

Sources: IMF, *International Financial Statistics*, Government Finance Statistics Yearbook; World Bank, World Debt Tables, EIU Country Profile.
* All levels of government.
** Exchange rates are for averages over period.

Table 2c

UNITED STATES	1986	1987	1988	1989	1990	1991	1992
Government Deficit*/GDP	5.04	3.31	3.23	2.78	3.99	4.84	5.72
Public Debt/GDP	42.80	43.10	42.80	42.70	45.60	49.40	51.9
M1 Rate of Growth	13.40	9.60	4.30	0.90	3.80	6.10	12.6
M2 Rate of Growth	8.60	6.50	5.60	3.40	4.30	3.30	2.3
Percent Change in GDP Deflator	2.70	3.20	3.90	4.50	4.30	4.00	2.6
Percent Change in CPI	1.90	3.70	4.00	4.80	5.40	4.20	3.0
90-Day Treasury Bill Rate	5.97	5.83	6.67	8.11	7.51	5.41	3.46
Long-term Government Bond Rate	7.68	8.38	8.85	8.50	8.55	7.86	7.01

Sources: IMF, *International Financial Statistics*, EIU Country Profile.
* All levels of government.

Table 3. Macroeconomic Indicators Affecting the Viability of an FTA

	Annual Inflation (1991) (%)	Real Exchange Rate Maximum Annual Change (1988-1990)b (%)	Trade Taxes end of the 1990s (% of Total Taxation)
United States	4.2	4.6	1.7
Canada	5.6	4.3	3.8
Mexico	22.7	n.d.	3.4
Andean Pact	21.0	23.7a	12.6
Bolivia	30.4	10.4	11.2
Ecuador	48.7	15.7a	n.d.
Peru	over 100	41.3	21.5
Venezuela	34.2	37.1	23.4
Central American Common Market			
El Salvador	n.d.	n.d.	21.1
Guatemala	33.2	n.d.	37.2
Honduras	n.d.	n.d.	n.d.
Costa Rica	28.7	3.7a	21.1
Nicaragua	n.d.	56.6a	16.9
Southern Cone			
Brazil	over 100	46.3	1.6
Argentina	84.0	15.9	10.3
Uruguay	over 100	10.7a	13.6
Paraguay	24.3	35.1a	12.0
Chile	18.7	3.8	9.9

Source: IMF, *International Financial Statistics*. J.P. Morgan. *World Financial Markets*.
Notes: *a* IMF *Government Finance Statistics Yearbook, 1990.*
   b This column measures the largest percentage change between the maximum and minimum values of the exchange rate for any pair of years in the period 1988-1990.

Table 4

COMMITTEES IN NAFTA

Committee on Trade in Goods	(Article 316)
Committee on Trade in Worn Clothing	(Annex 300-B, Sec. 9.1)
Committee on Agricultural Trade	(Article 706)
Advisory Committee on Private Commercial Disputes regarding Agricultural Goods	(Article 707)
Committee on Sanitary and Phytosanitary Measures	(Article 722)
Committee on Standards-Related Measures	(Article 913)
Land Transportation Standards Subcommittee	Art. 913(5)(a)(i)
Telecommunications Standards Subcommittee	Art. 913(5)(a)(ii)
Automotive Standards Council	Art. 913(5)(a)(iii)
Subcommittee on Labelling of Textile and Apparel Goods	Art. 913(5)(a)(iv)
Committee on Small Business	(Article 1021)
Financial Services Committee	(Article 1412)
Advisory Committee on Private Commercial Disputes	(Article 2022(4))

WORKING GROUPS IN NAFTA

Working Group on Rules of Origin	(Article 513)
Customs Subgroup	(Article 513(6))
Working Group on Agricultural Subsidies	(Article 705(6))
Bilateral Working Group (Mexico-United States)	(Annex 703.2(A)(25))
Bilateral Working Group (Canada-Mexico)	(Annex 703.2(B)(13))
Working Group on Trade and Competition	(Article 1504)
Temporary Entry Working Group	(Article 1605)

Others

Tribunal for Arbitration	(Article 1126)
Binational Panel	(Article 1904)

Figure 1. Monthly Changes in Consumer Price Index
1986 – 1993

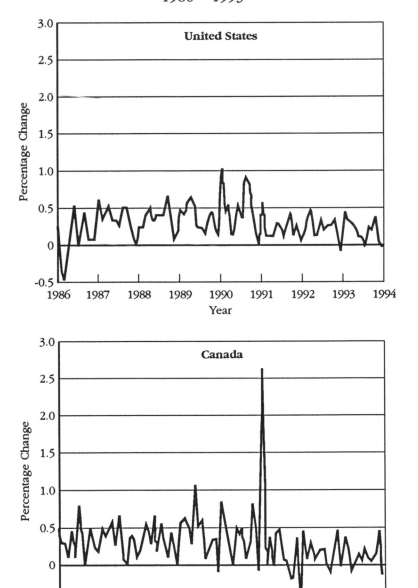

Source: Statistics Canada.

Figure 2. Monthly Changes in Exchange Rates
1986 – 1993

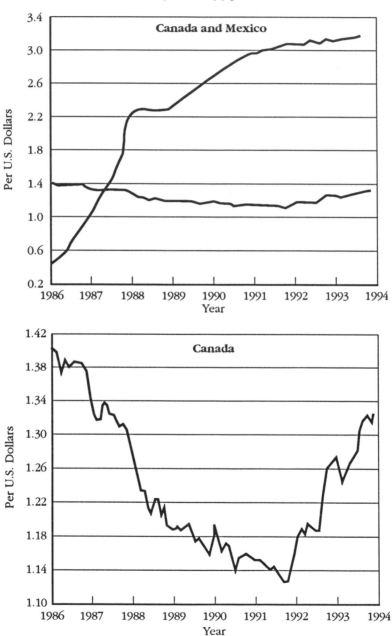

Figure 3. Treasury Bill Rates
1986 – 1993

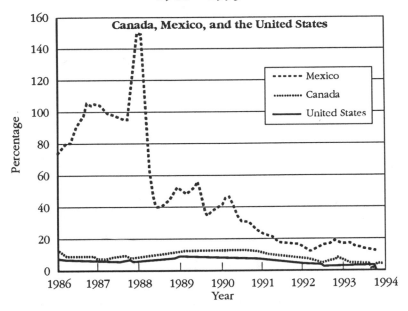

Source: Statistics Canada, International Monetary Fund, Banco de Mexico.

Figure 4. Unemployment Rates
1986 – 1993

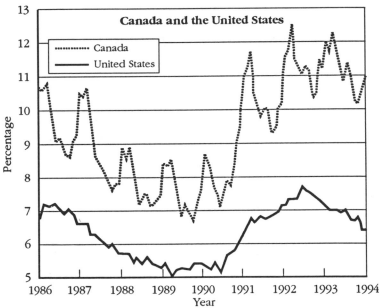

Source: Statistics Canada.

Notes

1   In this paper, I do not examine current trade and investment flows in North America or project changes or gains and losses under NAFTA. For these analyses and projections, see Globerman 1993, Schott and Hufbauer 1993, U.S. GAO 1993, and Waverman 1992.

2   As compared with economic unions, all free trade agreements do leave domestic policies in place.

3   Sylvia Ostry, in *Governments and Corporations in A Shrinking World* (1990), drew attention to the need to harmonize a set of domestic policies.

4   For the former view, see Harris 1993; for the latter view, see Reid 1993.

5   See Schwanen 1992, 1993.

6   U.S. General Accounting Office 1993, Vol. 2:14.

7   For many high-tech goods, no general internationally recognized Harmonized Commodity Description and Coding System (HS) exists. Thus, where agreement was possible, the three countries made up their own HS class for those goods. For other high-tech goods where agreement was not possible, specific rules were established. For example, a computer is of regional origin if 50 percent of its costs are regional and if the motherboard is regional.

8   Costs (for a rule-of-origin test) do not include sales promotion, marketing and after-sales services, packing and shipping, royalties, and interest costs above a reasonable ceiling.

9   All three countries are members of the International Energy Association (IEA). The IEA rules require the sharing of exports in times of IEA-determined shortages.

10 See Gestrin and Rugman 1993.

11 See Waverman 1993.

12 Canada feels cultural industries are exempt under CUSFTA. The United States feels it can challenge Canadian actions that damage U.S. interests. The countries appear to have agreed to disagree.

13 Mexico's review only holds if there is more than 49 percent foreign ownership and if the enterprise was originally controlled by Mexican interests.

14 This section draws on joint work with Alan Alexandroff on this subject.

15 See Krugman 1994.

16 Super 301 actions refer to provisions that were added to the Omnibus Trade and Competitiveness Act of 1988. These provisions made it mandatory for the U.S.

Trade Representative (USTR) to identify trade policy priorities with respect to the implementation of sections 301 through 310. The provisions required the USTR to prepare on schedule an inventory of foreign trade barriers, establish a priority list of countries and their unreasonable practices, and then set deadlines for their removal. The provision expired after 1990. It was renewed in 1994 by President Clinton by executive order.

17 Governor Bill Clinton and Senator Al Gore, *Putting People First: How Can We All Change America* (New York: Times Books), 1992, 13.

18 Trade expert and former economic policy adviser to the Secretary General of GATT Jagdish Bhagwati named this critique of the trading system and the criticism of Japan and other rapidly developing economies as the "diminished giant" syndrome in the United States. This approach, suggested Bhagwati, arose in response to the United States' declining economic dominance in the global economy. The attack on the rising economic states, in his view, paralleled the British reaction to their country's decline in the face of rapidly industrializing Germany and the United States in the late nineteenth century.

19 Again, this is a phrase that has been popularized by Jagdish Bhagwati. See Bhagwati 1991.

20 Section 301 of the 1974 Trade and Tariff Act directs the USTR to enforce U.S. rights under international trade agreements and to take other actions necessary to remove unfair foreign trade practices.

21 Sylvia Nasar, "The Risky Allure of Strategic Trade," *New York Times*, February 28, 1993, E1.

22 The exact nature of these FTAs, that is, how deep they are, is unclear.

23 However, any individual or company affected by a ruling on AD or CVD can ask for a review of the decision by a trinational panel under chapters 19 of CUSFTA and NAFTA. This review mechanism supersedes appeals to the Court of International Trade in the United States or the Federal Court of Appeals in Canada. A decision of the panel can be appealed by one of the governments to an extraordinary challenge committee.

24 See Steinberg 1993, 22. Countervailing duties have been based on a not-well-defined subsidies code agreed to in the Tokyo Round (the Interpretation and Application of Articles VI, XVI, and XXIII of GATT). In the Uruguay Round, it was generally the United States that was aggressively pursuing the defining and limiting of subsidies and foreign governments that were attempting to constrain attacks on subsidies. The new GATT agreement divides subsidies into four colors analogous to traffic lights (the level playing field is now a Grand Prix event) — green (nonactionable); red (prohibited); amber (permissible yet actionable); and dark amber (presumptuously prohibited). Both the "green" and "dark amber" classes have five-year sunset clauses. It will take some time to determine the impact that the new GATT subsidies code will have on U.S. actions against Canada and Mexico. This paper does not discuss subsidies and CVD; however, they are important issues.

25 The thirteen AD cases launched in 1992-1993 in Canada include four that are retaliations for the U.S. steel AD cases.

26 Trebilcock 1993, 78.

27   AD cases may provide some limited value even in a free trade area. The ability of private firms to initiate actions against foreign rivals in a known administrative process removes some protectionist pressures from the political arena. Not all political pressures are reduced — witness the extraordinary challenges launched by the U.S. government or the statements from the U.S. administration during the NAFTA debate of the desirability of attacking Canadian exports of durum wheat. AD cases are now brought in a system of due process which includes the ability of those accused to react and to appeal. Removal of this process might cause these protectionist forces to move into less obvious, less public venues.

28   See Staiger and Wolak 1993.

29   See especially Boltuck and Litan 1991.

30   See Murray 1991.

31   This analysis assumes standing in a dumping case — that the firm is acting on behalf of the industry. Besides dumping, injury must also be proved.

32   In the recent Brown & Williamson case (Brooke Group Ltd v. Brown and Williamson Tobacco Comp. 113 S. Ct. 2578 [1993]), the U.S. Supreme Court stated that to demonstrate predation, the plaintiff must prove 1) "that the prices complained of are below an appropriate measure of its rival's costs" and 2) "that the competitor had a reasonable prospect, or ...a dangerous probability, of recouping its investment in below-cost prices." Significantly, the Court noted: "Because the parties in this case agree that the relevant measure of cost is average variable cost, ...we again decline to resolve the conflict...over the appropriate measure of cost." Elaborating on the second element of this test, the Court said that "[f]or recoupment to occur, below-cost pricing must be capable, as a threshold matter, of producing the intended effects on the firm's rivals," such as "driving them from the market."

33   Contrary to the popular notion that dumping is "selling below cost," both in law and in economic theory, dumping is defined as international price discrimination or the practice of charging a higher price for sales in a foreign producer's home market than for export to the United States. Under current U.S. law, when comparisons to home market or other third-market prices are not possible or when U.S. investigators find that a large part of the home market sales are made "below cost," export prices to the United States are compared with a measure of production cost constructed from accounting data, through the use of statutory guidelines. In principle, all price comparisons are made at the "factory gate," or at the point when goods leave the plants — before any transportation or selling costs are incurred that would result in legitimate price differences among international markets. Once dumping has been found, U.S. law grants producers of a "like product" relief in the form of an antidumping duty if they then can prove to the ITC that they have been materially injured "by reason of the subject imports" (Boltuck and Litan 1991).

34   *New York Times*, February 15, 1994, C2.

35   See *New York Times*, February 3, 1994.

36   U.S. industrial leaders and politicians are convinced that Canada and its provinces subsidize a wide variety of industries. The potential for subsidies must be large in Mexico with significant state controls still in existence and with the exemption

from NAFTA of crucial sectors such as energy. Thus, changing CVD laws also becomes more difficult.

37 *New York Times,* December 3, 1993, C5.

38 Lepsoe 1993, 36.

39 Vantyghem and Pelkmans 1992, 87.

40 The Benelux countries have largely done away with borders among themselves.

41 See Vantyghem and Pelkmans 1992, 87. Vantyghem and Pelkmans point to one unfortunate fallout of truly removing internal border controls — the absence of statistics on imports and exports! The EC recognizes this and is moving toward a "common system of integrated economic accounts" and data on shipments from companies rather than from customs officials.

42 *Journal of Commerce,* November 23, 1992, 54.

43 LBJ School, *Texas-Mexico Multimodal Transportation,* 1993, 9.

44 See LBJ School 1993, chapters 3, 4, and 5 for a good discussion of the bottlenecks developing at the Mexico-Texas border because of inadequate roads, bridges, rail connections, and border guard stations.

45 A year is quick compared to pre-Uruguay Round GATT procedures.

46 "During 1990, 39 rulings [of the Court of Justice] were delivered on questions relating to the free movement of goods and the operation of the Customs Union," and "the Commission undertook 1326 investigations of possible infringements of articles 30 and 36 in 1990" Bohan 1992, 93, 94. The number of cases in NAFTA as compared with the EC will not be a good measure of the importance of technical barriers. In NAFTA, there are only borders and trade flows; in the EC, there are 11 borders and 132 internal trade flows.

47 See Bohan 1992, 94.

48 All these questions are from Bohan 1992.

49 The EU has been quite careful to state that non-EC products are treated identically to EU products. Thus, once a product has been accepted in, say, France, home country equivalence means that product is exportable across the EU. There seems to be no similar language in NAFTA.

50 The CSC runs four separate accreditation programs (for standards developers, certification organizations, testing laboratories, and registration organizations [the latter three are conformity assessment groups]); approves National Standards for Canada; and is the Canadian manager for international standards organizations (ISO and ITC).

51 Krugman and Obstfeld 1991, 479.

52 De la Dehesa and Krugman 1992; Harris 1993.

53 Since 1979, the European monetary system's exchange rate mechanism aimed at maintaining the twelve EC currencies within narrow bands. While enunciating the goal of a single currency, the ERM fell apart in July 1993 due to pressures on a number of currencies. These pressures were "a lack of full convergence of inflation," "the widening of current account deficits," "clear market perception of serious inconsistencies between, on the one hand, the domestic requirements for monetary policies in a number of countries with lackluster economic activity," "clear problems associated with cost competitiveness" and "rising unemployment" (IMF, *World Economic Outlook* (October), 1993, 30,32,32).

54 *The Economist* has stated that Luxembourg is the only country in the EU that meets these two criteria.

55 The Maastricht Treaty proposes a European Central Bank (ECB) and a European System of Central Banks (ESCB). The ESCB consists of national central banks (NCBs) and the ECB. The role of the ESCB is "to define and implement the monetary policy of the Community" and "to conduct foreign exchange operations...." Both the ECB and the NCBs will conduct open market transactions. The ECB is controlled by a governing council and an executive board. The ultimate aim is to have the ECB control the money supply and monetary policy in the EC. However, elaborate transitional mechanisms and derogations are included. As a step along this road toward an ECB with participation by all countries, the European Monetary Institute (EMI) is now in place. The goals of the EMI are to strengthen coordination of monetary policy "with a view to ensuring price stability" and to make preparations for the ESCBs and the creation of a single monetary policy and a single currency. The analogues to the EMI and the ECB in North America — the NAMI and NACB — are not visible, even on the distant horizon.

56 Coorey 1991, 37.

57 In May 1990, articles 28 and 123 of the constitution were amended to allow privatization of banks. Most Mexican banks are now private.

58 Most observers feel that the peso is overvalued.

59 "The Banco de Mexico's control over the monetary supply is greater than that exercised by its European counterparts" (*Banamex Review*, November 1993, 484).

60 *Banamex Review*, November 1993, 482.

61 For example, the Committee on Trade in Goods established in Article 316 "shall meet at the request of any Party to the Commission to consider any matters arising under this Chapter." Once a year (at least) a meeting of "officials responsible for customs, immigration, inspection of food and agricultural product, border expansion facilities and regulation transportation" shall meet to consider movements of goods through ports.

62 However, Article 2021 states that no right of private action in domestic law can be introduced.

References

Banamex. *Review of the Economic Situation of Mexico*. Various issues.

Bank for International Settlements. 1993. 63rd Annual Report. Basle. June.

Bhagwati, Jagdish. 1991. *The World Trading System at Risk*. Princeton, N.J.: Princeton University Press.

Brown, David A. 1993. "Developing and Enforcing Regulations and Standards: A Canadian Private Sector Perspective." Davies Ward & Beck. September.

Bohan, Niall. 1992. "Technical Barriers to Trade." Chapter 4 in *The Annual Review of European Community Affairs 1991*. London: Brassy's Centre for European Policy Studies.

Boltuck, Richard, and Robert Litan, eds. 1991. *Down in the Dumps: Administration of Unfair Trade Laws*. Washington, D.C.: The Brookings Institution.

Coorey, Sharmini. 1992. "Financial Liberalization and Reform in Mexico." In *Mexico: The Strategy to Achieve Sustained Economic Growth*. IMF Occasional Paper (99). Washington, D.C.: IMF. September.

de la Dehesa, Guillermo, and Paul Krugman. 1992. "EMU and the Regions." Occasional Paper (39), Washington, D.C.: Group of Thirty.

Eichengreen, Barry. 1990. "Is Europe an Optimum Currency Area?" CEPR Discussion Paper (438). London: CEPR.

Gestrin, Michael, and Alan Rugman. "The Impact of NAFTA Upon North American Investment Patterns." *Transnational Corporations*. Forthcoming.

Hufbauer, Gary, and Jeffrey Schott. 1993. *NAFTA An Assessment*. Washington, D.C.: Institute for International Economics.

Harris, Richard G. 1993. "Trade, Money and Wealth in the Canadian Economy." C.D. Howe Institute, Benefactors Lecture. September 14.

IMF. 1992. *Mexico: The Strategy to Achieve Sustained Economic Growth*. Occasional Paper (99). Washington, D.C.: IMF. September.

IMF. 1993. *World Economic Outlook*. Washington, D.C.: IMF. October.

Krugman, Paul, and Maurice Obstfeld. 1991. *International Economics, Theory and Policy*. New York: Harper Collins.

Krugman, Paul. 1994. "Competitiveness: A Dangerous Obsession." *Foreign Affairs* 73 (2): 28-44.

Lepsoe, Paul. 1993. "Dumping Side Agreement to NAFTA Adds Little." 14:4 Can. Comp. Rec.

Meller, Patricio. 1993. "Latin America's Stark Choice." *Policy Options* (January-February).

Reich, T.C. 1993. "Time for North-American Monetary Union: The Canadian Perspective." *International Economic Law Society Bulletin* 6(2): 18-20.

Staiger, Robert, and Frank Wolak. 1993. "Measuring Industry Specific Protection: Antidumping in the United States." Mimeo, Brookings Micro Panel. December.

Steinberg, Richard H. 1994. "The Uruguay Round: A Preliminary Analysis of the Final Act." Berkeley Roundtable on the International Economy, University of California at Berkeley.

Szymcrak, Philippe. 1992. "Mexico's Return to Voluntary International Capital Market Financing." *Mexico: The Strategy to Achieve Sustained Economic Growth.* IMF Occasional Paper (99), Chapter VII. Washington, D.C.: IMF. September.

Trebilcock, Michael. 1993. "The Case for Replacing Anti-dumping with Anti-trust." 14:4, Can. Comp. Rec.

U.S. International Trade Commission. 1993. *Potential Impact on the U.S. Economy and Selected Industries of the North American Free-Trade Agreement.* USITC Publications 2596. Washington, D.C.: USITC.

United States General Accounting Office (GAO). 1993. Report to the Congress, *North American Free Trade Agreement, Assessment of Major Issues*, Vol. 2. Washington, D.C.: GAO.

Vantyghem, Dirk, and Jacques Pelkmans, 1992. "Border Controls for Goods." In *The Annual Review of European Community Affairs 1991.* London: Brassy's Centre for European Policy Studies.

Waverman, Leonard. 1992. "The NAFTA Agreement: A Canadian Perspective." In *Assessing NAFTA: A Trinational Analysis*, eds. Steven Globerman and Michael Walker. Vancouver: The Fraser Institute.

Chapter 5

From NAFTA to a WHFTA?
The Summit May Tell

Albert Fishlow

Introduction

NAFTA, the North American Free Trade Agreement, came into effect on January 1, 1994. Its enactment has triggered wide speculation about the next steps in Western Hemisphere trade policy. Chile is already in a position to be the next entrant to NAFTA, but there is much speculation that economic integration could move farther and faster than had been foreseen. That conclusion derives substantially from the Washington announcement of a hemispheric assembly of heads of state in Miami at the end of 1994. Throughout the region, individual countries have begun efforts to prepare their positions. For the first time in close to thirty years, since the formation of the Alliance for Progress, the United States has again emerged as the undisputed leader within the region. Nations of the Caribbean and Latin America are looking northward for signals of real U.S. interest and commitment.

This meeting will be the first among hemispheric leaders since the Punta del Este encounter of 1967, at which President Lyndon Johnson offered U.S. support for a Latin America Free Trade Association (LAFTA). However, LAFTA excluded the United States, whereas today U.S. policy is one of direct and active engagement. U.S. strategy has now taken seriously President George Bush's 1990 vision of an Enterprise of the Americas, a position initially put forward largely to stimulate the moribund General Agreement on Tariffs and Trade (GATT) negotiations. Yet it was the affirmative NAFTA vote that helped to assure a final favorable GATT settlement. Ironically, Latin American policy, at least until the 1994 summit meeting, seems to have become more important for its indirect effects than for its direct results.

This chapter takes up the questions of the possible form and timing of future hemispheric integration. The focus is addressed to the pending summit meeting, but the subjects discussed may have continuing relevance.

The first section argues that the likely static effect of the extension of NAFTA, both for the United States and Latin America, is relatively small. By contrast, the two central dynamic implications of a broader free trade zone, a permanent increase in investment rates and a new commitment to macroeconomic stability and microeconomic competition, are much more profound for Latin America. For the United States as well, the dynamic gain is greater, but still small. Such a strategy also requires a simultaneous rise in Latin American domestic savings rates if it is to produce long-term growth within the region. And the substantial inequality that sadly places Latin America as the global leader in dismal domestic savings rates cannot be ignored. Income redistribution simply cannot be put off to a later stage after recovery.

The second section considers how NAFTA might be extended, with regard to both possible membership and the style of adherence. An argument is presented in favor of a major effort to include Brazil as the center of such a venture, a move that is contrary to current policy in Brazil and the United States, but stands out as a necessity if free trade is to be the center of future hemispheric policy. It foresees as well the use of a hub-and-spoke strategy for rapid expansion. While this strategy is generally rejected because of its economic deficiencies, the costs of long delay outweigh the temporary modest reduction of benefits from integration.

The final section weighs the gains and costs to the United States of such a different regional program as the basis of future Latin American policy. It is a design that recognizes realistically that the United States can no longer hold out promises of large-scale public assistance. At the same time, the potential benefits of renewed Latin American economic expansion, apart from possible gains on such other pressing issues as the drug trade and migration, more than merit the effort.

Gains from Regional Integration

As a result of many independent assessments typically using computable general equilibrium models, there has been widespread recognition that Mexico is the only country likely to achieve a measurable static gain as a consequence of NAFTA.[1] Those findings logically follow from the very high percentage of Mexican trade with the United States — more than two-thirds of Mexico's total — as well as from the large share of Mexican exports in relation to the country's gross national product (GNP). But even so, the benefit is limited. Most independent sources find that the gain is of an order of magnitude of 1 to 2 percent of Mexican gross domestic product (GDP). And much of this gain derives from the elimination of nontariff barriers of various kinds.

The consequence for Canada and the United States is trivially small — a gain of approximately 0.1 to 0.5 percent of their incomes — because prior to NAFTA's negotiation, Mexican tariffs had already been substantially reduced to about 11 to 12 percent. Indeed, what static gain emerges for these wealthier countries derives in part from higher growth in Mexico.

When the subject moves from NAFTA to the hemisphere more generally, these broad results are not much altered, according to one recent extension of NAFTA modeling.[2] The big surprise in this initial effort is the magnitude of the apparent gains achieved by Chile and Colombia, which are of the order of 1 to 2 percent of their incomes. But these gains seem to be accounted for by the presumed expansion of some key sectors, such as nonferrous metals for Chile and leather products and footwear for Colombia. In the case of other countries, such as Brazil and Argentina, the total effects are a much smaller share of income, 0.3 to 0.5 percent. Moreover, there is the puzzling decline in Argentine gains if Brazil is admitted. A much earlier calculation by Refik Erzan and Alexander Yeats, using the World Bank simulation model, differs slightly, precisely because after Brazil, gains for other countries, excepting those in Central America and the Caribbean, are irrelevant.[3]

Gains for the United States, Canada, and Mexico in the Drusilla Brown et al. hemispheric model remain virtually unchanged from the original NAFTA conclusions. In the case of all three countries, the gains are a measure of the limited amount of their trade with South America and, hence, of the minimal opportunity for static effects. Had Central American and Caribbean countries been included, they would have benefited more, but again the effects on the United States and Mexico would have been much smaller in a static trade model.

A flurry of similar modeling efforts in future months involving some changes in country coverage, the initial level of tariffs and quantitative restrictions, and other factors can be anticipated. Yet it is likely that the broad conclusion from earlier exercises will remain essentially the same: There is simply no significant static gain from the extension of free trade. At current hemispheric tariff levels of 20 percent and less, and after the additional concessions of the GATT's Uruguay Round, there is little room for benefit.

But more fundamentally, the correct lesson emerging from these exercises is the importance of related changes in evaluating the impact of freer trade. One evident conclusion that appears in some of the dynamic Mexican models is the consequence of increased investment on potential output. This change is partially the result of larger foreign capital inflow in response to the new trade relationship. Clearly, this effect is of considerable weight; various estimates suggest gains of 5 to 8 percent in the Mexican case once these capital inflows are taken into account, along with such additional factors as increasing returns, product differentiation, and the effect on migration. It is further clear that President Carlos Salinas de Gortari had such an impact clearly in mind when in 1990 he pushed ahead with the idea of integration and that Mexico has already been rewarded with quite large and continuous foreign investment in the three years after.

There is little question that equivalent dynamic effects are foreseen by other countries of the region as among the greatest real gains from integration. And these effects are very much a necessity. During the 1980s, Latin American investment rates fell from levels of 24 percent in 1980 to less than 20 percent in the early 1990s. Given these lower amounts, it is impossible to imagine adequate long-term recovery. Regional integration, in addition to providing recovery from the debt crisis, can offer powerful encouragement not only to foreign enterprises but also to local firms. Latin America is in search of a new strategy, and a coherent policy of trade liberalization can be one of its essential components.

Equally crucial, however, are the permanent changes required in macroeconomic and microeconomic policies in hemispheric countries. These changes seem to have begun. As one measure, inflation rates have fallen — in some cases, dramatically — in a number of countries in recent years. In 1993, the average unweighted increase in consumer prices, excluding Brazil, was 19 percent. "Moreover, countries with an annual inflation rate of under 15 percent became the majority in 1993."[4] If Brazil's current stabilization program works as it should, Latin America will finally have all its principal economies converted to new domestic stability. It is easy to miss the novelty of this shift in the midst of continuing regional pressure for renewed economic growth.

Behind such a radical conversion lie the important reductions in fiscal deficits that have been achieved. The fiscal balance has shifted from -7.8 percent of GDP in 1987-1989 to 0.7 percent in 1992 for countries undertaking formal stabilization programs. For others, it went from -5.1 percent to -2.8 percent, still a considerable decline. And in 1993, "roughly half of the 19 countries on which information is available improved their fiscal management...."[5] Such progress was due mainly to improved public sector revenues and has avoided the necessity of resorting to an inflationary tax as a means of balancing governmental accounts. It is apparent that continuing attention to fiscal accounts will be one required component of changed macroeconomic policy.

Two other components are also necessary. One is the avoidance of overvalued exchange rates; the second is closer attention to the recent large inflow of resources into the region. Both have recently become increasingly worrisome problems.

Exchange rates in Argentina, Mexico, and Chile all show signs of overvaluation. In the case of Argentina, committed to a fixed exchange rate, there is an immense difference in result depending upon whether the consumer or the wholesale price index is used: The former shows an increase in the value of the peso of 35 percent between 1990 and 1993, while the latter shows a decrease. The fact of zero volume increase in Argentine exports in the last three years, while exports have grown 25 percent for the region as a whole, gives some doubt to those who maintain that the rate is not overvalued.

For the other two countries, the problem is less severe, both as calculated as well as by export performance. By the end of 1993, Mexico's exchange rate had appreciated by some 20 percent, while Chile's had risen less than 10 percent. In both cases, however, the value of trade went up considerably: 28.5 percent for the former, 33.9 percent for the latter.[6]

What makes overvaluation easy to sustain in the short term is the renewed capital flow to Latin America of almost $160 billion in the last three years — 1991 through 1993. This inflow has come after a long period in the 1980s when Latin America was subject to outflows virtually every single year. One of the explanations of this phenomenon is the interest rate differential. As U.S. rates declined, partially as a result of a rapid fall in the rate of inflation, those in Latin America became quite positive in real terms. It is not rare to encounter real rates well above 10 percent in the region, and on occasion they have gone substantially higher — as in the current Brazilian effort to curb inflation or the Mexican intervention to sustain confidence after the assassination of ruling party presidential candidate Luis Donaldo Colosio, after which rates just about doubled within a month. The consequence of the interest rate differential has been an inflow of short-term resources for Latin America. Indeed, one of the problems with the current capital inflow has been its limited direct application to real investment: The stock market, which soared in 1993, and other financial uses have been strong competitors. And the huge accumulation of reserves in many countries that have sought to curb imports of consumer goods has been an unintended outcome.

Such a situation contributes to disequilibrium within the region. In almost all countries, real interest rates are much higher than the real rate of growth. This factor sets up a need for increasing obligations. The first implication is a rising internal debt to meet the larger current obligations of debt service; now, even external obligations have begun to increase again. Moreover, such a situation worsens the already poor distribution of income by rewarding asset holders, the wealthy, with very handsome returns. It is not only foreign investors who are eligible for the favorable interest rates but also the domestic public.

This imbalance is cause for concern about the future. Because foreign investment is only partially converted to real applications, there is no higher productivity to yield the much higher returns that are paid. There is also no later flow of exports, aided by more favorable exchange rates, to erase the earlier inflow. What may be lurking is not as severe as another debt crisis, but may involve a continuous bias against the increased investment that is needed to trigger real growth. Such a pattern of development, moreover, in which Latin America emerges as a large deficit region, tends to discourage requisite efforts to increase domestic savings. Current national savings rates amount to some 20 percent, well below the level now found in Asian successes. Chile has been the exception, experiencing a significant rise in recent years, a rise that is associated, it should be added, with efforts to restrain the entry of foreign capital. The ability to expand national saving capacity is very much a requirement of the future. Regional integration must not become a mechanism for easy imports of goods from the United States that wind up expanding consumption rather than encouraging investment. Nor must a focus on trade liberalization detract attention from the larger issue of increasing domestic savings as a centerpiece of development in the 1990s and beyond.

In the absence of adequate attention, there will only be renewed frustration as the future is mortgaged to repay present capital inflows. Developing countries around the world, especially in Asia, have managed to increase substantially their domestic savings over the past few decades. By contrast, the nations of Latin America, except for Chile, now display savings rates that are not much different from what they were thirty years ago. Given this long history, increased savings are unlikely to emerge suddenly from the private sector; it has already been seen that high interest rates in recent years have played little part in increasing national accumulation. Rather, the requirement is for much larger surpluses to be achieved through an excess of taxes over expenditures. This is a new role for the state in the region. Without success in accomplishing it, higher rates of sustainable development will remain a fanciful dream instead of becoming a positive reality.

Equally, greater attention must be paid to microeconomic competition. This question is largely ignored in discussions of Latin American development — and with some merit. The emphasis has rightly been upon performance, or lack thereof, at the aggregate level and with the failure to control deficits. Only in exchanges concerning the diminished future role of the state has there emerged a focus on rent seeking as the major deficiency in Latin America. If only rent seeking could be eliminated, prospects would look more promising. But "the rent-seeking model posits a static competitive Eden as the counterfactual alternative rather than the reality of powerful private interests and inadequate price signals."[7] It is the latter factor to which more attention must be turned and for which remedy must be sought, rather than focusing exclusively on rent seeking and its consequences.

The current process of denationalization is key. To the extent that firms are sold off to concentrated national interests, the process of monopolization is worsened rather than improved. The fact that such firms are private, and may even follow market signals in the determination of wages and costs of other inputs, does not make for market efficiency. For that, competition is also needed. Formerly nationalized firms are frequently large-scale enterprises. Thus, a critical virtue of market openness, especially for smaller countries, is the ability to utilize the benefits of international competition to assure price discipline. Foreign imports can provide a significant continuing degree of discipline to domestic firms.

Just as important is the role of domestic firms in assuring regular increases in productivity that are essential to continuing long-term growth. They translate the gains in efficiency accomplished globally. National firms joined in a regional scheme of integration involving the United States will have little alternative but to adopt better technologies and to assure that regular advances are made. There is no protective barrier to rely upon. And this unprotected environment applies much more widely than had been the case earlier; financial services, for example, are explicitly included as well as other service activities that formerly enjoyed de facto protection. The consequence of economic integration can thus have quite a profound impact on rates of productivity advance, as happened in Europe, where the realized gains have been much larger than originally predicted. It now remains to be seen whether the consequences can be as great for the developing countries of Latin America. Regional competition affords much more effective discipline than that found internally.

This new element of international discipline does not imply a nonexistent state. But it requires a changed role for the state, just as was the case in the Asian successes. The state must rid itself of former regulatory obligations and concentrate on the vital roles it retains: expanding domestic saving through public sector surpluses, stimulating productivity change and export growth in key sectors, and assuring adequate investment in areas such as education, health and nutrition, and housing where social returns have been quite high. This changed role for the state adds up to a significant, but somewhat altered presence that will prove indispensable to a successful policy of trade integration.

Extension of NAFTA

The questions of the direction and speed of the extension of NAFTA have now become central. Chile already has a commitment to begin negotiations to be the next entrant. Argentina has increasingly sought to emphasize its own claims for entry. The Caribbean and Central American countries have shown considerable interest for fear that their current special arrangements will be outdated by NAFTA. The announcement of the forthcoming meeting of regional heads of state has naturally heightened expectations. But the close vote on NAFTA, with victory in the end determined by Republican support, has made the Clinton administration somewhat reluctant to take a strong leadership role. Indeed, there is a chance that the summit will emphasize democratic governance and environmental concerns, among other topics, rather than focusing on the central issue of regional free trade that Latin America now sees as an essential step forward to renewed growth.

Here it seems appropriate to propose a somewhat novel stance. A major U.S. policy goal should be to obtain a firm commitment of Brazilian adherence to NAFTA; and conversely, Brazil should seek to play a more active role, not by striving for South American solidarity but by its own diligent pursuit of early membership. There cannot be an effective and sustained regional policy in which Brazil is not a full participant. It is too large a country to ignore. Equally, an essential assurance of the success of current Brazilian efforts to end inflation could be created by a commitment to adhere to NAFTA. That commitment can quickly and automatically supply the needed credibility for current efforts at Brazilian stabilization to work.

This position is different from both present U.S. policy and Brazilian conceptions of its foreign strategy. For too long, U.S. diplomatic emphasis has been on Brazilian compliance with U.S. concerns about intellectual property rights and trade restrictions rather than on assisting recovery to growth and stabilization. And Brazil, as closer U.S. relations have been progressively forged with Mexico, has tended to emphasize its independent foreign interests even more strongly in the GATT negotiations and elsewhere. Substantial changes are therefore required of both countries if they are to proceed effectively. The 1994 Summit of the Americas provides an unusual window of opportunity for such changes.

There are costs to such a strategy. For Brazil, it means eschewing any effort to substitute other foreign interests for the Mexico agreement in any significant way. This will not be an easy decision. But the reality is that after years of negotiation, including both political parties in the end, the basic principles are now defined. There is clearly the possibility of specific alteration. In the environmental area, for example, the Amazon region poses different issues from the border region, and Brazilian labor unions have been much more prominent than the Mexican. But there is little to be gained by expressing concern over the percentage of domestic value-added required in the automobile sector, for example, or for the gains achieved by the U.S. financial and insurance sectors. The acceptance of this strategy could speed the process of convergence quite substantially and avoid a long and potentially divisive set of discussions.

On the other side, the United States must be prepared to accept early entry rather than gradual accession into NAFTA. It will do little good for the summit to express the hope that over the next decade many other countries besides Mexico and Chile will be admitted. That would be equivalent to avoiding the issue. Such a short waiting period is also consistent with the lower level to which Brazilian tariffs have fallen in recent years.[8] Obviously, there are additional nontariff barriers on both sides that require elimination. Brazil has a higher proportion of manufactured exports than other countries, and several affect U.S. domestic producers, who can be expected to complain.

But there are also important benefits from such an approach. For Brazil, this means not only credible support for stabilization policy but also access to increased resources for investment. Until the last few years, Brazil stood out as the leading recipient of U.S. direct flows in the hemisphere, but the consequence of continuing inflation coupled with persistent low growth has changed that situation. Clearly, a new inflow could help spark another period of accelerated growth. Growth does not have to reach the level of the Brazilian "miracle" in the late 1960s to make a difference. For the United States, the principal economic gain would consist of an expanded market for exports that can contribute to productivity advance in this country. Brazil is a potentially large purchaser whose expanded demand for capital goods can make a positive difference.

Does such a focus on Brazil mean that the rest of the hemisphere should be discounted? Hardly. Indeed, it suggests that a broad regional free market is much more likely the outcome than otherwise. An excluded Brazil, after all, dramatically changes the result. The hemisphere ceases to be the target, and only specific, and smaller, trading partners become the objective of policy. That is a strategy in which content is solely economic and broader political objectives are subordinated. The United States should proceed with its commitment to Chile, as already scheduled, but focus on Brazil as the next major participant.

Beyond this emphasis on Brazil, U.S. policy should also give a simultaneous signal to Central America and the Caribbean for early adherence. This group of countries requires close attention. U.S. assistance efforts have been sharply reduced just as conflict has virtually disappeared. At the same time, the area is a source of immigration pressure that will continue to persist in the midst of limited and unsatisfactory economic growth. Yet because of size limitation, the impact on product markets in the United States remains a second order of significance. Costa Rica has already adhered to a separate free trade treaty with Mexico, and other such pacts can be anticipated. It is much simpler to proceed in a coordinated fashion within the NAFTA framework rather than outside it.

Coordinating through NAFTA would offer new possibilities of economic gain at relatively low cost to the United States. If the United States is unable to offer aid, at the least it can provide much freer opportunities for trade. To be sure, individual industries will complain, as they did when the Caribbean Basin Initiative (CBI) was first established. But the reality was quite modest U.S. investment overseas as a consequence. These economies are of such limited size that independent common markets among themselves make little sense; they involve higher costs of production and lack of capacity to exploit their one advantage of much lower wage rates. It is far better to accept the principle of full integration with a long time to implement it, especially in the absence of even minimal foreign aid.

With this thrust, the small as well as the large countries are taken care of. For the remaining intermediate countries of the region, there should be no serious problem. They will simply be able to join on an equivalent basis. Some will be more ready than others. But this time, because there are no major indirect benefits to the United States, pressures to establish special precedence are reduced.

There is a further advantage to such a suggestion. It clearly establishes U.S. concern for success. There is little reason for extended negotiation where the conditions are manifest and determined, as they should be, by the largest markets for U.S. exports in the hemisphere. The United States should also extend an invitation for other countries to join the market on an equivalent basis. The decision can be left to individual countries.

Moreover, to facilitate adherence and to avoid the complications of ever more intricate negotiations, accession can occur directly with the United States rather than with NAFTA. This hub-and-spoke pattern violates economic principles because it produces marginal losses to Canada and Mexico as a result of trade diversion.[9] But such a scheme is intended as an intermediate stage that will not long persist. The political gains from reaching out quickly to encompass the hemisphere as a whole have to be weighed against the modest economic costs. Moreover, since many countries within the region already have free trade relations with each other, privilege would automatically extend. Consequently, even without comprehensive free trade in the first instance, the degree of discrimination will be both small and temporary.

The ultimate objective is a broad free trade area, leaving to individual countries the determination of what tariffs to impose on the rest of the world. There will be no guaranteed free movement of people or the equivalent set of common institutions that are found in Europe. That is beyond present thinking. But there can be significant gains that go beyond calculations of general equilibrium models. These gains will come from a broad commitment to a freer flow of goods and services and the new discipline of a coherent macroeconomic policy. This change would be revolutionary within the hemisphere. Then it will be possible to get on with the really important needs of improved income distribution and much expanded domestic savings rates that will, in the end, prove determining.

What if such a strategy proves infeasible? Brazil, at the time of the December 1994 summit meeting, will have its present, rather than newly elected, president in attendance. It will be difficult, if not impossible, to put the aggressive strategy described here on the table. At the same time, the coherence of a Central American and Caribbean position is assumed, when there are real differences and problems in reaching agreement among the countries involved, and limited time to do so.

Under such circumstances, the Miami meeting may be seen as an initiating exercise, rather than as a decision mechanism. If the United States seeks to modify and structure its regional policy most effectively, it will offer a general vision of the future. That vision should emphasize the reality of a free trade zone without providing for detailed specifics. What is essential is the creation of a mechanism for subsequent early implementation that would allow for the possibility of the dual track strategy argued here. The main issue is what signal is given: slow, individual accession to NAFTA with the door open to Asian membership, or speedy and coordinated membership exclusively for hemispheric countries.

Is There a Possibility of Such a Hemispheric Strategy?

Thus far, the focus of this chapter has been upon a Western Hemisphere Free Trade Area (WHFTA). But such a regional outcome is hardly inevitable. The United States has simultaneously been playing a prominent role in the Pacific region; indeed, an international meeting of APEC in November 1993 barely followed the decisive vote on NAFTA. After Mexican and Chilean adherence, Korea or Taiwan might well be the next entrant. Indeed, that is a sequence that makes good economic sense: "To preserve the outward-looking image and reality of the WHFTA, countries outside the Western Hemisphere that met the preconditions should be welcomed."[10] Such a thrust is not only consistent with general trade liberalization but sustains the multilateral commitment that the United States has had for decades.

Yet this kind of movement implies a different relationship between the United States and the rest of the hemisphere. Instead of being rewarded for more than a decade of effort to gain control of their macroeconomics, Latin American countries have achieved only an equivalent status with other third countries. Being part of Latin America yields no special advantage or privilege. And there is no intent of U.S. policy to afford special gain.

Once again, economics and politics diverge. If the Clinton administration intends to use a Western Hemisphere model (and there are obvious goals that can be pursued such as encouraging good government or controlling the flow of drugs), it must offer some Latin American advantage of membership. In reality, the divergence can be small, but it still must be palpable. Otherwise, there is little logic to a hemispheric grouping. A free trade area establishes one and offers hope for greater regional solidarity than at any time since the Alliance for Progress was first proposed.

Regional free trade is the test for the administration as it plots its strategy for the 1994 Summit of the Americas. After the flurry of action on trade at the end of 1993, there is an understandable desire to move on to other agenda items, items for which much stronger support exists among Democrats. But the trade issue will not go away so readily. It is of central importance to Latin America, even if of marginal, but hardly trivial, significance to the United States. The United States can create a mechanism that will be of great consequence in defining a new strategy of expansion for those countries; or it can substantially ignore the issue. To do the latter would be to fail to understand the overriding necessity of economic expansion for the region and to forgo the opportunity to participate creatively in its resurgence.

Latin America has passed through a difficult decade and more. Within a changing world economy, the region must choose its options for the next decade. They are clear enough. Future success requires a much greater commitment to external markets than has been seen during the post-World War II period. However, success does not require the export-led growth of 10 to 15 percent a year that Asian countries achieved. An export-adequate strategy, where foreign sales regularly keep up with product growth and perhaps slightly exceed it, would represent a major stride forward. Success equally means much greater macroeconomic stability than was achieved in the past.

A WHFTA offers a common path in search of new directions for both parts of the region. It is a way to assure the continuity of policy changes within Latin America, as well as a means to attract the foreign capital and technology necessary to achieve higher rates of growth consistent with more equal income distribution. It is also a way for the United States to commit itself to freer trade as a mechanism for future expansion, while gaining at the same time a common commitment to the environment, population control, and other areas of joint concern. The concern initially heard about the inconsistency of U.S. regional and global objectives is overstated; the effects will be minimal as the United States continues to play its unique international role.

The future will be defined shortly. The 1994 Summit of the Americas will make clear whether regional integration is on the immediate agenda.

Notes

1   See the listing of the results of a number of independent studies in Nora Lustig, 1993, "NAFTA: Potential Impact on Mexico's Economy and Beyond. " Paper presented at the Conference on Economic Integration in the Western Hemisphere, University of Notre Dame, April, unpublished, Table 6.

2   Drusilla Brown, Alan Deardorff, David Hummels, and Robert Stern, 1993, "An Assessment of Extending NAFTA to Other Major Trading Countries in South America," Paper presented at the Conference on Trade Liberalization in the Western Hemisphere, Inter-American Development Bank, November.

3   Refik Erzan and Alexander Yeats, 1992, "U.S.-Latin America Free Trade Areas: Some Empirical Evidence," in *The Premise and the Promise: Free Trade in the Americas*, ed. Sylvia Saborio (Washington, D.C.: Overseas Development Council), 139-140.

4   Economic Commission for Latin America and the Caribbean (ECLAC), 1993, "Preliminary Overview of the Economy of Latin America and the Caribbean, 1993," *Notas Sobre la Economia y el Desarrollo* 552/553 (December): 1.

5   International Monetary Fund, 1992, "Fiscal Adjustment in Developing Countries," *World Economic Outlook* (May): Annex V, as well as subsequent IMF reports; ECLAC 1993, 2.

6   ECLAC, 1993, Tables 9 and 10.

7   Albert Fishlow, 1990, "The Latin American State," *Journal of Economic Perspectives* 4, 3 (Summer): 65.

8   Brown et al., 1993, 20, shows Brazilian tariffs toward the United States to be 16.9 percent and those of the United States to be 2.0 percent. While Brazilian rates are higher than those of other countries, where they average 11 percent or higher, they have come down significantly in recent years.

9   See, for example, Carsten Kowalczak and Ronald J. Wonnacott, 1992, "Hubs and Spokes, and Free Trade in the Americas," NBER Working Paper No. 4198, October.

10   Richard C. Lipsey, "Getting There," in ed. Sylvia Saborio, 1992, 114.

References

Brown, Drusilla, Alan Deardorff, David Hummels, and Robert Stern. 1993. "An Assessment of Extending NAFTA to Other Major Trading Countries in South America." Paper presented at the Conference on Trade Liberalization in the Western Hemisphere, Inter-American Development Bank, November.

Economic Commission for Latin America and the Caribbean (ECLAC/CEPAL). 1993. "Preliminary Overview of the Economy of Latin America and the Caribbean, 1993." *Notas Sobre la Economia y el Desarrollo* 552/553 (December): 1

Erzan, Refik, and Alexander Yeats. 1992. "U.S.-Latin America Free Trade Areas: Some Empirical Evidence." In *The Premise and the Promise: Free Trade in the Americas*, ed. Sylvia Saborio. Washington, D.C.: Overseas Development Council.

Fishlow, Albert. 1990. "The Latin American State." *Journal of Economic Perspectives* 4,3 (Summer): 65.

International Monetary Fund (IMF). 1992. "Fiscal Adjustment in Developing Countries." *World Economic Outlook* Annex V (May).

Kowalczak, Carsten, and Ronald J. Wonnacott. 1992. "Hubs and Spokes, and Free Trade in the Americas." *NBER Working Paper No. 4198* (October).

Lipsey, Richard C. 1992. "Getting There." In *The Premise and the Promise: Free Trade in the Americas*, ed. Sylvia Saborio. Washington, D.C.: Overseas Development Council.

Lustig, Nora. 1993. "NAFTA: Potential Impact on Mexico's Economy and Beyond." Paper presented at the Conference on Economic Integration in the Western Hemisphere, University of Notre Dame, April.

Chapter 6

MERCOSUR and Free Trade in the Americas

María Beatriz Nofal

The Southern Cone Common Market (Mercado Común del Sur — MERCOSUR) is at a turning point. There has been substantial progress in intraregional trade liberalization, but there are many difficulties ahead if MERCOSUR is to make further advances in economic policy coordination and harmonization. A number of objectives have already been defined. The ultimate goal is to reach a common market (CM); the immediate goal is to achieve a customs union (CU) by January 1995. In fact, the achievement by January 1995 is likely to be either an imperfect CU or a free trade area (FTA). Whether MERCOSUR will become a customs union or a free trade area has important economic implications for the partner countries, for their future trade relations with other countries in South America, and for future trade relations with countries in the North American Free Trade Agreement (NAFTA).

This chapter reviews the present state of MERCOSUR, its challenges and promise, and its relationships with schemes for future Western Hemisphere economic integration.

Regional Trade Liberalization in MERCOSUR: An Overview

The overall intraregional trade liberalization schedule is set forth in the bilateral agreement to form a common market in 1995 between Argentina and Brazil, which is the Latin American Integration Association (Asociación Latino Americana de Integración — ALADI) Economic Complementation Agreement No. 14 of 1990. The agreement between Argentina and Brazil and Uruguay and Paraguay is the MERCOSUR initiative (the Asunción Treaty of 1991 and ALADI Economic Complementation Agreement No. 18).[1] The original objective was to constitute a common market by January 1995. It is more likely, however, that free trade will be achieved by 1995, while the CU and the CM objectives are medium- and long-term propositions.

Free Trade by 1995:Automatic Mechanisms

Two automatic mechanisms have been established to achieve free trade by January 1, 1995.

1. An automatic progressive tariff reduction schedule.

   - Tariffs have already been reduced by 82 percent, as mandated by the schedule. After July 1994, the level of tariff reduction will be 89 percent and after December 1994, 100 percent.

   - The tariff reduction schedule was first applied in January 1991 (between Argentina and Brazil, ACE No. 14) with a 40 percent reduction from existing tariffs. Tariffs have since been reduced automatically by an additional 7 percent every six months, the purpose being to reach zero tariffs in January 1995.

   - The automatic progressive tariff reduction schedule is as follows:

Brazil-Argentina (ACE No. 14)		MERCOSUR (ACE No. 18)	
Date	% of tariff reduction	Date	% of tariff reduction
12/31/90	40	6/30/91	47
6/30/91	47	12/31/91	54
12/31/91	54	6/30/92	61
6/30/92	61	12/31/92	68
12/31/92	68	6/30/93	75
6/30/93	75	12/31/93	82
12/31/93	82	6/30/94	89
6/30/94	89	12/31/94	100
12/31/94	100		

2. A list of goods exempted.

   - There is a list of goods exempted from application of the across-the-board tariff reduction schedule.

   - In the case of Brazil and Argentina, this list has been reduced (as mandated) 20 percent annually in order to disappear by December 1994, at which time tariffs should be zero. Paraguay and Uruguay have one extra year to eliminate the list of goods exempted.

   - In January 1993, the governments of Argentina, Brazil, Uruguay, and Paraguay carried out the list reduction for exempted goods by the required 20 percent.

- In the case of Argentina, this was done despite the opposition of strong business interests, for example, in steel and textiles.

The governments of Argentina and Brazil have stated publicly that they will fully carry out the implementation of these two automatic mechanisms without any delays or exclusions.[2]

Given the record of timely implementation during the period from 1991 to 1993 of the automatic mechanisms to achieve free trade and the substantial progress already attained in intraregional trade liberalization, it seems certain that by January 1995 free trade or something close to it will be concluded between Brazil and Argentina.

The Customs Union and the Common Market: Medium- and Long-term Objectives

Both the economic integration agreement No. 14 between Brazil and Argentina and the MERCOSUR agreement No. 18 (Brazil, Argentina, Paraguay, and Uruguay) state as an objective the formation of a common market by January 1995.

The main differences between a common market and an FTA is that the CM option implies, in addition to the free movement of goods and services, a common trade policy and the free movement of the factors of production (capital and labor). The CU option entails free trade and a common trade policy, but it does not involve the free movement of capital and labor.

Forms of regional integration	Free movement of goods and service	Common trade policy	Free movement of factors of production (capital and labor)
Free trade area (FTA)	x		
Customs union (CU)	x	x	
Common market (CM)	x	x	x

x = Condition exists.

In both the MERCOSUR and the Brazil-Argentina trade agreements, there are automatic mechanisms to get to an FTA, while the formation of a CU or a CM requires additional negotiation on such issues as a common external tariff, macroeconomic policy coordination, and tax and sectoral policy harmonization. The government of Argentina has emphasized on several occasions that the process of economic integration to attain a CM is sequential — that is, in a first phase, an FTA will be achieved, then a CU, and after that a CM.

Therefore, for MERCOSUR to become a CU by January 1995, a common external tariff and additional instruments would first have to be formulated. This is not an easy task given the macroeconomic divergences between Brazil and Argentina and their different views regarding protection levels in the capital goods, electronics, and telecommunications sectors.[3] Argentina wants low external tariffs, and Brazil does not agree. These difficulties led to the postponement of decisions on the subject until June 1994 (decision No. 13/ 94 of the Common Market Council).

However, the two governments recently ratified their decision to form a CU by January 1995 "as an essential step to begin the common market building stage" (decision No. 13/94 of the Common Market Council). While it is certain that there will be free trade (or substantial free trade) between Brazil and Argentina by January 1995, there are still uncertainties about reaching a CU by then.

To conclude, the CU and CM options are medium- and long-term objectives because of the difficulties inherent in economic policy harmonization and coordination (as shown by the experience of the European Community); these are compounded in the case of Brazil and Argentina because of macroeconomic divergences.

Alternative Scenarios in MERCOSUR: Degrees of Probability

For planning purposes, it is convenient to evaluate the following three scenarios ranked by degree of probability, from the least to the most probable.

Case 1: MERCOSUR's Global Failure. This is the least probable scenario because substantial progress has been achieved in intraregional trade liberalization. The tariff reduction on intraregional trade is already 82 percent. In the case of Argentina and Brazil, this level of tariff reduction is applied to all but about 100 tariff positions, that is, to more than 8,000 tariff positions in the ALADI nomenclature. For Argentina, 81 tariff positions are still omitted, and for Brazil, 65 tariff positions. These exceptions should be completely eliminated by December 1994.

The likelihood of trade liberalization reversal is minimal. Whatever risk of reversal exists would be due more to contingent political events, such as the breakdown of democracy in one of the main partners, Brazil or Argentina, than to the economic effects of the trade agreements. The political risk of democratic breakdown in these countries is quite low at present.

Case 2: MERCOSUR's Deferral. The probability of deferring some aspects of MERCOSUR is higher than that of MERCOSUR's total failure. It has already been stated that the CM option is a long-term objective. To put it explicitly, it will take longer than until January 1995 to get to a situation of free movement of capital and labor. A prior condition is to reach a greater level of macroeconomic convergence between Argentina and Brazil. The economy of Brazil, in particular, needs to be stabilized before real progress can be made on factor flow liberalization.

The CU is a medium-term objective, although an imperfect CU can be achieved by January 1995. The MERCOSUR governments have announced that there is agreement on the common external tariff levels for about 80 percent of the tariff positions, within an overall tariff level that will be between 0 and 20 percent. A convergence path up to the year 2001 (or perhaps 2006) will probably be established in 1994 for the rest of the tariff positions. These delays do not, however, in any way endanger the main thrust of the economic integration effort: free intraregional trade.

Case 3: MERCOSUR as a Free Trade Area or as an Imperfect Customs Union by 1995. This scenario has the highest degree of probability, a conclusion supported by the timely implementation of the automatic mechanisms to achieve free trade and by the steady progress made in intraregional trade liberalization despite some strong business opposition. Agriculture and the agro-industrial sectors may be special cases. Sugar, for example, will not be fully liberalized within MERCOSUR because of the large subsidy program that the Brazilian sugar-alcohol program entails for the sugar-processing industry in that country.

But no deviations from the automatic tariff reduction schedule or from the elimination of manufactured products from the list of excepted goods are envisaged. However, in January 1994, the government of Argentina proposed to its MERCOSUR partners that transitory mechanisms be introduced to facilitate restructuring in a few sectors. These mechanisms could include measures to administer trade flows temporarily in the form of safeguard clauses. Along the same lines, a proposal was made to introduce new safeguard measures to protect against injury from import surges during the transition to the CM. The rationale given was the lack of macroeconomic coordination and of harmonization of sectoral policies.

One of the more contentious trade issues in the industrial sector will center around automobiles. Trade in vehicles and parts is the largest single sectoral component of bilateral trade between Argentina and Brazil, and the imbalance in bilateral sectoral automotive trade was one of the main factors underlying Argentina's trade deficit with Brazil in 1992 and 1993. The MERCOSUR countries have agreed that the common external tariff on motor vehicles will not be implemented until the year 2001. Finished vehicles remain on the list of goods exempted from tariff elimination by January 1995. Although there are pressures to continue this protection of finished vehicles in MERCOSUR, such an outcome is not foreordained.

Cross-border integration in the automotive industry between Brazil and Argentina is well under way. In this regard, the effects of the automotive free trade agreement (protocol No. 21) have been far-reaching. To take advantage of the opportunities of integration in a large regional market (in 1993, the joint market of Brazil and Argentina was about 1.6 million vehicles), companies with operations in both countries are unifying product lines, specializing in some models on a country basis, concentrating the regional production of some components in only one country (for example, gearboxes in Argentina), and allocating new investment on a regional scale. Thus, while the automotive industry of Argentina is smaller than that of Brazil, the Argentine industry is gaining higher volume production per model and greater economies of scale. Argentina is also able to lower the cost of model changeovers, that is, to shorten the amortization time and to introduce new model lines more rapidly.

Summary

The process of economic integration is advancing both steadily and progressively. The Argentina-Brazil integration process and trade liberalization in MERCOSUR are irreversible because 1) trade agreements are being implemented and 2) industry restructuring and specialization are advancing; moreover, a growing number of firms are developing regional strategies and organizations to position themselves in the regional market, as in the case of the automotive industry.

Consequently, there is a domestic constituency that benefits from the widening of the regional market and has interest in preserving open access to it. There will be free trade between Argentina and Brazil by 1995, and this is all that matters for strategic planners to take advantage of the opportunity of the enlarged regional market.

Trade Results

The process of economic integration between Argentina and Brazil, which started in 1986, and that in MERCOSUR, which began in 1991, led to a significant increase in intraregional trade flows. These flows were facilitated as well by the unilateral trade liberalization undertaken by Brazil and Argentina beginning in 1987, and further reductions in tariff barriers were made by Uruguay after 1991. It was the process of regional integration that stimulated the unilateral trade liberalization for Argentina and Brazil, rather than the other way around. The bilateral trade agreements were a stepping stone in the decisive shift toward unilateral trade liberalization of these countries.

Trade within MERCOSUR increased by 70 percent between 1991 and 1993, rising from $5 billion (all dollar figures are U.S. dollars) in 1991 to more than $8.5 billion in 1993. Bilateral Argentina-Brazil trade represented 75 percent of total MERCOSUR trade in 1993, and this trade grew by 112 percent between 1991 and 1993, or by more than total MERCOSUR trade. Bilateral

Argentina trade totaled $6.36 billion in 1993. In fact, if the period from 1986 to 1993 is considered, from the time bilateral trade agreements were implemented, total Argentina-Brazil trade grew by 358 percent. Although overall trade growth has remained high, the bilateral trade balance has been volatile. Also, the composition of Argentine exports to Brazil shows higher volatility than the composition of Brazilian exports to Argentina.

What factors lie behind bilateral and intraregional trade growth? Have regional trade agreements made a difference? What explains the bilateral trade balance volatility and the changing composition of Argentine exports to Brazil?

For the sake of simplicity, and since Argentina-Brazil trade represents about 75 percent of total MERCOSUR trade, the analysis will not cover the evolution of trade with Uruguay and Paraguay. Tables 5 and 6, however, give Argentina's and Brazil's trade figures with Uruguay and Paraguay for the period from 1988 to 1993.

Evolution of Argentina-Brazil Trade

The evolution of bilateral Argentina-Brazil trade in the post-1986 period has two different phases: the years from 1986 to 1990 and the period from 1990 until the present. Both phases are marked by distinctive trade agreements and different trade results.

In the first stage, reciprocal market opening was carried out under the Argentina-Brazil Integration Program, and bilateral trade growth was promoted by the increase in Argentine exports to Brazil. In the second stage, the bilateral and intraregional liberalization schedules were set out both in the agreement by Argentina and Brazil to form a CM in 1995 and in the MERCOSUR agreement between these two countries and Uruguay and Paraguay to reach the same objective. The growth in bilateral and intraregional trade was fueled by the increase in Brazil's exports to the region and by the expansion of Argentina's import demand.

First Stage: Argentina-Brazil Integration Program, 1986-1990. During the first stage, economic integration between Argentina and Brazil was promoted primarily by the following instruments: free trade sectoral agreements in the capital goods industry and the food industry and Preferential Trade Agreement No. 1 in ALADI (AAP No. 1). The ALADI agreement introduced partial tariff reductions across the board and the elimination of nontariff barriers for all goods covered by the agreement. The latter measure was a very important commitment to open market access, particularly from Brazil at that historic time. Brazil, in 1986, was an economy with high tariff and nontariff barriers that closed access to its domestic market even to neighboring countries such as Argentina.

One other principal instrument was the Treaty of Integration signed in November 1988; its objective was to free trade between Argentina and Brazil from all tariff and nontariff barriers within a ten-year period. The treaty was approved by the Congresses in both countries in 1989, but it was not implemented. In 1990, the new administrations in Argentina and Brazil decided to change the original objective of the treaty to constitute an FTA over ten years (which was modeled after the Canada-United States FTA negotiations). They decided instead to constitute a CM within a four-year period. Reality proved later that this objective was too ambitious and not necessarily a better option than that of an FTA.

During the period from 1986 to 1990, under the impulse given by the bilateral trade agreements, the trade evolution between Argentina and Brazil had the following positive outcomes:

- A sustained increase in bilateral trade at a cumulative growth rate of 93 percent, from $1.1 billion in 1985 to $2.1 billion in 1990 (see Table 1).

- A substantial expansion of exports from Argentina to Brazil showing a cumulative increase of 187 percent during the years from 1985 to 1990. This contributed to the partial redressing of the historic trade imbalances of Argentina with Brazil. More important, the positive trade balance experienced by Argentina in 1989 and 1990 helped to raise local business confidence about the capacity to profit from freer access to the Brazilian market. On the other hand, Brazilian exports to Argentina, which had increased during the period from 1985 to 1988 at a rate of 59 percent, decreased 26 percent during 1989 and 1990 as a result of the fall in Argentina's import demand due to the recession experienced by the economy (see Table 1).

- Bilateral trade became more balanced not just quantitatively but qualitatively in terms of trade composition. Historically, while Brazil's exports to Argentina were predominantly manufactured goods, in the case of Argentina, exports of manufactured goods of industrial origin represented only 20 percent of total exports to Brazil. By 1990, exports of manufactured goods represented 39 percent of total exports from Argentina to Brazil, having experienced a significant increase in relative and absolute terms (see Table 2).

- An intrasectoral pattern of trade and specialization emerged in many sectors, such as capital goods, that opened early to free trade. Intra-industrial trade entails both potential welfare gains from economies of scale and an increase in the variety of goods available, as well as lower adaptation costs than there would be under an intersectoral pattern of specialization.[4]

When the factors that explain the evolution of trade flows during the 1986-1990 period are considered, it is important to assess the impact of exchange rates. This study and others indicate that the correlation between the evolution of exchange rates and bilateral trade flows in this period is not very meaningful.[5]

Two other factors explain, to a larger degree, the positive trade outcomes in this period. First, an institutional factor: The opening of the Brazilian market through the Integration Program resulted in effective and wider market access for Argentine exports, particularly of manufactured goods. Access to Brazil's market for manufactured goods was almost closed before 1986, and in such a situation, not even a favorable exchange rate could undo trade barriers. Second, an economic factor: The level of economic activity declined. The studies show a significant correlation between the level of domestic economic activity and the evolution of import demand in bilateral trade. The fall in import demand of Argentina from Brazil in 1989 and 1990 is precisely related to the decline in the level of domestic economic activity.

Second Stage: MERCOSUR and the Common Market Program, 1991-1993. In the second stage, a CM project was announced. Accordingly, an automatic progressive intraregional tariff reduction schedule was implemented from 1991 onward to phase out all barriers to intraregional trade by December 1994.

During the 1991-1993 period, bilateral Argentina-Brazil trade experienced a substantially higher growth rate compared with the previous period. There was, however, a full reversal in trade results, with Argentina experiencing a large trade deficit with Brazil. In the years 1991 and 1992, there was a trend toward increasing trade imbalances that was partially corrected in 1993. Macroeconomic divergences were at the root of unbalanced trade flows during this period. Uncertainty about future unbalanced trade growth exists insofar as the source of macroeconomic disturbances is not eliminated.

1991-1992: Unbalanced Trade and Macroeconomic Divergences. During this period, changes in trade results were as follows:

- Bilateral Argentina-Brazil trade grew at a rate of 130 percent in the period, increasing from $2.1 billion in 1990 to $5 billion in 1992. Intraregional MERCOSUR trade grew at a rate of 79 percent in the same period, increasing from $4.1 billion in 1990 to $7.3 billion in 1992 (see Figure 1 and Table 1).

- The growth in bilateral Argentina-Brazil trade was due primarily to the increase of Argentina's import demand from Brazil or to the expansion of Brazil's exports to Argentina, since exports from Argentina to Brazil were comparatively stagnant. In the two-year period, Brazil's exports to Argentina grew by 365 percent, while exports from Argentina to Brazil increased by only 17.5 percent.

- Intraregional trade growth was promoted by the expansion in the imports of Argentina from the region; they increased 329 percent in 1992 compared with 1990, while Brazil's imports from MERCOSUR declined 4.4 percent in the same period. Consequently, Argentina's relative share in intraregional MERCOSUR trade, measured in terms of imports from the region, went up from 21 percent in 1990 to 51.2 percent in 1992. Paradoxically, Brazil, which has an economy about three times larger than that of Argentina, saw its relative share of imports in intraregional MERCOSUR trade drop from 56.7 percent in 1990 to 30.3 percent in 1992. Uruguay's and Paraguay's relative import shares from MERCOSUR also experienced a small decrease in the same period.

When the evolution of intraregional trade from the export side is examined, the situation is just the reverse. Brazil experienced an increase in its relative share of exports in intraregional trade, from 32 percent in 1990 to 56.3 percent in 1992, while Argentina saw its relative share drop from 44.4 percent in 1990 to 31.7 in 1992. Uruguay's and Paraguay's relative share of exports in intraregional trade also went down slightly. Nonetheless, all the partner countries' exports to MERCOSUR went up in absolute terms.[6]

- The unbalanced growth of trade flows led to Argentina having a trade deficit of $1.7 billion with Brazil in 1992 (see Table 1).

- The composition of exports from Argentina to Brazil showed a relative decline of high value-added exports, affecting both manufactures of industrial origin, except motor vehicles and parts and manufactures of agricultural origin, particularly nontraditional exports, such as those of industrialized fruits, vegetables, and cheeses (see Table 2). On the other hand, the composition of Brazil's exports to Argentina showed an increase in the exports of high value-added products — motor vehicles and parts, capital goods, and parts and consumer goods (see Table 3). As a result, the problem of qualitative imbalance in bilateral trade composition reappeared, threatening a reversal of the positive trends experienced in this regard during the 1986-1990 period.

In a nutshell, in the years 1991 and 1992, Brazil appeared as the winner, capturing the largest share of intraregional trade growth in terms of exports, while Argentina's import demand behaved as the main locomotive of intraregional trade growth. The pattern of unbalanced trade growth described was due mainly to the divergent macroeconomic evolution in the two countries and to divergent movements in exchange rates. Other contributing factors were microeconomic asymmetries in competitive conditions. These asymmetries arose from differences in national economic policies, with Argentina adopting a market-oriented approach and Brazil maintaining a more active industrial policy approach, and from the fact that Argentina's industry had embedded a higher tax burden in production costs than Brazil.

In that two-year period, Argentina experienced a growth recovery (with gross national product, or GNP, growth rates of 8.9 percent and 8.7 percent in 1991 and 1992, respectively), pushing inflation to moderately low rates (consumer prices increased 172.8 percent in 1991 and 23 percent in 1992) and lowering real interest rates. Conversely, Brazil's economy underwent a recession (with GNP growth rates of 0.9 percent and -0.9 percent in 1991 and 1992, respectively), with high and increasing inflation rates (consumer prices increased 440.8 percent in 1991 and 1,000 percent in 1992) and high real interest rates.

The comparative real exchange rate evolution of the Argentine peso and the Brazilian cruzeiro also showed a divergent evolutionary path (see Figures 2 and 3). In the period from March 1991 (when MERCOSUR was signed and the convertibility plan was implemented in Argentina) to December 1992, the peso appreciated relative to the U.S. dollar, while the cruzeiro became undervalued in relation to the U.S. dollar. Argentina's convertibility plan relied on a fixed exchange rate policy in relation to the U.S. dollar to stabilize prices, while Brazil's exchange rate policy resorted to frequent devaluations to promote export competitiveness.

The relationship between the peso and the cruzeiro real exchange rate movements was an important factor influencing trade results in this stage of the integration process. This was so because substantial progress had already been achieved in reciprocal and unilateral market opening and because exchange rate movements translated directly into relative prices. In 1992, the level of tariff reduction mandated by the automatic tariff reduction schedule was 54 percent up to July and 61 percent from July to December.

Macroeconomic divergences were, therefore, a key element underlying the evolution of unbalanced trade growth between Argentina and Brazil in the 1991-1992 period. The increase in Argentina's import demand from Brazil was due mainly to the demand-pull effects caused by the economic recovery in Argentina and the relative appreciation of the peso. On the other hand, the stagnation in import demand from Brazil was largely influenced by that country's domestic economic recession and the relative undervaluation of the cruzeiro.

1993: Smaller Trade Imbalances but Persisting Macroeconomic Divergences. During 1993, trade results indicated a sustained increase in intraregional trade and a partial rebalancing of trade flows, mostly due to the fact that Brazil's exports to Argentina slowed and its import demand picked up.

It must be noted that the level of tariff reduction on intraregional trade, as mandated by the automatic tariff reduction schedule, was 68 percent up to July 1993 and 75 percent from July 1993 to January 1994, when it became 82 percent. This high level of tariff preference brought down many residual tariff barriers that still remained and effectively widened access to the Brazilian market.

Overall, in 1993, the evolution of intraregional trade showed the following results:

- Bilateral trade between Argentina and Brazil increased 27 percent, rising from $5 billion in 1992 to $6.4 billion in 1993 (see Figure 1 and Table 1).

- The growth in bilateral Argentina-Brazil trade was due to 1) an increase of 67 percent in Argentine exports (leading to an increase in Argentina's share of total Brazilian imports from 8.2 percent to 10.3 percent) and 2) a smaller relative increase of 6.9 percent in Brazilian exports to Argentina (sales to Argentina were 9.4 percent of total Brazilian exports, up from 8.5 percent the year before) (see Tables 1 and 5).

- Bilateral trade resulted in Argentina's having a smaller trade deficit of $780 million with Brazil, half of the 1992 level (see Table 1).

- The growth of Argentine exports to Brazil was based on primary products, particularly wheat and fuels (oil), which increased at a rate of 37.4 percent and 306 percent, respectively; some industrial manufactures, particularly vehicles and parts, with an increase of 139.6 percent, and machinery and electrical equipment, with an increase of 84.5 percent; and some agro-industrial goods, such as fish and milk products, with an increase of 45 percent and 533 percent, respectively (see Table 2 for aggregate figures).

The rapid increase in Argentine exports to Brazil during 1993 was a positive outcome. It was stimulated primarily by demand recovery in Brazil during the first semester of 1993; there was an estimated gross domestic product (GDP) growth rate of 5 percent in this period. Also, administered trade decisions to improve Argentina's trade balance played a considerable role (for example, stimulating purchases from Argentina in the case of Petrobras — Brazil's public petroleum company — and enforcing trade compensation requirements in the case of the Argentine automotive industry).

Insofar as Argentine and other MERCOSUR countries' exports to Brazil continue to experience sustained growth, the problem of unbalanced growth of intraregional trade flows in MERCOSUR will be minimized.

The important question to answer, however, is whether Brazil's economy can go through a sustainable economic recovery given the fact that inflation in consumer prices accelerated to almost 45 percent monthly during March and April 1994.

Challenges, Prospects, and Future Expansion

Additional Measures Needed

MERCOSUR, at present, faces uncertainties about future unbalanced trade growth and difficulties in achieving economic policy coordination and harmonization. The situation of macroeconomic instability in Brazil is one factor slowing down progress on these issues.

Similarly, there are difficulties in reaching an agreement on the common external tariff that arise mainly from the different visions that the present Argentine and Brazilian administrations have on industrial policy: Brazil wants a more active policy stance and Argentina wants a more market-oriented approach. Indeed, at the core of these discussions, which involve Uruguay and Paraguay as well, is the central issue of trade diversion and trade creation effects. These problems imply a delay in the creation of a common market by 1995 but do not suggest a reversal of the regionalization process or a return to a closed-border situation.

In fact, at the presidential meeting of MERCOSUR, in January 1994, the governments of the partner countries agreed to redefine MERCOSUR objectives and to set January 1995 as the date for achieving a CU. In order to begin the CU by January 1995, not only should there be an agreement on the common external tariff, but a complex set of additional trade issues must be resolved (regarding export policy, contingent protection mechanisms, and the relations of MERCOSUR to ALADI and third countries) and new trade rules must be formulated accordingly.

The position presented by the Argentine government in the January MERCOSUR meeting was that in order to constitute a CU by January 1995, there must be either substantial advance in economic policy coordination and harmonization or new safeguard clauses must be introduced from that date onward to prevent injury due to the lack of policy harmonization. Along the same lines, Argentina proposed the formulation of mechanisms to facilitate sectoral structural adjustment based principally on some sort of sectoral safeguards for sensitive sectors during a period of no longer than a year and a half. These issues have been included on the MERCOSUR agenda for future discussions, and a final decision on them should be reached no later than December 1994.

In addition, some specific measures will have to be formulated to cope with the problems posed for regional trade liberalization by economies undergoing stabilization and market-oriented policy reforms at different rhythms. These measures need not be contemplated in the regional trade liberalization experiences of stable market-oriented economies as in the case of the Canada-United States FTA or in the European Community. As I proposed in an earlier work, the mechanisms should be designed to cushion the impact of macroeconomic disequilibrium on trade flows; in other words, they should play the role of shock absorbers. For instance, they could take the form of automatic trade balance safeguards or exchange rate safeguards to compensate for the unbalanced growth of trade flows. They should have a double function: to act as a deterrent to macroeconomic imbalances by penalizing them and to promote a dynamic rebalancing of trade flows primarily by expanding and not stopping trade.[7]

Prospects and Future Expansion

It appears that it will be difficult to achieve a CM by January 1995. Most likely, by that date, there will be an imperfect FTA or an imperfect CU. The alternative of achieving an FTA is a better option than that of a CM.[8]

Supporters of the CU option point to the benefits derived from becoming a trading bloc (basically, the increase in international bargaining power) and from simplifying border controls within the CU since there would be a common trade policy with other countries and, therefore, the opportunities for triangulation of goods will be reduced. Additional support for this argument is that members of the European Union recently expressed the importance of MERCOSUR's becoming a CU and of its acquiring international legal capacity in order to be considered a valid interlocutor by Europe.[9]

Contrarily, in my view, an FTA is preferable to a CU for several reasons. First, an FTA does not have a common trade policy and, therefore, does not behave internationally as a trading bloc. The central aspect of an FTA is that it allows free trade within the region while leaving each country free to formulate and change its own trade policy (tariff and nontariff barriers) with respect to the rest of the world. The formation of an FTA, compared with the CU option, allows a greater degree of individual freedom for partner countries to formulate present and future trade policy at the same time it reduces the risk of dividing the world into trading blocs.[10]

An FTA requires, however, the use of border controls and the definition of rules of origin to determine whether a product is made within the region. The setting of rules of origin is a crucial aspect that will determine the relative openness of an FTA. Complex and nontransparent rules of origin may become a protectionist device against nonpartner countries.[11]

Second, because an FTA does not have a common trade policy, it does not require the same degree of harmonization of economic policy or the coordination of macroeconomic policies as a CU or a CM. These requirements of policy harmonization look ideal when written but become idealistic in practice if, as in the case of MERCOSUR, the partner countries are at different stages in terms of stabilization and economic policy reforms (deregulation, privatization, trade and investment liberalization). Argentina is far more advanced than Brazil in the reform toward market-oriented policies. Brazil's restructuring lag makes the process of policy harmonization more difficult, particularly on issues that are central to a CU and a CM — for instance, the definition of a common external tariff (at the product level), compatible competition policies, and a subsidies discipline. And if competition policies and incentives are not harmonized, partner countries will be helpless against unfair competition practices in a CU, while an FTA will allow each partner country to maintain its own defense mechanisms in the forms of antidumping and countervailing duty policies.

Third, an FTA reduces the probability of negative trade diversion effects. When an FTA, a CU, or a CM is formed, two economic static effects take place: 1) trade creation — low cost imports from a partner country replace more expensive domestic production; and 2) trade diversion — low cost imports from the rest of the world are displaced by more expensive sources of supply from the partner countries. Trade creation is beneficial since it improves economic efficiency, while trade diversion results in welfare losses both to the importing partner country and globally.

In an FTA, the probability of suffering welfare losses from trade diversion is reduced because the affected partner country can solve the problem by unilaterally lowering tariff barriers vis-à-vis the rest of the world. Therefore, in an FTA, the pressures are to harmonize over time to the lowest tariff barriers among the partner countries. By contrast, in a CU or a CM, changes in the common trade policy cannot be introduced unilaterally by individual partner countries, and initial pressures are to harmonize tariffs to the highest existing level, particularly if the dominant trading partner in the area is a high tariff country.[12]

The preceding argument is well illustrated by the Chilean example. Under the administration of Patricio Aylwin Ozocar, Chile declined to be a partner in the MERCOSUR option of a CM, basically because the common external tariff of MERCOSUR will have a maximum level of 20 percent, or higher than the 11 percent uniform tariff level that Chile has today. Consequently, if Chile had to raise external tariffs because of joining the CM, the costs of trade diversion would outweigh the beneficial effects of trade creation.

Nonetheless, Chile can become a partner if MERCOSUR turns into an FTA rather than a CU or a CM. In fact, Chile has already expressed its willingness to enter into an FTA with MERCOSUR. This is a convenient move for Chile in order to preserve wide access to the regional market, particularly to the Argentine market that in 1993 became the third most important destination for its exports, the first most important destination for its manufactured exports, and the first most important destination for its direct foreign investment (see Table 7). Although Chile is not a member of MERCOSUR, it has advanced economic integration with Argentina. This process was promoted by bilateral preferential trade agreements and by unilateral trade liberalization and demand recovery in Argentina.

A recent study commissioned by the Chilean Ministry of Foreign Relations concludes that if Chile does not establish a closer trade relationship with MERCOSUR, it will lose $125 million in terms of exports and $170 million in terms of imports, all resulting from trade creation. Furthermore, this study establishes that reaching some form of association with MERCOSUR will accelerate the flow of foreign investment into Chile, investment attracted by the size of the wider regional market.[13]

It will be easier not only for Chile but also for Bolivia to enter MERCOSUR if it is an FTA. Bolivia has repeatedly expressed an interest in participating in the subregional integration scheme but has asked for some sort of special status (in terms of reciprocal obligations) that it has been denied. Nevertheless, in the January 1994 meeting, Bolivia was approved as an observer in MERCOSUR technical subgroups negotiations.

The Chilean and Bolivian cases lead to the fourth supporting reason for MERCOSUR's becoming an FTA. The prospect of joining forces with other countries and extending the movement of intraregional trade liberalization in South America is enhanced under an FTA, while a CU and a CM tend to be more exclusive by their very nature. Countries that want to join a CU or a CM must be ready to accept a more comprehensive set of rules and give up more degrees of freedom in the formulation of economic policy than they would in an FTA.[14]

For instance, in the January 1994 meeting, Brazil proposed extending MERCOSUR to form an FTA in South America: ALCSA (Area de Libre Comercio Sudamericana), or SAFTA (South American Free Trade Area). Argentina and the other MERCOSUR partners approved the direction of the initiative particularly because it would favor convergence between the Andean Group and MERCOSUR and because it would promote Chile's greater involvement in South America's regionalization movement. The main points of the ALCSA proposal were spelled out by Brazil in March 1994; the proposal is still pending final definition and agreement on its content.

There is, however, an apparent inconsistency here. Brazil is at the same time the promoter of an FTA in South America and the strongest supporter of the CU and CM options for MERCOSUR. Paraguay, Uruguay, and Argentina are more inclined toward the FTA option.

The inconsistency is based on the fact that while the smaller economies in MERCOSUR will have to pay trade diversion costs to have access to Brazil's large domestic market and to conform a wider regional market, other competing countries in the region, like Chile, by striking an FTA agreement, will benefit from freer market access to MERCOSUR without having to pay trade diversion costs. The inconsistency will clearly disappear if MERCOSUR becomes an FTA rather than a CU.

Similarly, the movement toward Western Hemisphere economic integration, either by the linking of subregional efforts such as NAFTA and MERCOSUR or by extending NAFTA, will be facilitated under the alternative of an FTA in the Southern Cone.

MERCOSUR, NAFTA, and Western Hemisphere Economic Integration

It is important to analyze whether MERCOSUR and NAFTA are divergent or convergent efforts from the standpoint of moving toward Western Hemisphere economic integration. In my opinion, MERCOSUR and NAFTA are convergent efforts. Convergence will be forthcoming if MERCOSUR sustains its record of outward orientation (openness) and of consistency with further multilateral trade liberalization. So far, the intraregional trade liberalization process in MERCOSUR has fed into the process of unilateral trade liberalization and market-oriented policy reforms. Although the common external tariff is not yet determined, the already agreed maximum tariff level of 20 percent is at present lower than the maximum tariff level of Brazil (the largest economy in MERCOSUR). Therefore, one of the two principles of open regionalism, not raising trade and investment barriers to nonmembers, is likely to be generally fulfilled. There may, however, be cases at the product level where the selected tariff for a commodity is higher than that maintained by the member with the lowest tariff for that commodity, given the fact that Paraguay and Uruguay have very low tariffs or even zero tariffs for some goods.

Therefore, it can safely be concluded that the completion of the process of subregional trade liberalization in MERCOSUR by January 1995 will strengthen rather than weaken the prospects of hemispheric trade liberalization and economic integration. Convergence will be enhanced under the alternative of MERCOSUR's becoming an FTA rather than a CU. This is primarily because an FTA is not a trading bloc. Its members have different external policies, and each can negotiate separately its own commercial policy in the General Agreement on Tariffs and Trade (GATT) and in other international forums. If MERCOSUR becomes a CU, the region will behave as a trading bloc in the sense that it will have a common trade policy, and any changes in that policy will have to be negotiated jointly by the member countries.

In my view, the most positive approach in proceeding toward Western Hemisphere economic integration is a mixed approach, one that includes simultaneous unilateral liberalization, subregional integration, and accession to NAFTA. Insofar as regional integration deepens and remains outward-oriented and consistent with multilateral trade liberalization (and GATT rules), there is likely to be an interdependence of liberalization efforts between regional subgroupings (or cross-feedback effects).[15] Viewed from this stand-point, MERCOSUR is thus far a building block rather than a stumbling block toward free trade in the Americas.

On the other hand, there is a time dimension that favors the mixed approach. While there is already pervasive progress in terms of regional (and unilateral) openness in the Southern Cone, NAFTA's implementation just started in 1994, and new accessions are not likely in the short term. There is time to complete the process of intraregional trade liberalization in MERCO-SUR before effective negotiations on access to NAFTA are entertained.

The official position of MERCOSUR with regard to formally asking for accession to NAFTA is not yet established. What is clear, however, is that if MERCOSUR becomes a CU by January 1995, none of the partner countries could seek individual accession to NAFTA. For this reason, it is very unlikely that Argentina—a potential candidate usually mentioned after Chile—will seek individual accession to NAFTA unless it is decided that by January 1995 MERCOSUR will become an FTA.

In conclusion, therefore, the achievement of a comprehensive FTA in the second half of the 1990s seems to be a more convenient objective for the Southern Cone countries than that of a CM. This alternative will facilitate the incorporation of Chile and Bolivia into MERCOSUR, the extension of MERCOSUR to form an FTA in South America, and the move toward Western Hemisphere economic integration by linking with NAFTA in the future. Clearly, this alternative is consistent with open regionalism because it will both reduce the degree of exclusivity of MERCOSUR and induce lower trade barriers against nonmembers over time. Thus, it is the best alternative to keep regional trade liberalization in MERCOSUR open, convergent with free trade in the region and in other regions, and consistent with further multinational trade liberalization.

Table 1. Argentina-Brazil Bilateral Trade
In millions of US$, FOB Values and Percent

Year	Argentina Exports to Brazil	Argentina Imports From Brazil	Total Trade	Bilateral Trade Balance
1980	765.0	1,072.3	1,837.3	-307.3
1981	595.1	893.3	1,488.4	-298.2
1982	567.7	687.7	1,255.4	-120.0
1983	358.3	666.8	1,025.1	-308.5
1984	478.2	831.2	1,309.4	-353.0
1985	496.3	611.5	1,107.8	-115.2
1986	698.1	691.3	1,389.4	6.8
1987	539.3	819.2	1,358.5	-279.9
1988	607.9	971.4	1,579.3	-363.5
1989	1,124.1	721.4	1,845.4	402.7
1990	1,422.5	717.9	2,140.4	704.6
1991	1,488.6	1,526.3	3,014.9	-37.7
1992	1,671.4	3,338.8	5,010.2	-1,667.4
1993	2,790.5	3,569.9	6,360.4	-779.4

PERCENT CHANGE

Year	Argentina Exports to Brazil	Argentina Imports From Brazil	Total Trade	Bilateral Trade Balance
1981/80	-22.2	-16.7	-19.0	
1982/81	-4.6	-23.0	-15.7	
1983/82	-36.9	-3.0	-18.3	
1984/83	33.5	24.7	27.7	
1985/84	3.8	-26.4	-15.4	
1986/85	40.7	13.0	25.4	
1987/86	-22.7	18.5	-2.2	
1988/87	12.7	18.6	16.3	
1989/88	84.9	-25.7	16.8	
1990/89	26.6	-0.5	16.0	
1991/90	4.6	112.6	40.9	
1992/91	12.3	118.8	66.2	
1993/92	67.0	6.9	26.9	
1990/85	186.6	17.4	93.2	
1993/90	96.2	397.3	197.2	

Source: ECO-AXIS SA based on INDEC (Argentina).

Table 2. Composition of Argentina Exports to Brazil
In Millions of US$ and Percent

	1985	1986	1987	1988	1989	1990	1991	1992	1993
TOTAL EXPORTS	**496.3**	**698.1**	**539.3**	**607.9**	**1,124.4**	**1,422.7**	**1,488.5**	**1,671.4**	**2,790.7**
Primary Products	178.7	317.4	218.1	210.4	346.8	560.0	592.0	711.2	865.5
Manufactures of Agricultural Origin	148.7	206.7	113.1	93.7	259.3	306.2	335.0	242.3	343.3
Industrial Manufactures	104.1	150.3	207.8	299.3	498.7	550.2	533.1	596.4	1,088.2
Fuels & Energy	64.5	23.4	0.1	4.1	18.5	5.7	28.4	121.5	493.7
Primary Products	36.0*	45.5*	40.4*	34.6*	30.8*	39.4*	39.8*	42.6*	31.0*
Manufactures of Agricultural Origin	30.0*	29.6*	21.0*	15.4*	23.1*	21.5*	22.5*	14.5*	12.3*
Industrial Manufactures	21.0*	21.5*	38.5*	49.2*	44.4*	38.7*	35.8*	35.7*	39.0*
Fuels & Energy	13.0*	3.3*	0.0*	0.7*	1.6*	0.4*	1.9*	7.3*	17.7*

	86/85	87/86	88/87	89/88	90/89	91/90	92/91	93/92
Primary Products	77.6*	-31.3*	-3.6*	64.9*	61.5*	5.7*	20.1*	21.7*
Manufactures of Agricultural Origin	39.0*	-45.3*	-17.2*	176.8*	18.1*	9.4*	-27.7*	41.7*
Industrial Manufactures	44.4*	38.2*	44.0*	66.6*	10.3*	-3.1*	11.9*	82.5*
Fuels & Energy	-63.7*	-99.6*	4731.8*	349.7*	-69.1*	397.0*	327.8*	306.3*

Source: ECO-AXIS SA based on INDEC (Argentina).
* = Numbers in percent

Table 3. Composition of Argentina Imports from Brazil in Millions of US$ and Percent

	1990	1991	1992	1993
TOTAL IMPORTS	**717.9**	**1,526.6**	**3,338.7**	**3,569.9**
Capital Goods	64.1	167.4	414.4	472.8
Intermediate Goods	474.7	801.1	1,333.9	1,346.1
Fuels	0.6	5.1	23.4	89.4
Parts of Capital Goods	129.9	291.4	721.9	874.7
Consumer Goods	41.2	171.9	480.0	567.4
Motor Vehicles (*)	0.1	87.3	360.7	214.0
Others	7.3	2.4	4.4	5.5
Capital Goods	8.9%	11.0%	12.4%	13.2%
Intermediate Goods	66.1%	52.5%	40.0%	37.7%
Fuels	0.1%	0.3%	0.7%	2.5%
Parts of Capital Goods	18.1%	19.1%	21.6%	24.5%
Consumer Goods	5.7%	11.3%	14.4%	15.9%
Motor Vehicles	0.0%	5.7%	10.8%	6.0%
Others	1.0%	0.2%	0.1%	0.2%
		1991/90	1992/91	1993/92
Capital Goods		161.2%	147.6%	14.1%
Intermediate Goods		68.8%	66.5%	0.9%
Fuels		750.0%	358.8%	282.1%
Parts of Capital Goods		124.3%	147.7%	21.2%
Consumer Goods		317.2%	179.2%	18.2%
Motor Vehicles		87200.0%	313.2%	-40.7%
Others		-67.1%	83.3%	25.0%

(*) Fully assembled cars only. Argentine imports of motor vehicles and parts from Brazil in 1992 were over US$ 880 million.

Source: ECO-AXIS SA based on INDEC (Argentina).

Table 4a. Argentina: Exports to MERCOSUR, Chile, LAIA, USA & Total in Millions of US$

	Brazil	Paraguay	Uruguay	MERCOSUR	Chile	LAIA	USA	Total
1988	607.9	79.9	187.4	875.3	259.3	1,760.6	1,185.5	9,134.8
1989	1,124.4	96.3	207.7	1,428.4	350.3	2,388.0	1,151.8	9,579.3
1990	1,422.7	147.4	262.6	1,832.6	462.3	3,128.1	1,665.2	12,352.5
1991	1,488.5	178.0	311.0	1,977.5	487.7	3,368.7	1,210.1	11,977.8
1992	1,671.3	271.9	383.6	2,326.8	580.9	3,917.6	1,349.4	12,234.9
1993	2,790.5	357.8	512.7	3,661.0	590.8	5,262.4	1,273.4	13,090.4

Percent Total

	Brazil	MERCOSUR	LAIA	USA
1988	6.7%	9.6%	19.3%	13.0%
1989	11.7%	14.9%	24.9%	12.0%
1990	11.5%	14.8%	25.3%	13.5%
1991	12.4%	16.5%	28.1%	10.1%
1992	13.7%	19.0%	32.0%	11.0%
1993	21.3%	28.0%	40.2%	9.7%

Source: ECO-AXIS SA based on INDEC (Argentina).

Table 4b. Argentina: Imports from MERCOSUR, Chile, LAIA, USA & Total in Millions of US$

	Brazil	Paraguay	Uruguay	MERCOSUR	Chile	LAIA	USA	Total
1988	971.4	67.6	130.9	1,169.9	146.8	1,774.5	908.2	5,321.6
1989	721.4	48.8	98.9	869.1	111.3	1,389.2	880.5	4,203.2
1990	717.9	41.6	116.1	875.6	111.9	1,403.3	861.6	4,076.7
1991	1,526.3	42.8	235.2	1,804.3	381.4	2,748.4	1,845.2	8,275.5
1992	3,338.8	64.7	351.2	3,754.7	645.8	4,981.3	3,226.3	14,871.8
1993	3,569.9	72.9	570.8	4,213.6	706.0	5,434.2	3,858.6	16,786.0

Percent Total

	Brazil	MERCOSUR	LAIA	USA
1988	18.3%	22.0%	33.3%	17.1%
1989	17.2%	20.7%	33.1%	20.9%
1990	17.6%	21.5%	34.4%	21.1%
1991	18.4%	21.8%	33.2%	22.3%
1992	22.5%	25.2%	33.5%	21.7%
1993	21.3%	25.1%	32.4%	23.0%

Source: ECO-AXIS SA based on INDEC (Argentina).

Table 5a. Brazil: Exports to MERCOSUR, Chile, LAIA, USA & Total in Millions of US$

	Argentina	Paraguay	Uruguay	MERCOSUR	Chile	LAIA	USA	Total
1988	976.5	340.8	321.2	1,638.5	—	—	—	33,789.0
1989	725.0	321.0	333.6	1,379.6	694.4	3,487.9	—	34,383.0
1990	645.2	380.5	294.6	1,320.3	483.7	3,193.7	7,762.1	31,414.0
1991	1,476.2	496.1	337.1	2,309.4	677.3	4,938.7	6,760.5	31,620.0
1992	3,039.8	543.3	514.2	4,097.3	922.6	7,591.9	7,058.6	35,861.5
1993	3,661.5	960.6	774.8	5,396.9	1,110.4	9,144.0	8,023.8	38,782.7

Percent Total

	Argentina	MERCOSUR	LAIA	USA
1988	2.9%	4.8%	—	—
1989	2.1%	4.0%	10.1%	—
1990	2.1%	4.2%	10.2%	24.7%
1991	4.7%	7.3%	15.6%	21.4%
1992	8.5%	11.4%	21.2%	19.7%
1993	9.4%	13.9%	23.6%	20.7%

Table 5b. Brazil: Imports from MERCOSUR, Chile, LAIA, USA & Total in Millions of US$

	Argentina[1]	Paraguay	Uruguay	MERCOSUR	Chile	LAIA	USA	Total
1988	706.0	117.4	313.9	1,137.3	—	—	—	14,605.0
1989	1,248.0	358.8	596.1	2,202.9	515.1	3,391.8	—	18,263.0
1990	1,412.4	329.7	584.6	2,326.8	485.4	3,805.9	4,876.5	20,661.0
1991	1,614.7	219.6	434.1	2,268.4	493.6	3,667.6	5,945.1	21,041.0
1992	1,687.1	184.6	342.9	2,214.6	474.5	2,672.7	5,441.6	20,542.0
J-Jun 92	1,098.1	102.8	146.0	907.3	—	—	—	9,379.7
J-Jun 93	1,924.4	110.5	187.9	1,629.7	—	—	—	16,493.4

Percent Total

	Argentina	MERCOSUR	LAIA	USA
1988	4.8%	7.8%	—	—
1989	6.8%	12.1%	18.6%	—
1990	6.8%	11.3%	18.4%	23.6%
1991	7.7%	10.8%	17.4%	28.3%
1992	8.2%	10.8%	13.0%	26.5%
J-Jun 92	7.5%	9.7%	—	—
J-Jun 93	10.3%	9.9%	—	—

(1) Argentina 1992/1993: January-September.
Source: ECO-AXIS SA based on DTIC (Brazil) and NTDB (USA).

Table 6. Argentina and Brazil:
Changes in Foreign Exchange Rates and Prices
March 1991 - December 1993

CHANGES IN NOMINAL VARIABLES

		Argentina	Brazil
Exchange Rate	(1)	3.6%	134,215.5%
Consumer Prices	(2)	52.9%	140,783.4%
Wholesale Prices	(3)	6.1%	127,839.8%
Combined Prices	(4)	29.5%	134,411.6%

CHANGES IN REAL EXCHANGE RATE RELATIVE TO THE DOLLAR DEFLATOR

		Argentina	Brazil
Consumer Prices – (1)/(2)	(5)	-26.1%	3.9%
Wholesale Prices – (1)/(3)	(6)	6.4%	14.4%
Combined Prices – (1)/(4)	(7)	-9.9%	9.1%

CHANGES IN THE BILATERAL REAL EXCHANGE DEFLATOR

	Peso/Cruzeiro	Cruzeiro/Peso
Consumer Prices – (5)/(5)	-28.9%	-7.0%
Wholesale Prices – (6)/(6)	40.7%	7.5%

Source: ECO-AXIS SA based on Central Banks of Argentina and Brazil,
        INDEC (Arg), FGV (BRA).

Table 7. Argentina and Brazil Real Exchange Rates
March 1991 = 100

| | Real Exchange Rate of Argentina and Brazil (1) | | | | Argentina Bilateral Exchange Rate Relative to Brazil Deflator | |
| | Argentina Deflator | | Brazil Deflator | | | |
	CPI	WPI	CPI	WPI	CPI	WPI
1982	228.70	103.83	71.70	92.33	319.14	112.57
1983	240.29	103.40	101.30	120.07	239.93	86.53
1984	223.15	101.94	119.49	119.65	186.94	85.20
1985	252.61	119.65	132.95	127.49	189.96	94.01
1986	210.24	114.05	121.93	116.17	172.51	98.22
1987	215.82	123.33	116.73	116.26	184.95	106.18
1988	220.76	109.50	123.30	107.63	179.46	101.66
1989	344.98	147.11	105.94	92.99	329.15	159.31
1990	212.17	117.75	84.32	75.47	248.51	157.62
1991	100.89	103.60	104.36	106.84	97.24	97.64
1992	79.24	100.69	115.53	121.90	68.58	82.65
1993	74.50	103.17	106.87	118.01	69.78	87.46
Mar 91	100.00	100.00	100.00	100.00	100.00	100.00
Apr	96.74	100.67	100.56	100.17	96.20	100.50
May	95.25	100.86	102.89	104.04	92.57	96.94
Jun	93.20	100.69	101.30	105.21	92.00	95.70
Jul	90.85	100.34	99.34	103.97	91.45	96.51
Aug	89.86	100.92	98.02	102.48	91.67	98.48
Sep	88.21	100.40	99.43	105.49	88.71	95.17
Oct	87.20	99.87	111.37	115.04	78.30	86.81
Nov	87.04	100.93	116.10	119.77	74.97	84.27
Dec	87.22	102.81	119.39	125.50	73.05	81.92
Jan 92	84.13	101.77	116.73	122.07	72.08	83.37
Feb	82.66	101.68	117.58	120.67	70.30	84.26
Mar	81.55	100.93	119.22	123.58	68.40	81.67
Apr	80.45	100.74	119.80	126.59	67.16	79.58
May	80.05	100.91	115.89	124.39	69.08	81.13
Jun	79.71	100.46	114.28	124.90	69.75	80.43
Jul	78.57	99.82	115.94	124.92	67.77	79.91
Aug	77.57	99.42	114.01	120.02	68.04	82.83
Sep	76.93	98.92	112.97	117.95	68.10	83.87
Oct	76.20	99.11	112.35	118.98	67.82	83.30
Nov	76.23	101.50	113.70	118.77	67.04	85.46
Dec	76.78	103.09	113.92	119.94	67.39	85.95
Jan 93	76.35	102.53	111.44	120.28	68.51	85.24
Feb	76.00	102.02	98.17	120.89	77.42	84.39
Mar	75.63	102.94	110.91	119.72	68.19	85.98
Apr	75.05	102.40	109.50	120.17	68.54	85.22
May	74.30	102.26	109.20	117.92	68.04	86.73
Jun	73.90	102.84	107.42	118.23	68.79	86.72
Jul	73.93	103.06	107.88	117.36	68.53	87.82
Aug	74.12	102.88	106.04	117.39	69.89	87.63
Sep	73.71	103.12	106.20	116.04	69.41	88.87
Oct	73.50	103.00	106.57	117.08	68.96	87.97
Nov	73.65	104.89	105.54	116.62	69.79	89.94
Dec	73.86	106.40	103.54	114.41	71.34	93.00

Source: ECO-AXIS SA based on Central Banks of Argentina and Brazil.
(1) Using the CPI Index of USA/CPI = Consumer Price Index and WPI = Wholesale Price Index.

Figure 1. Argentina-Brazil Bilateral Trade
1980–1993

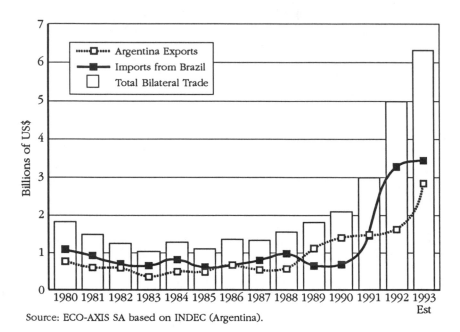

Source: ECO-AXIS SA based on INDEC (Argentina).

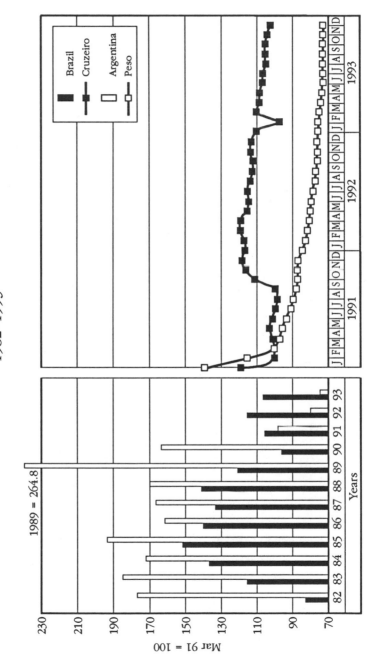

Figure 2. Argentina-Brazil's Real Exchange Rates Relative to the Dollar. Deflated by Consumer Prices. 1982–1993

Source: ECO-AXIS SA based on Central Banks of Argentina and Brazil.

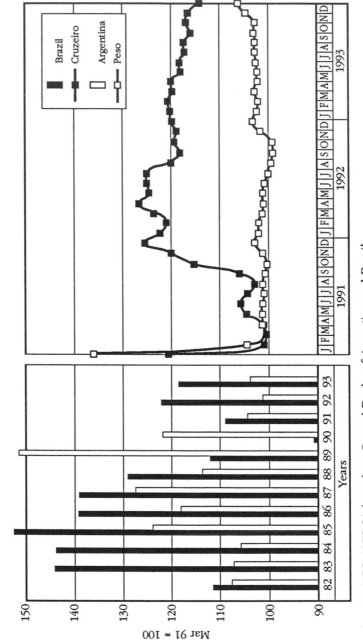

Figure 3. Argentina-Brazil's Real Exchange Rates Relative to the Dollar. Deflated by Wholesale Prices. 1982–1993

Source: ECO-AXIS SA based on Central Banks of Argentina and Brazil.

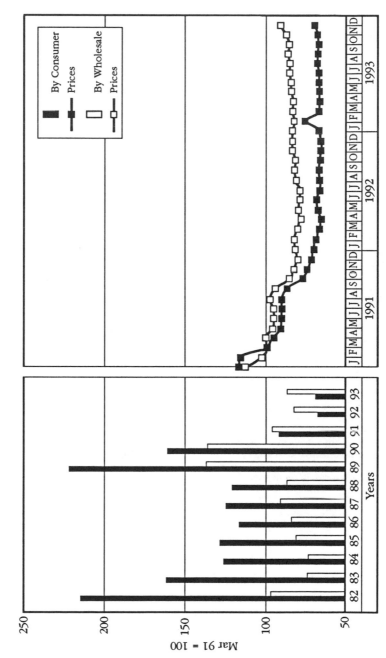

Figure 4. Argentina's Real Foreign Exchange Rate Relative to Brazil.
1982–1993

Source: ECO-AXIS SA based on Central Banks of Argentina and Brazil.

Notes

1   Asociación Latinoamericana de Integración (ALADI), or Latin American Association of Integration (LAIA).

2   On January 18, 1994, the Secretary of Trade, Investment and Commerce of Argentina, Dr. Sanchez (virtually the vice-minister of economy), stated in a meeting with various important representatives of the private sector that the automatic mechanisms would be implemented in a timely manner and that by January 1995 trade between Brazil and Argentina should be completely freed from tariff or nontariff barriers.

3   The large difference in inflation rates between Argentina and Brazil clearly shows the macroeconomic divergences. In 1993, Argentina's inflation rate as measured by the consumer price index was 7.4 percent, while that of Brazil was 2,299.7 percent.

4   For research on the subject of intra-industrial trade between Argentina and Brazil, see Sourrouille and Lucángeli (1992) and Lucángeli (1993).

5   I have done econometric studies for the private sector to predict intraregional trade flows and their impact on different markets (for example, transport by railways). The econometric analysis of the determinations of bilateral trade flows showed a large, positive correlation between the evolution of import demand and the evolution of the level of economic activity (gross national product, or GNP) of the importing country and a smaller nonsignificant relation between the evolution of trade flows and the evolution of real exchange rates (particularly during the period from 1985 to 1989). Only in the case of the evolution of exports from Brazil was a significant relation with real exchange rate evolution found. Similar results were arrived at in an econometric study by Heyman and Navajas (1993) from the UN Economic Commission for Latin America (ECLA) office in Buenos Aires.

6   MERCOSUR intraregional trade data is based on statistics from Instituto de Integración Latinoamericana (INTAL) collected from each of the partner countries.

7   See María Beatriz Nofal (1993a).

8   The vision that a free trade area is at present a better option of integration than a customs union or a common market for the countries in the Southern Cone oriented the integration treaty signed between Argentina and Brazil in 1988.

9   See Félix Peña (1994).

10   See Richard G. Lipsey (1993).

11   Nora Lustig (1994) calls for attention to the central issue of rules of origin to determine the degree of openness of regional trade agreements.

12   See Lipsey (1993).

13 "Chile mira al MERCOSUR," *Ambito Financiero*, Buenos Aires, April 13, 1994.

14 Nora Lustig (1994) emphasizes that regional trade agreements tend to be more exclusive when they have ambitious objectives, i.e., those that want to create a Common Market.

15 See Nofal (1993a).

References

Ambito Financiero. 1994. "Chile Mira al MERCOSUR." Buenos Aires. April 13.

Heyman, Daniel, and Fernando Navajas. 1993. "Interdependencias macroeconómicas entre Argentina y Brazil: los flujos comerciales." In *Estudios Argentinos para la Integración del MERCOSUR.* Buenos Aires: Centro de Economía Internacional (CEI).

Lipsey, Richard G. 1993. "Laying the Foundations: The Main Paths to Hemispheric Free Trade." Paper presented at the Conference on Designing the Architecture for a Western Hemisphere Free Trade Area at the North-South Center, University of Miami, January 28-29.

Lustig, Nora. 1994. "The Future of Trade Policy in Latin America." In *Integrating the Americas: Shaping Future Trade Policy,* ed. Sidney Weintraub. Coral Gables, Fla.: North-South Center, University of Miami.

Lucángeli, Jorge. 1993. "Integración comercial, intercambio intra-industrial y creación y desvío de comercio: el intercambio comercial entre Argentina y Brazil en los años recientes." Buenos Aires: Secretaría de Programación Económica. Subsecretaría de Estudios Económicos - PNUD.

Nofal, María Beatriz. 1993a. "Economic Integration of Argentina-Brazil, MERCOSUR and Regionalization in the Southern Cone Market." In *NAFTA and Trade Liberalization in the Americas,* ed. Elsie Echeverrie-Carrol. Austin: University of Texas.

Nofal, María Beatriz. 1993b. "Brazil no es Unico culpable del Desequilibrio Comercial." *Ambito Financiero,* December 24.

Nofal, María Beatriz. 1992. "El Problema no es el Déficit sino los Flujos de Comercio." *Ambito Financiero,* February 11.

Nofal, María Beatriz. 1991. "Argentina y Brazil: Asimetrías de Política Industrial y de Comercio Exterior." *Revista IDEA.* (November) No. 159.

Nofal, María Beatriz. 1990a. "The Argentine-Brazilian Integration Process: Achievements, Problems and Prospects." The Wilson Center Working Papers, No. 181. Washington, D.C.

Nofal, María Beatriz. 1990b. "Industria Siderúrgica Argentina: Competitividad Respecto de Brasil y Políticas de Integración." *STRAT Parte II Competitividad y Alternativas Estratégicas de Desarrollo para la Industria Siderúrgica Argentina (1900-2000).* November.

Peña, Félix. 1994. "Clara Señal de Menem para la Integración Regional." *El Cronista Comercial,* Buenos Aires (May 3).

Sourrouille, Juan V., and Jorge Lucángeli. 1992. "El Intercambio Comercial Argentino-Brasileño. Un Exámen del Comercio intraindustrial." Buenos Aires: Instituto para la Integración de América Latina (INTAL).

Weintraub, Sidney. 1992. "Western Hemisphere Free Trade: Getting from Here to There." IDB/ECLAC Working Papers on Trade in the Western Hemisphere, No. 13. November.

Chapter 7

Japan's Future Trade and Investment Policies in the Western Hemisphere

Ippei Yamazawa

Evolving New Trade Regime in the 1990s

Toward the end of 1993, a series of trade regime arrangements in the North American and Asia-Pacific regions went into effect. The North American Free Trade Agreement (NAFTA) enabling legislation was passed by the U.S. Congress in the middle of November, and immediately thereafter the Asia Pacific Economic Cooperation (APEC) had a successful meeting in Seattle. Three weeks later, the Uruguay Round of the General Agreement on Tariffs and Trade (GATT) negotiations was concluded.

Since the beginning of 1994, three regional trade arrangements have been launched: NAFTA, the Association of Southeast Asian Nations (ASEAN) Free Trade Area (AFTA), and the European Economic Area (EEA). Regional economic integration has been accepted as long as it is consistent with GATT principles. However, if the Uruguay Round had failed, there would have been serious concern about the potential negative effects of these new arrangements on trade. The success of the Uruguay Round has brightened the prospect for the compatibility of these regional integration arrangements with the multilateral system.

NAFTA, APEC, and the Uruguay Round all got off the ground because of a strong but flexible initiative by the United States. Other countries also contributed to their achievement, but none of the three would have succeeded without the U.S. contribution. At times, the likelihood of success for each was rated below 50 percent. The Clinton administration may well be credited for its "triple play." The trading environment for American firms will be improved, and the recent active movement of American firms to Asia will be accelerated. Asia-Pacific firms will also gain from the improved trade environment through the Uruguay Round and APEC. However, with respect to NAFTA, Asians watch the intensified integration in the Western Hemisphere with both expectation and concern. Will NAFTA develop in conformity with the "open regionalism" adopted in APEC?

This chapter deals with the policy interests of Japan's government and business firms. Since the Western Hemisphere covers a vast area, the analysis will focus on Japanese economic relations with Mexico and the possible impacts of NAFTA on these relations. The following section gives an overview of the economic relationship between Japan and North America (the three NAFTA countries). Starting with a bird's-eye view of the findings in a consolidated trade matrix covering the Asia-Pacific region as a whole, the section focuses on the main characteristics of the Japan-Mexico relationship. The third section analyzes the core elements of the Japan-Mexico relationship and the strategy of Japanese firms in foreign direct investment (FDI) and also provides details of Japanese investment in Mexico over the past decade and discusses NAFTA's effects on this investment.

The fourth section describes how the NAFTA proposal was perceived in Japan before NAFTA was approved, with occasional references to other Asian perceptions. The fifth section reports on the recent responses by both business and government and comments on future prospects.

The establishment of NAFTA has made clear the U.S. commitment to the development of the Western Hemisphere, enhanced prospects for accomplishing this end, and improved the business atmosphere in the region. The countries on the other side of the Pacific welcome the emerging regime in the Western Hemisphere but are concerned about whether it will continue to be compatible with the new direction of APEC's open regionalism. Mexico was admitted to APEC at the Seattle meeting, and all three NAFTA countries are now members of the community. All Asian participants are inevitably worried about how this NAFTA subgroup will behave. The final section discusses the possible impacts of NAFTA in the broader context of the APEC vision.

Japan's Relationship with the Western Hemisphere

What follows is an overview of trade relationships across the Pacific. Table 1 presents trade data for the three major regional areas. In order to grasp the trend of the 1980s, figures are shown for the years 1980, 1986, and 1990. The three broad groups shown are East Asia (EA, consisting of Japan; newly emerging Asian economies, or NIEs; ASEAN; and China), North America (NA3, consisting of the United States, Canada, and Mexico), and the European Community (EC12).

The overall intraregional trade shares of EA and NA3 were by and large similar, while EC12's figure was almost twice as high. The share of intraregional trade increased in all three groups between 1980 and 1990 but were much higher in EC12 than in the other two groups.

In 1980, transpacific and transatlantic trade values were almost the same — $110 billion. However, throughout the 1980s, the former expanded by 2.7 times, while the latter just doubled. In 1990, transpacific trade recorded a large surplus on the EA side, while transatlantic trade was balanced. Disaggregating the figures of EA into Japan and Other EA, Japan's total exports were 70 percent of Other EA, while its total imports were 90 percent of Other EA. But both Japan and Other EA exported the same amount, $100 billion, to the United States in 1990. In the same year, 34 percent of Japan's exports went to the United States and 29 percent to the countries of Other Asia, while 27 percent of Japan's imports were from the United States and 29 percent from Other EA.

Turning to Japan-Mexico trade, both exports and imports expanded at two-digit growth rates in the years 1987 to 1989. Since 1990, export growth from Japan has accelerated, while imports into Japan stagnated, thus resulting in a sizable trade imbalance between the two countries.[1] Japan is the second-largest trade partner of Mexico. The United States, of course, is predominant in Mexican trade, accounting for almost two-thirds of the total. In 1990, Japan's share was 7 percent of Mexico's exports and 5 percent of Mexico's imports, almost equal to the combined share of the United Kingdom, France, and Germany and three times as big as Canada's.

As regards the pattern of trade, three-quarters of Japan's exports to Mexico are machinery (electronic, industrial, and transport), and three-quarters of Japan's imports from Mexico are raw materials, particularly crude oil (55 to 61 percent), followed by silver and salt (5.5 and 5.2 percent, respectively). This pattern reflects close complementarity in natural resource endowment between the two countries. However, it is misleading to ignore Japan's indirect trade with Mexico, that is, Japan's exports of machinery parts to Mexico and Mexico's export of assembled machinery to the United States — a trade pattern that reflects another complementarity of human resource endowments between Japan and Mexico.

Japan, together with the United States, has been one of the biggest suppliers of financial resources to Mexico. In fact, Mexico received more than half of all Japanese funds going to Latin America. Japan's Export-Import (Ex-Im) Bank, other government banks, and commercial banks contributed financially to Mexico to carry out the Brady Plan — the 1989 U.S. initiative to reduce debts for foreign commercial loans, which was named for then-Treasury Secretary Nicholas Brady.

Japanese firms were investing actively in manufacturing in Mexico before Mexico's *maquiladora* program got under way and have continued to do so. Nissan, the second-largest car manufacturer of Japan, was an early investor in Mexico and is regarded almost as an indigenous firm. Japanese investment in *maquiladora* plants has accelerated since the middle of the 1980s. There were 14 Japanese *maquiladora* firms in 1985, and their number increased to 50 in 1989. These firms are engaged in the indirect trade of importing parts and materials from Japan and exporting their assembled products (typically, household electronics) to the United States.[2]

There is an indirect form of Japanese investment in *maquiladoras*; Japanese subsidiaries in the United States adjacent to Mexico invest in subcontracting *maquiladora* firms to take advantage of lower wages and cheaper processing costs. They are "grandchild subsidiaries" of Japanese firms, but they are not captured in Japanese FDI statistics. They are also engaged in border trade between the United States and Mexico. The two forms of Japanese investment in Mexico are illustrated below.

NAFTA will add a major new element to the future relationship between Japan and Mexico. There is no doubt about its stimulative effect in the long run, but its short-run impact is complicated and as yet uncertain. In order to analyze that impact, it is necessary to look into the changing behavior and strategy of Japanese investors and how they have been responding to the evolving policy environment in the world, especially to regionalization in Europe and North America.

Patterns of Japanese FDI

In the latter half of the 1980s, Japanese FDI continued to grow and reached a peak of $67.5 billion in 1989, but it decreased consistently over the period 1990 to 1992 and almost halved, to $34.1 billion, in 1992.[3]

Several factors explain the increase of FDI during the 1980s. Japan accumulated huge surpluses in its trade and current account, and the resulting excess liquidity at home provided funds for FDI. Furthermore, the rapid appreciation of the yen expanded Japanese purchasing power of overseas assets. As a matter of fact, the deficit in the long-term capital account (the net outflow of investment abroad) exceeded the surplus in the current account for the years from 1987 to 1990.

The boost of Japanese FDI in the late 1980s also reflected the restructuring of Japanese firms. The restructuring originated as a response to the global adjustment common to all industrialized economies during the last two decades, that is, the responses to the changing pattern of Japan's comparative advantage resulting from such factors as wide fluctuations of energy and raw material prices, increased labor cost, the process of catch-up by late-starting Asian neighbors, and the dramatic increase in value of the yen. These changes began in the early 1970s and accelerated in the late 1980s.

The restructuring effort of Japanese firms took three forms: rationalization, diversification, and globalization of their business activities. The rationalization was carried out typically by metal and chemical firms affected adversely by higher energy and material prices and low utilization of their large-scale factories under slowed growth after the oil shock of 1973. Many firms scrapped obsolete machinery and equipment and reduced employment so that they could run at competitive capacities under reduced scales. Saving of energy and material use, which was practiced by Japanese steel firms, was another aspect of the rationalization effort.

The diversification consisted of the upgrading and increasing of the sophistication of production toward higher value-added goods and the switching of higher technological requirements with related industries. The success of this effort depended on product innovation, which was promoted actively in Japan throughout the 1980s. The upgrading was helped by emerging new consumer tastes resulting from higher incomes.

The globalization was characterized by a shift from domestic production toward combined domestic and overseas production and then combined with exports to third countries. Such globalization is feasible only for firms with superior technology and efficient managerial resources.

FDI is a core element of the globalization effort. Japanese FDI has been directed mainly to three regions: North America, Western Europe, and East Asia. Of the Japanese FDI stocks accumulated during the 1951-1991 period, 44 percent was in North America, 19.5 percent in Western Europe, and 15.2 percent in East Asia. Regional composition of FDI in 1992 was almost the same: North America, 40.5 percent; Europe, 20.7 percent; and East Asia, 18.2 percent. Japanese FDI has decreased in total amount during the past three years, but its regional composition has shifted more toward Asia. FDI to North America and Europe has decreased by 23 to 24 percent and to Asian NIEs by 12.8 percent, while FDI to ASEAN has gained by 3.7 percent and to China by 84 percent.[4]

The motivation and pattern of investment in the United States and Europe differs from that in Asia. In Asia, Japanese investors are more concerned with cost reduction, mainly labor cost, as well as with better access to raw materials, while in the United States and Europe, FDI was forced initially by severe trade conflicts, that is, a switch from export to local production, and by growing markets. Since the late 1980s, Japanese firms have been relocating their production under their global strategy, which reflects the fact that they have realized a mature stage for global operations. However, low costs in Asia and trade friction and market access in the United States and Europe are still major incentives in the global strategy of Japanese firms.

Japanese FDI has also been affected by regional integration, most notably in Europe. The 1985 announcement of the drive toward a European Single Market stimulated FDI in Europe and thus increased Europe's share in the regional composition. The impact of NAFTA is yet to be seen in the FDI statistics, but the Ex-Im Bank (1994) predicts the beginning of the change mentioned below. The impact of regional integration may differ among industries. In contrast to the general tendency of globalization, regional integration may lead some firms to establish self-contained production-cum-marketing subsidiaries within the region if demand and supply characteristics allow.

How Was the NAFTA Proposal Perceived in Japan?

The NAFTA proposal was received calmly in Japan in comparison with a stronger reaction in other East Asian countries concerned about its possible adverse effect on their exports to the United States. First, because the other two NAFTA countries have long been integrated with the United States in both trade and investment terms and because policies along this line have been implemented for many years, the Canada-U.S. Free Trade Agreement (CUSFTA) and NAFTA were perceived in Japan as natural extensions of this long-term trend. Second, Japanese firms had already invested in the three countries, and it seemed unlikely that their business would be seriously affected immediately.

A distinctive feature of the trade among the three North American countries is the heavy dependence of both Canada and Mexico on the United States. In 1992, some 75 percent of Canada's exports went to the United States, and 65 percent of its imports came from there. In Mexico's case, 70 percent of the country's exports and 65 percent of the country's import trade was with the United States that year. For the United States, by contrast, trade with Canada accounted for only 21 percent of its total trade and trade with Mexico for just 7 percent. In other words, more than 70 percent of U.S. trade is conducted with countries outside North America. The United States trades on a truly global scale, and its trade relations with other North American countries are, in this respect, atypical. Trade between Canada and Mexico is fairly limited. It is clear that the United States constitutes the center of trade in the North American region, while Canada and Mexico effectively feed this center in a sort of radial, or hub-and-spoke, pattern.

The trend toward integration in North America has been in evidence for some time. Canada and Mexico naturally viewed their neighbor's massive market and high incomes with envy, while the United States dreamed of expanding its market to take in the whole of North America. Lying to the north and south, respectively, of the United States, Canada and Mexico both share extremely long land borders with their neighbor. These border areas are considered to have formed natural economic territories of their own. Canada and the United States, in particular, have a great deal in common — a shared language, social system and culture, and economic and political outlook. The two thus formed a de facto FTA even before the formal FTA was instituted. In the case of Canada, at least, there are still more restrictions on trade between provinces than there are on trade with its southern neighbor. From Canada's point of view, one of the chief reasons for formalizing the FTA was to institutionalize the process of settling trade disputes with the United States, thereby preventing the unilateral imposition by the latter of import restriction measures such as antidumping and countervailing duties.

There was also considerable integration of the United States with Mexico. In the wake of the debt crisis of 1982, Mexico moved, under the leadership of President Miguel de la Madrid and subsequently of President Carlos Salinas de Gortari, to stabilize and restructure its economy. Part of this restructuring involved a lowering of customs tariffs and a relaxation of nontariff import restrictions. The *maquiladora* system, which was initiated in the late 1960s, flourished, and in the 1980s, there was a proliferation of U.S. manufacturing and processing plants across the border in Mexico. Taken together, these measures encouraged the development of a sort of horizontal division of labor under which goods are processed in Mexico for export back to the United States, thus promoting a higher level of trade and investment activity. Among the main incentives behind a U.S.-Mexico FTA are, for the United States, the opening up of the Mexican market and, for Mexico, the assurance of access to the U.S. market.

The formation of the U.S.-Canada FTA and then of NAFTA represented attempts to institutionalize these growing trends toward integration. Both agreements were probably given additional impetus by an increasing awareness of the economic strengths of other regions of the world and by a desire to elevate the level of economic activity in North America as a means of countering the move toward a single market in the EC and the rapid growth of the East Asian economies.

Being an FTA, NAFTA will have a discriminatory impact on nonmember producers in competition with member producers. ASEAN producers are most anxious about the possible increase in competition with Mexican producers in the U.S. market, but Japanese and Asian NIE producers welcome the potentially larger North American market and wish to participate in it. They claim that they are not infringing on rival producers within NAFTA, but rather conveying competitive stimulus, new technology, and new products indispensable for the competitive development of NAFTA industries.

NAFTA's rules of origin are a prime concern of East Asian countries. The rules were introduced in order to encourage local production using higher local content, but their measurement involves some arbitrariness. For example,

1) no international standard has been agreed, and individual countries apply different rules; 2) the system is complicated, and different rules are applied to different sectors within a country; and 3) a definition such as "substantial processing" lacks clarity and often leads to arbitrary application. A well-known recent instance of this arbitrary application was that the Civic automobile produced by Honda in Ontario, Canada, was rejected by U.S. Customs as a non-North American product. (This incident occurred before NAFTA altered the rule used in considering this case under the U.S.-Canada FTA.)

It is reported that the U.S. public was uneasy about the switch of Japanese investment from the United States to Mexico and the resulting unemployment in the United States. However, in the middle of aggravated frictions between the United States and Japan, both the Japanese government and business firms are sensitive enough to avoid aggressive responses. A Japan External Trade Organization (JETRO) survey conducted in October 1991 of the Japanese manufacturing subsidiary firms operating in the three North American countries conveyed their subdued response to NAFTA in this respect (see Tables 2 and 3).

Generally speaking, more Japanese subsidiaries in the United States are expected to benefit from NAFTA (through internal liberalization and deregulation and the enlarged market) than to lose, and more Japanese subsidiaries in Canada are expected to be affected adversely by NAFTA (through increased competition from imports from Mexico) than to gain. Japanese subsidiaries in Mexico are divided into both "merit" and "demerit." Nevertheless, of the three categories considered, the highest number was in the "no impact" column. Modest responses by the Japanese subsidiaries are also observed in Table 3. Only a few reported either anticipated relocation or building of new factories, while 70 percent reported no plans for relocation of offices and factories even after NAFTA was implemented.

Responses in Recent Months and Future Prospects

While the fierce discussion of the NAFTA legislation in the U.S. Congress was under way last year, the Asian response was ambivalent. Some countries wished to see it fail out of fear of being excluded from the North American market, but in Japan there was a desire to see it succeed lest its failure discourage U.S. efforts for a new trade regime, leading the United States to become more inward-looking. At the same time, many Japanese were annoyed by the news report that both those who favored and those who opposed NAFTA based their position on the desire to prevent Japan from taking advantage of the North American market.

After the NAFTA legislation was approved, the Japanese government announced that it welcomed the result and expected that NAFTA would give birth to the world's biggest integrated market in North America, would help foster North American development, and would be managed consistently with GATT principles. However, the authorities also commented on the discriminatory effects on firms in nonmember countries. The start of NAFTA should make clear the U.S. commitment to the Western Hemisphere and thereby enhance the potential of the region's future and encourage both member and nonmember firms to increase production and employment in the region.

Questionnaire surveys conducted recently by Japan's Ex-Im Bank have shown no significant changes in the investment plans of Japanese firms but reported an increasing interest of those firms in the newly enlarged market in North America.[5] The surveys also predict that although Japanese firms are still cautious about overseas investment in the near future, they are resuming interest in FDI over the longer term.

A proposal for a NAFTA-Japan quadruple economic consultative body was made early in 1994.[6] The proposal originated from the *Final Report of the Japan-Mexico Commission for the 21st Century*, cochaired by Ambassador Nobuo Matsunaga and Minister Julio Rodolfo Moctezuma, published in March 1992. Anticipating the establishment of NAFTA, the *Final Report* made the following recommendation:

> In concrete terms, it is hoped that the establishment of NAFTA will lead to the expansion of economic exchange in both private and public sectors among the four nations. This would ensure the development of smooth economic interactions between the North American region and Japan, based on free trade principles.
>
> The four countries could establish a "North Pacific Economic Forum" as a place where multilateral dialogue could be conducted by representatives of the private and public sectors. This would no doubt shed light on problems for which solutions are not immediately forthcoming under bilateral negotiating frameworks. This type of joint effort could not only be profitable for the member countries, but could also contribute to the maintenance of a free trade regime and the steady development of the world economy as a whole.[7]

The report stated that the Ministry of Foreign Affairs would reconsider this recommendation after NAFTA was launched.

Economic Integration in the Western Hemisphere and the Vision for APEC

The establishment of NAFTA has made clear the U.S. commitment to the development of the Western Hemisphere and improved the business atmosphere in the region. We, on the other side of the Pacific, welcome the evolving regime in the Western Hemisphere, but are also concerned whether the development of NAFTA will continue to be compatible with the new direction of APEC under its open regionalism. Mexico was admitted as a new member of APEC at the Seattle meeting and all three NAFTA countries are now members of APEC. Asian members are concerned about how this NAFTA subgroup will behave. To conclude this chapter, I would like to raise this issue in the broader context of the APEC vision.

The 1993 APEC Economic Policy Group (EPG) Report recommended the broad vision of moving toward an economic community, but there still remain differences in approach between Asian and North American participants. In APEC's 1993 *Declaration on Trade and Investment Framework*, the concept of open regionalism was adopted and top priority was given to global liberalization, while liberalization within APEC was assigned a supplementary role. As the Asia-Pacific economies have been actively engaged in and realized gains from freer trade and investment, these economies believe there is scope for further liberalization beyond the GATT Uruguay Round.

> APEC would in essence seek to 'ratchet up' the process of global trade liberalization: push for a maximum multilateral accord, then work out new regional agreements that incorporate both the items that fail to win global approval and new issues that were not yet attempted in the GATT, and complete the cycle by putting its own agreements on the global agenda for multilateral adoption.[8]

Here, however, two approaches are identified in applying the liberalization achieved within APEC to nonmember countries. In the popular concept of open regionalism, the trade and investment liberalization achieved within APEC should be applied to non-APEC countries as well, consistent with the GATT principle of general most-favored-nation (MFN) treatment.[9] Conversely, there is a view that seems to prevail, especially in the United States, of applying APEC liberalization to nonmembers on a conditional MFN basis. This is based on the fear of a free rider position that would be enjoyed by nonmembers, a position consistent with the provision of GATT Article XXIV on free trade areas. "Open regionalism" is defined here as regional integration open to any country that meets the membership requirements.

If the Uruguay Round had failed last December, the Asia-Pacific countries might have been inclined to the FTA approach. With the successful conclusion of the Uruguay Round, Asians now feel that the outlook for the nondiscriminatory application of APEC liberalization has become more realistic. Although agreement was reached in the Uruguay Round, some areas are left unsettled; further negotiations may be needed. Is it certain that the textile and agricultural sector agreements of the round will be implemented on schedule? The commencement of a new round with an environmental theme and the inclusion of a competition policy will most likely be proposed in a few years. In a situation in which interest in worldwide negotiation toward global liberalization continues, negotiations on liberalization consistent with GATT's general MFN treatment will become the core of the Asia-Pacific position, and regional liberalization will play a supplementary role.

On the other hand, now that NAFTA is in effect, the United States has apparently gained confidence in extending the FTA approach to include other Latin American and some Asian countries in parallel with APEC liberalization. This extended NAFTA approach was rejected in the EPG report but still prevails in speeches by U.S. opinion leaders. NAFTA has already been accepted as a subgroup of APEC, and countries outside the subgroup have no choice except to strengthen APEC surveillance over NAFTA's possible restrictive management against nonmembers.

Asians understand that trade and investment liberalization is necessary to make their industries competitive in the world market, and, in fact, they have followed such a policy unilaterally for the past decade. They prefer to achieve APEC liberalization on a gradual and voluntary basis. Ratcheting up is accepted in principle, but they do not wish to see it happen at once.

The GATT report for 1992-1993 listed the autonomous trade liberalization measures that have been undertaken by seventy-two contracting parties since the start of the Uruguay Round.[10] All APEC member countries are among the contracting parties. Although some Asian members did not join the GATT Tokyo Round negotiations (whose agreements were implemented from 1980 to 1986), these countries undertook trade liberalization voluntarily.

This gives an encouraging indication of how to solve the problem of keeping NAFTA consistent with the APEC's open regionalism. The NAFTA countries can liberalize trade and investment rules unilaterally so as to reduce barriers against nonmember firms even as they reduce them for member firms. This is exemplified perfectly by the move by the Mexican government to liberalize the foreign investment act immediately after NAFTA was ratified. Under NAFTA, Mexico will give firms from other NAFTA member countries national treatment and exempt those firms from performance requirements. Under the new foreign investment act, the same liberalization will be applied to nonmembers. Mexico has the highest tariffs and nontariff barriers among the three NAFTA countries. However, as long as Mexico remains prepared to liberalize unilaterally, the development of the Western Hemisphere under NAFTA will be consistent with the objectives of APEC.

Table 1. Intraregional Trade Shares

	1980	1986	1990
EA	36.5	36.8	42.2
NA3	31.8	33.3	38.1
EC12	53.7	58.2	65.6

Table 2. Anticipated Impacts of NAFTA by Japanese Subsidiary Firms

Impact/Country of Operation	Total	USA	Canada	Mexico
Total	71	48	13	10
Receive Merits	20	16	1	3
Receive Demerits	20	8	1	3
No Clear Impact	33	26	5	2

Table 3. Responses to NAFTA by Japanese Subsidiary Firms
Number of Respondents

Response/Country of Operation	Total	USA	Canada	Mexico
No Relocation of Main Offices or Factories	35	27	3	5
Increase Sales Offices	11	5	3	3
Build New Factories	10	4	4	2
Relocate Factories	4	3	1	0
(Multiple answers are allowed.)				

Sources: Japan External Trade Organization (JETRO), Survey of Japanese Subsidiary Firms Abroad, October 1991.

Notes

1   Ministry of International Trade and Industry, 1993, *White Paper on International Trade for 1992*, (in Japanese) Part 2 (Tokyo).

2   Japan External Trade Organization (JETRO), 1993, *White Paper on Foreign Direct Investment* (Tokyo), January.

3   JETRO 1993.

4   JETRO 1993.

5   Japan Export-Import Bank, 1994, Foreign Investment Research Institute, "Report of the Questionnaire Survey on Foreign Investment for 1993," *Kaigai Toushi Kenkyujoho*, (in Japanese).

6   *Nihon Keizai Shinbun*, January 8, 1994.

7   *Final Report* of the Japan-Mexico Commission for the 21st Century, 1992, cochaired by Ambassador Nobuo Matsunaga and Minister Julio Rodolfo Moctezuma, 48, March.

8   Asia Pacific Economic Cooperation (APEC), 1993, "A Vision for APEC: Towards an Asia Pacific Economic Community," in the *Report of the Eminent Persons Group to APEC Ministers* (Singapore), 31, October.

9   General Agreement on Tariffs and Trade, 1993, *International Trade and the Trading System*, Report by the Director General for 1992-1993 (Geneva), Article I.

10   General Agreement on Tariffs and Trade 1993, Article I, 30-31 and 38-47.

Chapter 8

The European Community's Future Trade and Investment Policies in the Western Hemisphere

Eckart Guth

Introduction

This chapter touches on a wide range of issues integral to the future expansion of the European Union (EU) and to its relations with countries in the Western Hemisphere. It covers developments in Europe that have an impact on trade and growth. Trade and investment depend on the political, social, and economic situation at home and in the partner countries as well as on the multilateral framework for the conduct of these activities. The first section of this chapter describes the EU's current economic and political challenges and the opportunities resulting from developments within the Union, such as the completion of the internal market, the aftermath of the Maastricht Treaty, and the economic recession. Then reference will be made to the enlargement of the EU and to the openings arising from the successful conclusion of the Uruguay Round Multilateral Trade Negotiations (MTN). The conclusion deals with new challenges for international trade and investment. Against this background, the trade and investment relation of the EU with the countries of the Western Hemisphere will be examined.

Unjustified Fears about "Fortress Europe"

Contrary to the fears of many third countries, the vast legislative program of almost three hundred regulations and directives that was necessary for the establishment of the European Community's (EC's) internal market was largely completed on time. This was a staggering legislative achievement and showed a unique ability for action and compromise by the twelve member states. The EC's decision to set up an obstacle-free internal market across the Community by the end of 1992 is one of the most significant events of its recent history. It has made firms both inside and outside the Community rethink their production, marketing, and investment strategies. The 1992 project speeded up the removal of the remaining national barriers to the EC's internal market so that European firms could benefit from a home market of truly continental dimensions and take advantage of the economies of scale thus generated to increase their worldwide competitiveness. The internal market also has many ramifications for the Community's trading partners. At a technical or institutional level, the completion of the internal market required the formulation of a common commercial policy. In concrete terms, this has meant that individual import restrictions of member states had to be dismantled.

At the macroeconomic level, the completion of the internal market will have positive effects on growth, job creation, and European competitiveness. Overall, it will stimulate the world economy and open up new market opportunities for its suppliers all over the world.

The uniform (or mutually recognized) set of standards and procedures put in place means that exports to the EU can now reach over 340 million consumers. Exporters to the EU, like local EU firms, will need to manufacture to only one set of standards in order to market their product anywhere in the Community. They will no longer have to face twelve different national requirements. Foreign firms, like Community operators, can also enjoy economies of scale and greater market flexibility.

The fears concerning the creation of a Fortress Europe were dispelled by the EU's unequivocal commitment to ensure that the internal market should not close in on itself and that it should be fully in conformity with the provisions of the General Agreement on Tariffs and Trade (GATT). The first year of practical experience clearly demonstrates that none of the fears expressed by some third countries was justified. The formation of the single market has now been complemented by a major reform of the European Union's Import Regime, accompanied by significant changes in the operation of the Union's commercial defense instruments. The EU has finally completed its commercial policy by adopting uniform rules and procedures for all import and trade instruments. The unilateral removal of a large number of national quantitative restrictions, which have been in existence for thirty years or more, is proof not just of the EU's openness to trade but also of its determination to complete the external dimension of the internal market.

Furthermore, new commercial defense instruments mean that business in and outside the Union will benefit from more streamlined and transparent rules that will minimize market disruption and enable the Union to take effective action against unfair trading practices. The key elements of this commercial instruments defense package are as follows:

1. The final elimination of all residual national quantitative restrictions. All these restrictions predated the accession of the member states to the European Community, and they cannot now be reintroduced. The only remaining restrictions concern a limited number of textile products and a handful of Community-wide quotas for China.

2. A new, streamlined decision-making procedure for the Union's commercial defense — making it more effective in dealing with unfair trade practices that could disrupt an open trade regime. The main change is that although the European Economic Council retains the power to impose definitive antidumping and countervailing duties, these can now be decided by a simple majority rather than by a qualified majority of member states.

3. The Council's agreement also means that there will be binding deadlines and greater procedural transparency for all the Union's commercial policy instruments. These deadlines will considerably improve the legal certainty for those economic operators concerned, thereby eliminating unnecessary market disruption.

4. An accessory, but still meaningful practical point is that these new, uniform rules will simplify import formalities for both EU traders and exporters to the EU.

It is now possible to use a single import document valid throughout the Union for importing industrial goods. Economic analysis and the first year of experience show that the establishment of the internal market has created many opportunities for trade with and investment in the EU. Obviously, a number of positive factors will only become fully effective once the general economic crisis is overcome.

Further Steps toward Economic and Political Integration

Following the completion of the internal market, the EU took an even more important step toward economic and political integration and cooperation — the ratification of the Maastricht Treaty. Two driving forces incorporated in the Maastricht Treaty will push forward the process of further integration. The first is the movement toward monetary and economic union. The ratification of the treaty illustrates that the Community is ready to embrace fundamental changes and to take on more internal and external responsibilities. With such high stakes on the table, it was only to be expected that the negotiations would be difficult. Nor was it surprising that the ratification procedures were more delicate than anticipated — after all, the treaty constitutes changes of a most fundamental and ambitious nature.

Besides the creation of an economic and monetary union, the other major innovation — the second driving force — in the Maastricht Treaty is progress toward a common foreign and security policy, which should enable the European Union to act more cohesively and decisively and to become a more equal partner of the United States on the world stage. History will probably show that the unprecedented problems arising from the turmoil in the former Yugoslavia will considerably enhance this process.

One specific Article of the EC Treaty, the impact of which appears to be of paramount importance for companies from third countries doing business in the EU, should be mentioned. Article 58 puts companies on a par with natural persons with respect to the freedom to provide services within the Community. The nationality requirement is replaced by the following two conditions: 1) a company must be established under the laws of one member state of the EU, and 2) the seat of the company or its principal place of business must be within the EU.

Once these criteria are fulfilled, there is no further issue about the nationality of the owners of the company. The question as to who is controlling a company (control theory) is irrelevant. Thus, a 100 percent third-country-controlled company incorporated under the laws of France, having its seat or principal business within the Community, enjoys the right of establishment in any other member state, as well as the freedom to provide services throughout the Community, as if this company were a national of one of the member states. With the internal market in place, the opportunities provided by this article should now bear full fruit. It will be a difficult task for the European Commission to preserve the dynamic elements of Article 58 and to fight vigorously any attempts to undo the great achievement of setting up an internal market of 340 million —hopefully soon more than 360 million — consumers.

All these developments in the EU should lead over time to even greater economic and political stability in Europe and thus provide a fertile ground for further improvements for trade and investment.

The Economic Crisis

For the time being, it appears, however, that the positive effects emanating from these developments are to be overshadowed by the economic crisis prevailing in many industrialized countries. Most of the industrial world has felt the effects of the current recession. This is especially true in Europe, which is in a period of low or negative growth and rising unemployment. The Community grew by only 1.1 percent in 1992, then contracted by -0.5 percent in 1993, and is forecast to grow by only 1.2 percent in 1994. Perhaps most disturbing, EU unemployment hit 11.5 percent in 1993 and is projected to rise still further, to 12.0 percent in 1994. In other words, there will soon be a staggering nineteen million people out of work. In addition, Europe's competitiveness is continuing to deteriorate. The Community's share of world manufactured exports has fallen by one-fifth since 1980.

However, the Community has shown itself ready to respond to these challenges. In December 1992, the twelve member states launched a growth initiative at the Edinburgh European Council meeting; the initiative was given a boost in Copenhagen in June 1993 and in Brussels in December, when the Council decided on an action plan based on the Commission's white paper on growth, competitiveness, and employment.

The white paper outlines a strategy for expanding the EU's economic growth and restoring its competitiveness, and it aims to create fifteen million new jobs by the year 2000. The paper attributes the current slump to rigidities associated with the regulation of the European labor market and to the high indirect costs of employment. It proposes a variety of strategies to tackle these problems, including initiatives to increase investment in the workforce, to improve training and education, and to reduce non-wage costs.

High levels of unemployment are not unique to Europe — in November 1993, the unemployment rate in the United States was 6.4 percent. President Bill Clinton has stressed that if this problem is to be solved, Europe and the United States must learn from each other. His proposal to set up a transatlantic exchange of ideas to discuss employment creation, up to and beyond the job summit in March 1994, is a useful contribution that the EU welcomes.

There is much shared thinking between the EU and the United States. Both recognize the extent to which the EU and the United States have substantial overlapping interests, and both recognize the value of working together in order to develop common strategies and actions.

Europe's Approach to Economic Integration

The EU is not only committed to removing the impediments to free trade with the major world economic powers, it has been looking closer to home as well. The European Economic Area (EEA), which includes Austria, Finland, Iceland, Liechtenstein, Norway, and Sweden as well as the EU, came into force on January 1, 1994 — on the same day as the North American Free Trade Agreement (NAFTA). The EEA established an integrated economic area of more than 360 million inhabitants and will allow for the free movement of goods, services, and capital within it. Moreover, vast cooperation possibilities now exist in many fields, including research and development (R&D), environmental, social, and consumer policy. The EEA has opened up new opportunities for people and economic operators in a region reaching from the Arctic Ocean to the Mediterranean Sea. Operators from third countries will also benefit from easier access to this enlarged internal market. The completion of the EEA in no way diminishes the determination to finish the accession negotiations with Austria, Finland, Norway, and Sweden on time. The conclusion of the EEA was a big step toward this goal, and the target date for the accession of European Free Trade Association (EFTA) countries remains January 1, 1995.

Regional integration is encouraged in the EU, as well as elsewhere in the world, as long as its conformity with the multilateral trading system is assured. The EU has welcomed NAFTA and also takes a positive attitude toward the Asia-Pacific Economic Cooperation (APEC). Because the EU has important trade and investment ties with all the APEC countries, involvement, in the form of constructive dialogue, is desirable. Unfortunately, APEC has not yet responded affirmatively to this request.

The Multilateral Framework

The primary basis for the EU to improve trade and investment remains that of the multilateral system provided by the GATT, which has now been further enhanced through the successful conclusion of the Uruguay Round negotiations. The outcome of the Uruguay Round should reinforce EU cohesion and cooperation well beyond the economic sphere. No single member state, however rich or powerful, could possibly have faced the United States, Japan, and the Cairns Group on equal terms and secured the outcome that the EU as a whole was able to achieve. More generally, the GATT success marks the reaffirmation of the European and worldwide commitment to the multilateral system and to the benefits that flow from successful transatlantic cooperation.

As the GATT is replaced by the World Trade Organization (WTO), due to come into operation in 1995, the business and administrative communities of the world have to come quickly to terms with some far-reaching new rules. First, the conclusion of the Uruguay Round is in itself a resounding confirmation of the primacy of open trade rules. After decades of excessive subsidy and protection, it is difficult to overstate the importance of binding agreements both to reduce subsidy and protection in the field of agriculture and to remove the quotas applied for most of the postwar period to almost all trade in textile products.

The second major theme to come out of the Uruguay Round is the strengthening of multilateral dispute settlement disciplines and the removal of any scope for unilateral action. The WTO dispute settlement process will be more automatic, thanks to the abolition of the virtual power of veto that has applied to GATT dispute settlement. As a counterpart guarantee for the parties to disputes, the legal findings of WTO panels will be subject to review by a separate appeals body. For the first time, there will be definitive rules on the timetable for dispute settlement, on the implementation of panel findings, and on the steps to be taken in cases of nonimplementation.

Further, there is explicit reaffirmation that WTO members will not take it upon themselves to determine a breach of international rules or to apply unilateral sanctions. An improved dispute settlement system along these lines is essential to the strength and predictability of the open trading system. Without it, the rules alone would offer business people no guarantee of a stable working environment.

The third important achievement is that the Uruguay Round for the first time embraced the fields of services, intellectual property, and foreign direct investment.

Services

There is now a framework of open trade rules (transparency, most-favored-nation — MFN, and national treatment), together with the first package of market-opening commitments. Much remains to be done, but the inclusion of this area in the negotiations represents a huge step forward down the road of progressive liberalization.

Intellectual Property

The agreement will provide protection for a range of forms of intellectual property and will bring significant benefits for a wide spectrum of European industries: consumer goods, textiles and clothing, processed food, wines and spirits, pharmaceuticals, chemicals, computer programming, and entertainment.

Foreign Direct Investment

The most widespread handicaps on investors arise from local content or export requirements imposed by the host government as a condition of investment approval. The EU wanted clearer rules prohibiting such trade-impeding rules in other countries. Some advances were made, but again, more remains to be done.

Another achievement was the strengthening of the institution charged with the promotion of harmonious economic relations — we can now speak of a World Trade Organization.

- The WTO will be more political than the GATT. There will be more hours of ministerial attention to the WTO, not only during the regular meeting but in general.
- The WTO will have the authority necessary to be more active in cooperation with other key international bodies such as the International Monetary Fund (IMF) and the World Bank.

- The WTO will be a more transparent organization, combining the higher political profile that the GATT has earned from the successful conclusion of the Uruguay Round and a new statutory openness. The WTO will take more frequent initiatives to steer world economic cooperation toward greater openness and less friction.

Finally, there are, of course, the successes emanating from the most traditional GATT activity — tariff reductions. The Uruguay Round, while producing a final market access package not quite as ambitious as hoped for at the Tokyo summit, has nonetheless concluded the biggest liberalization deal in trade history.

The efforts of the final year of the Uruguay Round have certainly been worthwhile. Overall, developed country contributions reduce import duties by between 35 and 40 percent, bettering the targets set earlier in the negotiations. U.S. import duties on EU exports will be cut by nearly half, while Japan's trade-weighted tariff cut is around 60 percent.

The round promises notable trade and investment benefits partly because GATT liberalization is in harmony with the established trend toward global economic interdependence. More comprehensive and better enforced international rules for services as well as goods, for investment as well as trade, are essential in a world where the critical marketplace for an ever-growing number of products is worldwide rather than regional, where smaller companies depend on worldwide markets for their survival, and where the factors determining international economic relations are increasingly found in domestic rules and procedures rather than in border controls. The Uruguay Round may have overrun its timetable, but its results are precisely what are needed in today's economy.

The Next Generation of Trade Issues

With the conclusion of the Uruguay Round, the international economic agenda has opened up, and new substantive issues can begin to be tackled. Some of the most exciting new developments are related to trade and environment, trade and competition, and trade and social aspects.

As regards the question of trade and competition, the EU is in favor of initiating discussions with the United States and other parties. It is, however, only at the beginning of what looks like a long, arduous way to success. At present, the approach consists primarily of identifying the main difficulties with international antitrust rules, with the enforcement of such rules, or with the introduction of possible institutional arrangements. As far as the issue of trade and environment is concerned, the EU very much welcomes the GATT Trade Negotiations Committee decision of December 1993. This decision provides a solid basis for future work within the World Trade Organization. The EU will now have to provide the necessary input to shape the future WTO environmental work program. One of the prime objectives will be to keep the developing countries on board. It will be imperative to allay their concerns that environmental issues will serve as a back door for protectionism.

With respect to trade and social questions, the EU supports initiatives that constitute an expression of its commitment to human rights and to the pursuit of improving social conditions worldwide. But it must be stressed that the EU is equally as sensitive to humanitarian concerns as it is in opposing their use for trade protection purposes. Therefore, the most fruitful way to obtain an improvement of social standards worldwide remains through economic development, including the expansion of trade.

The EU does not see unilateral trade measures as an appropriate means to reach possible objectives in the above-mentioned areas. It would prefer to take a cautious multilateral-based approach.

The EU believes that the active involvement of developing countries in this clarification process is an absolutely necessary condition. It has to deliver the message that the industrialized world does not seek to impose new trade barriers or to reduce or eliminate the comparative advantage of developing countries, but rather wants to help their governments improve the social conditions in their respective countries.

Trade and Investment Relations with Countries of the Western Hemisphere

It has often been said that the EU and the United States have the most important political and economic relationship in the world. Each side has major overlapping interests in the other, and both sides share fundamental political principles and have a common interest in promoting them around the world. The EU and the United States have a common cultural heritage, a similarity of security interests, and close economic and trade relations; these bonds form the cornerstone of their relationship.

The unique partnership between the EU and the United States is reflected in the Transatlantic Declaration of November 23, 1990, which provides the institutional framework for transatlantic dialogue. In it, both sides agreed to have regular and intensive consultations and to make full use of and further strengthen existing procedures.

With the end of the Cold War, new economic and political challenges have emerged. The EU, together with the United States, is bound to remain in the forefront of regional crisis management, especially in the framework of the United Nations (UN), in contributing to stability and constructive change in Central and Eastern Europe and the former Soviet Union and to the achievement of peace in the former Yugoslavia. At the same time, the principal industrialized countries need to revitalize global economic growth to stimulate world trade and cut unemployment.

In a time of such unpredictability, it is not surprising that EU-U.S. relations have been subject to some strain. However, President Clinton's 1994 trip to Europe helped to revitalize the transatlantic relationship. Clinton said that the United States regarded the European Union as a strong and equal partner.

It is also difficult to overestimate the importance of EU-U.S. trade relations. The EU and the United States are each other's largest trading partners; their two-way trade in goods and services amounted to about $280 billion in 1991. Indeed, the United States sends about a quarter of its total exports to the EU, and the EU exports a similar amount of its total exports to the United States. Trade between the EU and the United States will be further facilitated by three recent developments: the establishment of the internal market, the completion of the EEA, and the successful conclusion of the Uruguay Round.

A similar pattern exists where direct investment is concerned. The Community is by far the main foreign investor in the U.S. economy and is the biggest recipient of U.S. direct investment abroad. Cumulative direct investment by EU firms in the United States stood at $219 billion in 1992, representing 52 percent of total foreign investment stock in the United States. The U.S. investment stock in the Community was valued at £200 billion.

But in spite of their close economic and political interdependence, there are still bones of contention between the EU and the United States that can seriously affect the overall trade and investment climate.[1] For one thing, the persisting unilateral elements in U.S. trade legislation continue to be of major concern to the EU. No other major trading partner of the EU has similar trade legislation. The comprehensive multilateral dispute settlement mechanism that has been agreed upon in the framework of the new World Trade Organization will restrain the contracting parties from having to resort further to unilateral determinations in trade disputes and will oblige them to bring their domestic legislation into conformity with all the Uruguay Round agreements.

The enforcement of U.S. legislation that also has an impact on trade outside U.S. territory is closely linked to the aspect of unilateralism. The extraterritorial reach of national legislation may not only provoke a dispute about the sovereignty of trading partners but may also lead to unsolvable legal conflicts for economic operators. In these circumstances, trade as well as investment may be negatively affected.

The United States continues to put forward national security considerations to justify trade and investment restrictions that pursue protectionist objectives. Measures range from limits on market share to procurement restrictions and from unilateral export controls to the screening and possible prohibition of foreign direct investment. There is no question of the right of every sovereign country to take necessary measures in defense of its national security. However, the EU is increasingly concerned that the rather vague U.S. concept of national security embraces more and more aspects of domestic economic security.

Another concern relates to the trend in the United States toward the proliferation of conditional national treatment legislation, particularly in the research and development field. The principle of national treatment is one of the pillars of liberalization of the world economy. It is a well-established legal standard used in international treaties and other multilateral instruments. This principle had also been incorporated in, and continues to be fundamental to, the GATT. It has been included within the framework of the Uruguay Round in the Agreement on Trade-related Investment Measures (TRIMS), Trade-related Aspects of Intellectual Property Rights (TRIPS), and the General Agreement on Trade in Services (GATS).

The European Commission services are now concerned about a growing tendency in the U.S. Congress to pass legislation conditioning the principle of national treatment and providing for the possibility of enhanced discrimination against European economic operators in the United States. In the past, legislation was aimed only at non-U.S. companies' participation in federally funded R&D and related activities, but it now extends to a growing number of sectors.

The discrimination against non-U.S. companies is mainly brought about in two different ways:

1. The conditioning of national treatment by requiring reciprocal treatment of U.S. companies. It is important to note that the reciprocity conditions are not always related to the sector in which the non-U.S. parent company is active in the United States but may also relate to other sectors (cross-sectoral reciprocity).

2. Distinctive operative conditions either in the form of a definition of the notion "U.S. company" or in the form of additional performance requirements for non-U.S. companies. In general, the performance requirements formally apply to all economic operators whether or not they are domestic or foreign-controlled. However, foreign-controlled enterprises can be faced with indirect, de facto discrimination insofar as they may face more difficulty — or a greater burden — than U.S. firms in fulfilling the performance requirements.

It is imperative to be aware that 1) the proliferation of conditional national treatment legislation could undermine an essential principle of multilateral trade and investment relations; 2) the investment climate in the United States could deteriorate, thus having a negative impact on overall trade relations; and 3) the U.S. legislation could easily provide a precedent for other countries to follow.

The economic crisis that currently plagues most industrial countries provides opportunities as well as risks for the future development of trade and investment. As far as economic recovery is concerned, both the EU and the United States are willing to generate as much of a synergistic effect as possible by staying in close contact about what each side is undertaking and by trying to learn as much as possible from each other. It is, however, equally important not to put the positive impact of such activities on the overall trade and investment climate into jeopardy by giving in to protectionist pressure, which traditionally gains influence when the economy is not doing well.

With respect to other countries of the Western Hemisphere, the EU's trade and investment policy is based on the following elements:

First, the EU welcomes regional economic integration agreements such as NAFTA, the Andean Common Market (ANCOM), and Mercado Común del Sur (MERCOSUR). The EU is built upon a similar approach and has no objection to the fact that other countries try to gain from closer economic and political integration or cooperation. The overriding principle, however, must be that the establishment of free trade zones or custom unions is primarily trade-creating and not trade-distorting. Therefore, the EU follows closely their implementation and monitors carefully their conformity with the relevant GATT provisions.

Second, the EU makes full use of the possibility provided for under GATT to grant preferential tariffs to the Central and Latin American countries.

Under the EU's general system of preferences (GSP) scheme, the Central and Latin American countries receive 1) duty-free access for all processed and semiprocessed industrial products (including textiles and European Coal and Steel Community items) subject to strict fixed amounts or flexible ceilings for a certain number of sensitive products; 2) reduced preferential duty rates for a certain number of agricultural products, without quantitative limitations except for five items, but subject to a safeguard clause; and 3) a 50 percent reduced levy on a limited number of agricultural products.

Four Andean countries — Bolivia, Colombia, Ecuador, and Peru — enjoy an exceptional and temporary preferential regime as part of the Community action to help them in their fight against drug trafficking. They are granted duty-free access for all the industrial products mentioned above without any quantitative limitation and for a much larger list of agricultural products.

In order to step up cooperation with Central American countries in the fight against drugs and to consolidate diversification of their exports, the EU also granted trade concessions to six countries in the region: Costa Rica, El Salvador, Guatemala, Honduras, Nicaragua, and Panama. These concessions were accorded for three years beginning on January 1, 1992, and will exempt the region's agricultural and fishery exports to the Community from customs duties (except in the case of bananas). Manufactured exports from the region already have a similar exemption under the GSP. Representing some ECU500 million a year, the chief exports covered by the decision are coffee, ornamental plants, tropical fruits and spices, cut flowers, and certain fishery products. In granting these concessions, the Council has shown its desire to take into account the considerable similarity between agricultural exports from Andean countries and those from Central America, as well as its concern not to prejudice the latter's economic and social development.

Finally, the EU recognizes that the performance of the Latin and Central American countries in terms of trade and investment is not yet satisfactory. Therefore, a program has been established to provide financial support for closer economic cooperation. These funds are used to promote exports to and investments from the EU. In the same spirit of better trade and investment cooperation, the EU had provided for advanced improvements in trade with tropical products in the framework of the Uruguay Round. This strengthened relationship is further enhanced by the expansion of diplomatic representations of the EU in the region.

The overall positive relationship between the EU and the Latin and Central American countries has, however, been overshadowed for some time by the banana dispute. It would take too much time to discuss here all the economic, legal, and political factors that determine the EU's position on bananas. From the point of view of the countries of the Western Hemisphere, however, it is important to realize that a major concern of the EU in creating a common import regime for bananas is to strike a fair balance between the highly competitive producers of so-called Dollar bananas and the traditional suppliers of so-called ACP (Africa-Caribbean-Pacific) bananas from the Caribbean countries.

Conclusion

Albert Einstein said, "I never think about the future, it comes soon enough." But perhaps economists should be guided by the advice given by the famous French writer Antoine de St. Exupéry, who said that our task is not to foresee the future but to enable it.

The EU is doing its homework in this respect. It has achieved an unprecedented degree of economic and political integration, which will soon be extended to new members of the Union. Its members are convinced that the internal market will continue to provide additional opportunities for trade and investment within as well as from outside the EU. As there are no signs that the EU will become inward-looking in the future, there is no reason why the very positive climate for traders and investors from third countries in the EU should change radically in the time ahead. On the contrary, the willingness of the EU to provide improved market access to its eastern neighbors demonstrates that it sees trade and investment as a two-way street.

This statement has been proved even more correct since the successful conclusion of the Uruguay Round negotiations on December 15, 1993. The EU is certain that the outcome of this round will provide all governments with a better framework to resist the temptation of protectionist and unilateral measures and, thus, to stick firmly to the multilateral rules. For companies, this outcome should foster a much more stable and transparent climate in which to do business, which is probably the maximum result that traders and investors around the world can expect to obtain from their governments.

Notes

1   A detailed list of U.S. barriers to trade and investment is published each year by the Services of the European Commission.

Production Notes

This book was printed on 60 lb. Glatfelter Natural stock with a 10 point C1S cover stock, film laminated.

The text of this volume was set in Garamond for the North-South Center's Publication Department, using Aldus Pagemaker 5.0, on a Macintosh IIci computer. It was designed and formatted by Susan Holler.

The cover was created by Mary M. Mapes using Quark XPress 3.3.

This volume was edited by Jayne M. Weisblatt.

Printed by Edwards Brothers in Lillington, North Carolina.